Developing Thinking and Understanding in Young Children

An introduction for students

Sue Robson

 Routledge
Taylor & Francis Group

LONDON AND NEW YORK

First published 2006
by Routledge
2 Park Square, Milton Park, Abingdon, Oxon OX14 4RN

Simultaneously published in the USA and Canada
by Routledge
270 Madison Ave, New York, NY 10016

Routledge is an imprint of the Taylor & Francis Group

Typeset in Times by
Newgen Imaging Systems (P) Ltd, Chennai, India
Printed and bound in Great Britain by
TJ International Ltd, Padstow, Cornwall

British Library Cataloguing in Publication Data
A catalogue record for this book is available from the British Library

Library of Congress Cataloging in Publication Data
A catalog record for this book has been requested

ISBN10: 0–415–36107–9 (hbk)
ISBN10: 0–415–36108–7 (pbk)

ISBN13: 9–78–0–415–36107–1 (hbk)
ISBN13: 9–78–0–415–36108–8 (pbk)

Developing Thinking and Understanding in Young Children

How do chil

From the ꜱ to
explore and ꜱhose
around them ꜱren's
thinking and ꜱ the
activities the ꜱren's
understandin

This esseꜱ ꜱdies
programmes ꜱples
from practiꜱ ꜱs of
young childr

- models ꜱkers
  such as
- neurosci
- the sociꜱ ꜱsion
  of 'emoꜱ
- languageꜱ ꜱk in
  pretend p
- the relatiꜱ
- whether cꜱ
- young chilꜱ

Throughout the b ꜱping
young children's

Developing Thꜱ ꜱlatest
research and writing from a number of areas, including education, social care, psychology and health. Any student, practitioner or parent looking for the key to understanding and encouraging young children's thinking will find this textbook an invaluable starting point.

Sue Robson is Senior Lecturer in Early Childhood Studies at Roehampton University, UK.

Contents

Illustrations

Figures

Boxes

Preface and acknowledgements

The field of early childhood is a vibrant and dynamic area, which is increasingly cross-disciplinary in outlook and multi-professional in practice. In writing this book I have tried to reflect this richness and diversity, drawing on a variety of disciplines, including education, ethnography, health, psychology and social care, for the contributions they each make to the study of young children's thinking and understanding. I have found myself exploring just about every aspect of young children's development. As a consequence, one of my greatest challenges has probably been in trying to draw some boundaries around the subject. The chief joy of writing has undoubtedly been in having the opportunity to look more deeply at the thoughts and actions of young children.

Throughout this book I draw upon data from the Froebel Research Fellowship Project *The Voice of the Child*. This project looks at how the thinking of young children aged 3–5 years is being supported and developed in early childhood settings and at the ideas and practices of practitioners working with them. The colleagues with whom I have been privileged to work on the project have forced me, in the most positive way, to try to think as clearly as I can about the area, and I thank them all – Kevin Brehony, Hiroko Fumoto, David Hargreaves and Veronica Towers. I am also indebted to all of the practitioners and children who have been involved in the three-year project, and I am particularly grateful for their enthusiasm and commitment. I should also like to thank the National Froebel Foundation and the Froebel Research Committee for their funding of the research project and Roehampton University for giving me some time to write.

The original idea for this book arose out of work on the BA Early Childhood Studies programme at Roehampton University. In developing this, I had invaluable help from Deborah Albon and John Griffiths, practitioners and researchers whose own research and experience has taught me a great deal. In addition, I should like to thank Pat Gura and Ann Bridges, and the staff, children and parents of Vanessa Nursery School in the London Borough of Hammersmith and Fulham, for their permission to reproduce material which formed part of the Final Report of the School Improvement Project *Thinking and Learning Skills*, Hammersmith and Fulham, 1997–1998. I am also grateful to Alison Kelly for her comments on part of the manuscript.

I should particularly like to thank all of the students whom I have taught, who have helped me to think about children's thinking, especially those whose work is reproduced or referred to here – Lynn Bartlett, Philippa Cooper, Jo Dabir-Alai, Lisa Frank, Lisa Guy, Yvonne Hatton, Joanna Johnson, Kirsty McLelland, Lucy Parker, Frances Pearmain, Janet Roberts, Meg Roberts, Jo Short, Sam Segar, Rebecca Shuttleworth, Rachel Spencer, Angela Streek,

Kathryn Torres and Esther Whalley. I am also extremely grateful to the children who feature in the observations throughout the book and for their consent to their ideas, words and actions being recorded. In most cases their names have been changed, apart from where they asked for the observation to keep their own name.

Finally, I must give my greatest thanks to my husband, Ken Robson, for his constructive comments on the manuscript, his unfailing encouragement, patience and endless supplies of meals and drinks, and to my daughters, Charlotte and Isabella, great thinkers all.

Chapter 1

How can we think about young children's thinking?

> Where do the days of the week come from? Do they come from the sun or from the clocks?
>
> (Isabella, aged 3 years 7 months)

Who would not be intrigued by Isabella's thinking? The puzzling mind of a young child comes through loud and clear in her question, as she tries to understand an everyday (literally!) event. It makes a fitting opening for a book which is about young children as active, persistent thinkers driven by a desire to make sense and meaning in their lives, to connect what they know and understand to what they do not yet understand. In this first chapter some fundamental, underpinning ideas about thinking are considered, posed as questions which set a context for the book as a whole. What do we mean when we talk about 'thinking' and 'understanding'? What activities might we describe as thinking, and is it different from learning? Do children and adults think in different ways? What parts are played by the environment and our genetic inheritance in developing our thinking and understanding? What is the role of memory? In considering these questions links are also made to many other parts of the book emphasizing a model of thinking as an activity which connects every part of young children's experience.

What is thinking?

Thinking is a fundamentally human characteristic, an activity in which we all engage, from the moment we are born and even before. As a child in Fisher (1990:1) says: 'If we didn't think there'd be no us.' What, though, do we mean when we use the language of thinking, for example, when we say 'I'm thinking about it'? How do we feel when we get a card that says 'thinking of you'? Wilson identifies three different meanings of the word 'think'. First, she suggests, there is an everyday meaning, where think is effectively a synonym for 'believe' or 'suppose'. Second, she suggests we use it as a way of suggesting we are paying attention to something: 'I'm thinking about it.' The final meaning is the main, though not exclusive, focus here: the special sense of thinking as an 'intellectual/high level process' (Wilson 2000:6).

White sets out four characteristics of thinking. First, he says, thinking is intentional; it is always '*of* or *about* something, or thinking *that* something is the case' (2002:101, emphasis in original), which suggests the important role of knowledge and experience for thinking. Second, he says, it is an activity. We engage in it deliberately; it does not happen to us. Sometimes thinking is directed towards an end, and at other times it may be an end in itself.

White's third proposal is that thinking employs concepts, whatever the context or activity in which the thinking is happening. His final suggestion is that thinking is a skill. As we shall see later, however, particularly in Chapter 10, and as White himself emphasizes, it is not just a skill, important though this is. Equally important is the development of the disposition to make use of this skill, to want to be a thinker and to enjoy thinking.

What does thinking mean to you? How would you describe it, and what kinds of activities would you include? Practitioners in one nursery identified words such as predicting, representing, recalling, considering, wondering, planning, deciding, modelling and evaluating as useful words related to the practice of thinking. They also suggested other, perhaps initially less likely words, including pretending, playing, picturing and dreaming (Ann Bridges and Pat Gura, in collaboration with the staff, children and parents of Vanessa Nursery School). All of these are important in the context of extending young children's thinking. Let us take three possible words that often come up in discussions about thinking and consider them in a little more depth: 'intelligence', 'knowing' and 'learning'.

Intelligence

Intelligence very often crops up in discussions about thinking. The idea that thinking is related to intelligence is a very pervasive one. It finds its expression in approaches to intelligence testing and IQ scores, an aspect of measuring individual difference that is considered in more detail in Chapter 6. For the general public 'intelligence' has often assumed the role of a badge of social approval (White 2002). As Pollard suggests:

> The concept of intelligence is very powerful, since it has passed into our culture to denote a generalized form of ability. It is part of our language and it influences our ways of thinking about children. For instance, parents often talk about their children in terms of 'brightness' or 'cleverness', and teachers routinely describe children and classroom groupings in terms of 'ability'. The concept of intelligence is important too because it is often used in the rhetoric of politicians and the media when they communicate with the public. It is thus routinely assumed both that there *is* a generalized trait of intelligence and that it is possible to measure it objectively.
>
> (Pollard 1997:128)

Defining what we mean by intelligence is, however, tremendously difficult, although this has not stopped people from trying. Francis Galton, developing mental testing in the nineteenth century, saw intelligence as fixed, inherited and underlying all cognitive activity (Meadows 1993). Those who came after him, including Eysenck and Burt, thus defined it as 'innate, general cognitive ability' (Burt in White 2002:78). This looks very different to Claxton's definition of intelligence as 'knowing what to do when you don't know what to do' (1999a:4). Gardner (1983), as we shall see, argues for the existence of multiple intelligences (MIs) identifying eight (or even eight and a half) forms of 'intelligence' and not just one. Nunes (2005) records the teachers in her studies assessing and defining the children's intelligence almost exclusively in relation to their verbal and literacy ability. Thornton suggests that intelligence is 'the capacity to solve problems and interact with the world in adaptive ways' (2002:179), a wide-ranging definition that, as she says, views intelligence as the product of all of an individual's knowledge, strategies and 'mental tools'.

Knowing

Knowing is often seen as a prerequisite to thinking in that we need to have something to think about but Duckworth suggests:

> of all the virtues related to intellectual functioning, the most passive is the virtue of knowing the right answer. Knowing the right answer requires no decisions, carries no risks, and makes no demands. It is automatic. It is thoughtless.
>
> (Duckworth 1987:64)

Gopnik *et al.* (1999) suggest that young children behave in much the same way that adult scientists do constructing their knowledge about the world and developing theories such as the children in Box 1.1 have about weight. They often persist in ignoring counterevidence to those theories for some time as do the children here. This leads Paley to conclude: 'I can't seem to teach the children that which they don't already know'(1986:126). However, eventually, it becomes impossible to ignore or reinterpret the new experiences, and children's knowledge and theories change as a result. Gopnik *et al.* (1999) suggest that this has an impact on children's understanding of more than just the particular element of knowledge and experience in question. This idea is also looked at in more detail in Chapter 8, in particular, in relation to young children's scientific understanding.

Learning

In thinking about thinking, it can be difficult to steer a clear path between it and learning, and the two are sometimes used interchangeably as if they were one and the same. It is, nevertheless, important to try to retain a clear distinction between the two. Perkins (1992), for example, suggests that learning is a consequence of thinking.

Claxton (1999a) argues for an approach which he calls learnacy or learning to learn. This, essentially, is what he means when he says that, for him, intelligence is knowing what to do when you don't know what to do. Crucially, for Claxton, this learning is not confined to 'the articulate, the numerate, the explicit and the measurable' (1999a:11). Rather, it is about taking a broad view of learning, which includes the use of the imagination, a playful disposition, persistence and the ability to learn with and from others.

Much attention has been focussed in recent years on the idea of learning styles and the view that we all have preferred ways of learning. In particular, approaches such as VAK (Visual, Auditory and Kinaesthetic) have gained popularity in early childhood settings (Bayley 2002, Dowling 2002). Bayley (2002) suggests that the extent to which an individual learns through each style will differ from person to person but that at least a part of a child's thinking may be lost if their opportunities to learn do not take account of their preferred learning style. Dowling (2002) cites statistics that point to the use of all three styles by all of us. These suggest that 29 per cent of our learning is through visual means, 34 per cent through listening or auditory means and 37 per cent through movement or kinaesthetic means. While it is questionable how verifiable such precise statistics can possibly be, it does at least highlight the idea that we may learn and remember in different ways.

What is the evidence for the claims of those who advocate learning styles approaches? The Learning and Skills Research Centre, or LSRC (2004), identify 71 different approaches. Much of the evaluation of these is small-scale, often conducted by the programme developers themselves (LSRC 2004) and tends to refer to older children and adults.

Box 1.1 Ben, aged 3 years 7 months, Oliver, aged 4 years 1 month and Jasmine, aged 3 years 8 months, at nursery school, sitting at a table with a teacher

TEACHER: We are thinking about which objects are heavy and which are light. We have a sponge and a brush. (The children are shown a large sponge and a brush.) Can you think about which one will be heavier?

BEN: The sponge.

TEACHER: Why do you think that?

BEN: Because it's big.

TEACHER: Oliver, which one do you think will be heavier?

OLIVER: The sponge.

TEACHER: What about you, Jasmine?

JASMINE: That one (points to the sponge).

TEACHER: Ok, so we are going to feel them now and see if we can feel which one is heavier. Can you all hold out both of your hands like this (shows them both hands, palms up). Oliver, here's the sponge (places it in his hand) and here is the brush (places in other hand). Which one do you think is heavier?

OLIVER: The sponge, because the brush is going down. (His hand holding the brush is lowering down and the hand holding the sponge remains in the same place.)

TEACHER: Why is the brush going down?

OLIVER: Because the sponge is going up.

(Jasmine is given both objects to hold.)

TEACHER: Jasmine, which one feels heavier?

JASMINE: This one. (Nods to the sponge.)

TEACHER: (Both objects are now placed in Ben's hands.) Which one do you think is heavier, Ben?

BEN: The sponge, because the brush is down. (His hand holding the brush is lowered below the sponge.)

TEACHER: If your hand has dropped down, it means you are carrying something heavy. The brush is heavy and the sponge is so light because it is full of air. Let's see if the balance scale show the brush is heavier. If it is heavier, the scales will go down on that side. (The objects are placed on the scales and the side with the brush on it goes down.) Has the brush gone down?

ALL CHILDREN: Yes, yes, yes.

TEACHER: So which one is heavier?

ALL CHILDREN: The sponge, sponge, the sponge.

By estimating through sight alone which object will be heavier, the children must rely on their own concepts of weight to come to a conclusion. In this case, it appears that their schema (Piaget 1962) of weight depends on their experiences of big objects being heavy. The children remain convinced that the sponge is heavier, even after first hand experience. In an attempt to develop their understanding the children are told the brush is heavier, and shown both objects on the scales. In this case, telling them seems less than effective, as questioning reveals that the children still believe the sponge to be heavier at the end of the episode. As Paley says, 'I can't seem to teach the children that which they don't already know' (1986:126).

Abridged and reproduced with permission of Frances Pearmain

Nevertheless, the LSRC do suggest that there is considerable variability between the different learning styles approaches and that it is difficult to be clear about the impact of any of them. With regard to VAK they suggest that, rather than it being a model for learning, it is a tool for instruction in that teaching is directed at identified learning styles. In addition, they quote one student describing herself thus: 'I learned that I was a low auditory, kinaesthetic learner. So there's no point in me reading a book or listening to anyone for more than a few minutes' (LSRC 2004:56). The dangers of children (and adults) labelling themselves in this way are a potential problem. In support of VAK, the report suggests that it is a user-friendly model.

Claxton (cited in Revell 2005) suggests that there are dangers in uncritical recommendation of learning styles approaches, stressing the need for further research in the area. Gardner has also emphasized that his MI theory 'begins from a different point and ends up at a different place from most schemes that emphasize stylistic approaches' (1993:44). He suggests that learning styles are not generic, but context- or subject-specific. Overall, the LSRC report emphasizes the value of approaches which target metacognition, considered in Chapter 5 in this book.

Are there different kinds of thinking?

The short answer to such a question is yes, of course, but a fuller answer would be that there may be different ways of looking at differences in thinking. White (2002) draws distinctions between undirected thinking, or daydreaming, and directed thinking, which he further elaborates into theoretical and practical thinking, and a category he calls contemplation or thinking done for its own sake.

Gardner (1983), in particular, has been responsible for suggesting that we think in different, domain-specific, ways. He outlines a number of 'intelligences', which differentiate between linguistic, logical–mathematical, musical, spatial, bodily-kinaesthetic, interpersonal, intrapersonal, naturalist and existential domains of thinking (Gardner 1983, 1999). These are looked at in more detail in Chapter 2.

Claxton (1998) differentiates thinking from the perspective of speed of thought. He suggests that the mind has three different processing speeds, which are responsible for different kinds of thinking:

- faster than thought – unselfconscious, instantaneous reaction;
- thought itself – the 'intellect' or deliberate 'd-mode' – what he calls the 'hare brain';
- less immediately purposeful, more leisurely, playful and contemplative ways of knowing – the 'tortoise mind', or 'undermind' (analogous to White's undirected thinking and contemplation).

(Claxton 1998)

Western culture in particular, he suggests, has tended to focus largely on the *d-mode* or *deliberate-mode* at the expense of what he calls the undermind or 'intelligent unconscious' (1998:7). The blame for this emphasis he lays partly at the door of Piaget. The undermind is, Claxton suggests, about implicit know-how or learning by osmosis and is analogous to Piaget's first stage of development (see Chapter 2), which is overtaken by other, more powerful, abstract and increasingly intellectual forms of thinking. The influence of Piaget's stage theory, Claxton suggests, carries with it an assumption that these later forms of thinking are the highest forms of development. Consequently, parents and adults working with young children may see their role as moving children on from the more intuitive forms of thinking and encouraging them to become deliberators and explainers as fast as possible. Claxton warns against the narrowness of over-reliance on d-mode and suggests a range of benefits of what he regards as intuitive thinking. This idea is looked at in more detail in Chapter 10. Perhaps the most important message he stresses is one of knowing how to think, of having a range of ways of thinking available to us for use in the most appropriate ways possible whatever the context.

In the context of the development of children's thinking, emphasis is often placed upon so-called higher order thinking. Resnick (cited in Meadows 1993) suggests that the key features of higher order thinking are as follows:

- it is nonalgorithmic: the path of action is not fully specified in advance;
- it is complex;
- it often yields multiple solutions;
- it involves nuanced judgement and interpretation;
- it involves the application of multiple, and sometimes conflicting, criteria;
- it often involves uncertainty;
- it involves self-regulation of the thinking process;
- it involves imposing meaning and finding structure;
- it is effortful.

(Adapted from Meadows 1993:334)

As Meadows points out, this includes knowing whether it will soon be teatime just as much as it is about more complex situations and ideas. It certainly characterizes, in my view, the kinds of thinking that young children engage in every day of their lives.

Do children think differently from adults?

Implicit in any kind of developmental theory – and many of the theories about children's thinking are developmental – is the idea of change over time. The stage theory developed by Piaget, discussed in Chapter 2, suggests that children's thinking changes in qualitative ways as they develop (this leads to the Piagetian idea that we develop in order to learn). Thus, the thinking of a 2-year-old is qualitatively different from that of a 10-year-old, and, importantly, the thinking of children is different in kind from that of adults. The major characteristics of this difference are ones of logic and abstraction. In the past 30 years, however, much evidence has been offered to suggest that children's thinking may not be as qualitatively different as Piaget believed. The work of Donaldson (1978), Tizard and Hughes (2002) and many others suggests that differences between children's and adults' thinking are more attributable to lack of knowledge and experience than to qualitative change. In situations where children have relevant knowledge and experience – whether it is playing chess, caring for goldfish or knowing about dinosaurs – they behave more expertly and display more mature thinking than many adults who are novices in the same area (Thornton 2002). As Siegler suggests: 'Differences between age groups tend to be ones of degree rather than kind. Not only are young children more cognitively competent than they appear, but older children are less competent than we might think' (1998:22). Just what those differences are is explored throughout this book.

Box 1.2 Magical thinking in *A Child's Work*

> On this day, Kostos is shouting out directions to anyone who will accept the premises of his plot. Even Vijay is drawn into the drama. 'Don't go there, Vijay! It's a poison river.'
> 'Did my feet get poisoned?' Vijay asks.
> 'Don't worry, I'm making you invisible. Touch this paper. Now I got you unpoisoned. It's invisible writing.'
> 'What does it say?'
> 'That you're invisible. No one can see you except me.'
> 'That's good. I was almost dead.'
> 'You mean poisoned. Now you're unpoisoned.'
>
> (Paley 2004:60)

Paley suggests that one characteristic form of young children's thinking is 'magical'. For young children, she suggests, it is 'the common footpath from which new trails are explored' (1981:4), as in Box 1.2.

Is thinking a solitary or a collective activity?

A search on the internet for images related to 'thought' and 'thinking' produces large numbers of a very similar image of a solitary figure resting his chin in his hand, invariably in a pose similar to Rodin's *Thinker* (although the image predates Rodin by a considerable period). Is thinking like this, however? The answer to such a question will depend very much on the kind of models of cognition (see Chapter 2) to which you subscribe. For Piaget (1950, 1959), thought is internalized action, and the child is a 'lone scientist' constructing understanding as a result of individual discovery. In so doing, children are viewed as self-regulating, learning when they are ready. Attempts to 'teach', show or explain things to children before they are ready will result in the learning of empty procedures with little impact on thinking. For Vygotsky (1978), however, children learn as they engage with others, as part of a culture. These are two very different viewpoints about the process of thinking discussed, along with others, in Chapter 2.

Nature or nurture, biology or experience?

The extent to which human growth and development is a matter of genetic inheritance or the result of experience, sometimes referred to as 'nature versus nurture', continues to be a cause of discussion and controversy. Cohen neatly summarizes the dilemma when he poses the following questions:

> 'Do parents who read more to their children improve IQ by providing a better environment? Or do children whose genes make them brighter insist their parents read to them more?'
> (Cohen 2002:158)

The philosopher John Locke, writing in the seventeenth century, was responsible for the idea that children are 'blank slates' at birth waiting to be written on by their experiences.

[handwritten margin note: Good quote for Nurture ✶]

A similar view is characteristic of a behaviourist approach to learning (see Chapter 2), which rests upon control of the environment as a determinant in children's development. The blank slate idea cannot entirely account for development, however. If this were so and babies were truly 'empty' they would have no basis for making sense of the kaleidoscope of experiences they encounter and no ability to progress beyond their empty state.

Research in genetics in recent years has tended to emphasize the predetermined nature of our development. As Thornton (2002) points out, every aspect of human beings must have a genetic basis starting from the fact that we grow into baby humans rather than ducklings! However, as she and many other psychologists stress, it cannot be the case that all cognitive ability is entirely inherited. The environments within which children live do have an impact on all aspects of their development. For example, we know that higher levels of nutrition enhance growth. Looking at cognition we see that higher levels of atmospheric lead pollution have been shown to have a negative effect on children's cognitive development (Cohen 2002, Meadows 1993), and research by Cutting and Dunn (1999) suggests a relationship between social class and the development of 'Theory of Mind', discussed in Chapter 5. The existence of interventions such as High Scope and Head Start in the United States and Sure Start in the United Kingdom are evidence of the assumption that environment can have an impact on young children's development. LeDoux puts it neatly when he says that 'Learning involves the nurturing of nature' (2003:9).

It seems reasonable to conclude that the two elements, nature and nurture, are inextricably linked. Rogoff suggests that it is 'a false dichotomy to focus on "nature" and "nurture" as separable influences on human development' (2003:65). For Rogoff, human biological development works together with cultural institutions and practices in mutually influential ways. For example, she suggests that the growth in the rate of births by caesarean section for mothers whose babies' heads are too large for the birth canal is a cultural practice which may lead, over a long period of time, to the evolution of larger heads in those populations.

Most recently, Pinker has emphasized the role of innate systems for development saying that 'Intelligent behavior (*sic*) is learned successfully because we have innate systems that do the learning' (2002:41). These innate systems form a 'universal complex human nature' (2002:73), which allow humans to behave flexibly in response to their experiences precisely because they are programmed with 'combinatorial software that can generate an unlimited set of thoughts and behaviours' (2002:41). Critics of Pinker's ideas suggest that he relies too strongly on particular 'sciences of the mind', notably cognitive science, behavioural genetics and evolutionary psychology (Midgeley 2002), and makes controversial use of other evidence from psychology and neuroscience (Blackburn 2003).

What we do not know is the relative balance between the two influences. In particular, given the subject of this book, what proportion of a child's cognition is inherited and what proportion is the result of experience? Thornton (2002) suggests that this will, in any case, vary as a result of each child's situation. Cohen (2002) points to research evidence that also suggests that it varies over time with the influence of the environment being at its strongest between 7 and 14 years, while Meadows (1993) highlights the small amount of useful data in the area on which to base any conclusions.

What is the relationship of memory to thinking?

Memory plays a vital role in all aspects of life, throughout life. Memories are central ingredients in our definitions of ourselves helping to 'make us what we are'

(Cohen 2002:110) and supporting an 'enduring and developing sense of self' (White 2002:189). While thinking is clearly not merely a matter of recalling memory, it is, as Meadows (1993) suggests, difficult to think of an aspect of human cognitive activity which does not involve memory in some way even if it is to conclude 'I've never met this situation before.'

Kuhn (2000) stresses the importance of situating the study of memory and memory strategies in the broader context of general cognitive development. She points, for example, to the vital part played by knowledge, looked at earlier in this chapter. It is useful to very briefly highlight a number of other aspects of children's thinking linked to memory which are looked at in the following chapters. All of the models of cognition outlined in Chapter 2 include memory processes. Memory is central to Information Processing theories, as well as having implications for Vygotskian (1978) ideas about the joint construction of meaning and collective memory making and the modular theories of Gardner (1983) among others. Kuhn emphasizes the ways in which memories arise out of social and cultural contexts, and children's 'everyday activities' (Kuhn 2000:23): the subject of Chapter 3. Memory development is also related to the physiological development of the brain: the subject of Chapter 4. Metamemory, the aspect of memory which is concerned with the ability to think about one's own memory processes, is inextricably linked with the development of metacognition looked at in Chapter 5. Kuhn (2000) suggests that memories are often represented in narrative form, an aspect of children's thinking that is discussed in both Chapters 7 and 8. In Chapter 8 the development of children's concepts is seen to be dependent, in part, upon their memories of past experience. Finally, in Chapter 10 memory is suggested as an element in the development of problem-solving in children. While this list is not exhaustive, it nevertheless highlights the central role of memory in the development of thinking and understanding.

Storing memories

A common way of thinking about memory is to see it as being structured according to how long we hold onto particular memories. Information is initially taken in through the sensory register, and much never passes beyond that. If it does, it becomes a memory. Some memories are short-term, that is, we do not remember some things for very long periods of time – exactly how long is short-term is disputed, some psychologists suggest a matter of seconds, others that short-term memory can be measured in minutes (Cohen 2002). When you stop someone in the street and ask them directions to a restaurant your interest is in remembering these for long enough to get you to the restaurant and such memories are usually short-term. At the other end of the spectrum are things that we need or want to remember for an indefinite period, for example, the kinds of memories that, at the start of this section, I suggested were what make you what you are. This is referred to as long-term memory. Smith *et al.* (2003) suggest that the idea of short-term memory has effectively been replaced by that of 'working memory', which focuses on processing capacity, and is thus much more than just a form of temporary storage. Baddeley, however, suggests that working memory is a distinct category, which sits between both short-term and long-term memory (Baddeley cited in Cohen 2002). However it is described, what is of interest are the ways in which short-term or working memory is transferred to long-term memory. Key to this process may be some of the strategies discussed in the following paragraphs.

Memories and memorizing

Kuhn (2000) suggests that in studying memory it is necessary to draw a distinction between two aspects of memory: *memories*, which she describes as knowledge structures that are the product of our efforts to understand and know, and *memorizing*, which she suggests is 'a socially situated activity undertaken in the service of individual or social goals' (Kuhn 2000:21). In relation to the first aspect, that of memories, there is evidence to suggest that foetuses have some capacity for memory (Cohen 2002), and that, from birth, babies can recognize something or someone familiar (Thornton 2002). Without this recognition memory every situation would be novel and unique and it would be impossible to learn from experience (Thornton 2002). An important developmental step forward, however, is the ability not just to recognize events but also to recall them thereby necessitating the retrieval and reconstruction of a memory stored somewhere. Eliot (1999) suggests that physiological development in the brain supports the development of this ability at around eight months. Thornton (2002) and Cohen (2002) point to research suggesting an earlier appearance, by about 2–3 months of age. Whenever it appears, there is clear evidence that children's ability to recall things develops over time.

A major factor in this development is the amount of knowledge we all have both about the world in general and also about the specific topic or domain in question (Kuhn 2000, Thornton 2002). This domain-specific knowledge seems to be particularly important for memory enabling us to make connections and see links and relationships that we might not otherwise notice. In young children, a lot of the knowledge they acquire is about everyday events, and they develop what are known as 'scripts' for experiences such as going shopping or going to a birthday party. This script knowledge helps them to remember and recall the likely sequence of events for such experiences. Other knowledge may be less script-like, for example, learning about the world or the rules of a game. Both cases, Kuhn (2000) suggests, account for the development of domain-specific knowledge structures that support memory. As we shall see in forthcoming chapters, knowledge and experience are key factors in the development of thinking and understanding.

In these everyday contexts, children's memories are formed as part of the meaningful, social context of the situation. Kuhn (2000) believes that it is in these situations that the best evidence for children's competence in memorizing, the second aspect of memory, is to be found. Claxton suggests:

> Anything which improves comprehension also improves memory. Trying to remember things that don't make much sense is a thankless task, and the effort of searching for some kind of meaningful 'glue' is usually well repaid.
>
> (Claxton 1999b:143)

When asked to deliberately recall things, that is, when they are asked to memorize something for the purpose of recalling it, young children's abilities may be much worse (Thornton 2002). Why should this be? Thornton (2002) suggests that one reason may be that children do not understand the point of such memory tasks. She recounts how her own son effectively refused to play the game of remembering objects on a tray, saying that the tester could look for herself if she wanted to know what was there.

The most significant factor that may account for young children's relatively poor performance in tests of deliberate recall is the strategies they use for remembering. These include the three encoding strategies of rehearsal, which refers to the mental repetition of information; organization, which involves structuring and grouping information in some way helpful to memory and elaboration, which involves making associations between items in order to help recall. Claxton (1999b) emphasizes how important language is in this process. Other types of strategy are concerned with retrieval, that is, approaches to trying to remember something which you cannot immediately recall. At age 4 children rarely make spontaneous use of the simplest strategies to aid recall. By the age of 7 the majority of children do, although they may tend to overestimate their capabilities (Thornton 2002). Thornton (2002) suggests that the difference between older and younger children is that the younger children do not yet have sufficient knowledge about how their memories work (part of what is referred to as metamemory and metacognition – see Chapter 5) in order for them to recognize the value of strategies. Smith *et al.* (2003) also suggest that older children's greater general knowledge may be important because it can help them to think of useful associations between ideas, and also that general processing capacity may increase over time, although Thornton (2002) and Meadows (1993) dispute this last possible reason. Meadows (1993) suggests that it is the efficiency with which memory capacity is used which may increase over time, rather than its basic capacity.

There is strong evidence that young children can be taught successfully to use memory strategies (Kuhn 2000 and Chapter 5, this book), although when they do so they may not recognize their value, and may not apply them outside the specific context in which they have been taught (Kuhn 2000). Interestingly, Claxton also focuses on *not* trying to remember as an important tool. Letting the unconscious take over or allowing your mind to 'come at it sideways' (1999b:145), he suggests, is also beneficial to memory. Alongside training in the use of encoding and retrieval strategies, children may benefit from knowing about, and using, other ways of remembering. In Chapter 6 the use of video and still photography is discussed as a way of stimulating recall. Brooks (2004) suggests the use of children's drawings of past events as prompts, that can act as tools for remembering, and as the starting points for discussion that supports shared memory.

Further reflection

1   Fisher (1990:1) suggests that thinking is about orchestrating the 'basic cognitive skills' of perception, memory, concept formation, language and symbolization'. Do you agree? How would you define 'thinking'?

2   Look back at Perkins' comment that 'learning is a consequence of thinking'. Do you agree? Is learning *always* a consequence of thinking?

3   Think about yourself and your family. Are you ever compared to other family members and told that you are 'just like them'? Do you see yourself as having inherited family traits? In what ways do you think you are unlike others in your family?

4   Do you have strategies for remembering? Do you think that you remember different kinds of things in different ways?

Further reading

Claxton, G. (1998, 1999a,b)
Cohen, D. (2002) pp. 28–30 and chapters 6 and 8
Dowling, M. (2002)
Duckworth, E. (1987) chapters 2 and 5
Gardner, H. (1983, 1993)
Kuhn, D. (2000)
Meadows, S. (1993) pp. 49–67
Paley, V.G. (1986)
Pinker, S. (2002)
Thornton, S. (2002) chapter 4
White, J. (2002) chapters 5 and 6

refinement of an existing schema or may require a rather larger shift in thinking. At what point, however, can we say that accommodation occurs? Meadows suggests that:

> the assimilation of new information must lead to some degree of accommodation in the old system of knowledge, if only to the minor degree of 'ah, here's another X: I've seen at least a hundred of those in my time, so now I've seen at least a hundred and one.'
>
> (Meadows 1993:199)

Anning and Edwards (1999) suggest that problem-solving play is particularly valuable for encouraging accommodation of new information.

The processes of assimilation and accommodation are held together by 'an even more important (and mysterious) process' (Meadows 1993:202) called equilibration. Siegler (1998:29) describes this as the 'keystone' of developmental change within Piaget's system, with long-term implications whereby the child's model of the world comes increasingly to resemble reality. Essentially, when children encounter new experiences or concepts their existing frameworks or schema have to adjust. This causes a state of disequilibrium or cognitive conflict, which acts as a motivation to learning until a state of equilibrium is restored.

Piaget's stages of cognitive development

Piaget suggests that cognitive, or intellectual, development is a continuous process, which proceeds through a universal, invariant series of stages in children. Children's thinking in each of these stages is qualitatively different both to what has come before and to what follows. According to Piaget there are four such stages (Figure 2.1).

Whereas the order of these stages is invariant their duration is not, and Piaget does not suggest that there is a fixed time span for each stage. He also believes that children may show evidence of more than one stage at a time, for example, elements of both the preoperational and concrete operational stages simultaneously. He refers to this phenomenon as décalage.

An important element of Piaget's stage theory is the idea of 'readiness' – that is, the idea that children cannot progress to the next stage of their development before they are ready, as a result of having gone through the stage before. Trying to 'teach' children something before they are ready to discover it for themselves, Piaget believes, involves them in learning procedures, and not the development of understanding, with lasting consequences for their development.

The first two of Piaget's stages are within the age focus of this book. The sensorimotor stage is characterized by the ways in which children come to know the world in terms of the

Sensorimotor stage (birth to about 2 years)
↓
Preoperational stage (2 years to about 7 years)
↓
Concrete operational stage (7 years to about 12 years)
↓
Formal operational stage (adolescence onwards)

Figure 2.1 Piaget's stages of cognitive development.

physical acts they can perform. At first such acts are inadvertent but they become increasingly intentional and coordinated. A common characteristic of babies in the sensorimotor stage is their lack of understanding of the permanence of objects. A 6-month-old baby, Piaget suggests, thinks that, if an object is removed, it ceases to exist. This first sensorimotor stage is followed by the preoperational period which marks the beginning of the means for representing the world symbolically, particularly in thought and language. However, this representational skill is limited to the child's own perspective. Piaget describes this behaviour as egocentric on the part of the child, not in the sense that it is selfish, but meaning that the child is simply unconscious of anything but his own needs. Thus, for Piaget, children under the age of 7 cannot 'de-centre' or see things from another person's point of view and cannot think about things from a perspective other than their own. This problem of centration is well illustrated by the 'three mountains task'. In this experiment, Piaget asked children to look at a model of three mountains and to identify what a doll, placed in a position different to themselves, would be able to see. Piaget found that children of 4 and 5 years often chose the view that they could see themselves, rather than that of the doll. As a result, he concluded that young children were egocentric and could not see something from the perspective of another person.

The two following stages, concrete operations and formal operations, are characterized by increasingly systematic, logical thinking, first as rooted in the present, and then later, and increasingly, in abstract, hypothetical terms, although Meadows (1993) suggests that the models given for both of these stages remain controversial.

In the years since Piaget first began to publish his work, many psychologists and educationalists have further developed, and modified, his ideas. They include both 'neo-Piagetians', and 'post-Piagetians'. Sutherland (1992) suggests that Case (1992) is a neo-Piagetian, who, like Piaget, rejects the idea of domain-specific structures, but who also suggests a greater role for adult intervention to support children's development. Karmiloff-Smith suggests a more modular approach, at least for specific subjects such as language and also places more emphasis on innate mechanisms than did Piaget (Wood 1998). The American High Scope programme is one well-known approach in early childhood which explicitly acknowledges the influence of Piaget on its development (Hohmann and Weikart 1995).

Critiques of Piaget

An early critic of Piaget's ideas was Susan Isaacs (see Chapter 6), who, working at the same time as Piaget, suggests a more positive view of young children, emphasizing what they can do rather than what they cannot, and concluding, as a result of her observations, that young children are capable of logical thought and of taking on the perspective of others. The majority of the critical reappraisal of Piaget's theories has occurred since the 1970s.

A fundamental basis on which Piaget's theories have been criticized is their suggested universality. This is seen as problematic in a number of ways. First, there is considerable scepticism about whether all development subscribes to a single pattern, across time and across cultures (Cohen 2002, MacNaughton 2003), a question which is considered in more depth in Chapter 3. Evidence across cultures suggests different rates of progress through any possible sequence, varying by culture, and amount and level of formality of schooling (Meadows 1993). Bidell and Fischer (1992) suggest that a model which suggests a singular developmental pathway may tend to disadvantage children who are not from the particular cultural group typified in the model. Gardner (1983), along with others, suggests that development is not even universal within an individual, and, as part of his theory of MIs (see later in the text) asserts that people have different levels of development in different domains, simultaneously. In recent years, we have also moved away from a view of learning as proceeding in any smooth, orderly direction, and the developmental ladder implied by Piaget's model has been replaced with a view of cognitive development as a much messier business, typified by a metaphor of a spider's web, or overlapping waves (Siegler 2000, see later in the text).

Related to these criticisms are others which point to Piaget's lack of acknowledgement of the parts played by social and emotional factors in children's development. Young children are born into a social world, which shapes their development in countless ways (Siegler *et al.* 2003). As we shall see, this is one of the most fundamental differences between Piaget's model and that of Vygotsky (1978).

Piaget emphasizes the importance of readiness in children's development, suggesting that there is little that an adult, or other person, can do to accelerate children's development. Cohen (2002) and Donaldson (1978) both suggest that, on the contrary, children can effectively be taught skills. Bidell and Fischer point to the difficulties for adults of waiting for just the 'right' moment before they 'pounce' in some way with a child who is deemed to be ready (1992:16). In this they echo Duckworth's dilemma: 'Either we're too early and they can't learn it, or we're too late and they know it already' (1987:31). They also highlight readiness as a potential issue for equity and social justice. Readiness, they suggest, may function well for the majority of white middle-class children, in whom mainstream literacy skills, for example, are presumed to develop as part of an unfolding process. Children whose cultural contexts support other kinds of skills may be disadvantaged while the adults working with them are waiting for them to become ready for literacy development. MacNaughton (2003) also points to issues around race, gender and culture and suggests that it may be problematic if adults view negative comments from children about these areas as something they will naturally develop out of without supportive interventions.

Donaldson (1978), while she acknowledges her indebtedness to Piaget and shares with him a belief in children as active and powerful thinkers, provides a range of evidence which suggests that children are much less egocentric thinkers, and are capable of disembedded or abstract thinking from a much younger age than Piaget himself believed. She and many others including Cohen (2002), Smith *et al.* (2003), Whitebread (2000a) and Wood (1998) suggest that as a result of his methods of gathering data Piaget may have underestimated children's competence. The problem, Donaldson (1978) suggests, is that Piaget's tests do not make human sense to children, and are couched in ways to which they cannot relate. Wood suggests that there are three possible main criticisms in this area:

1   Piaget may have underestimated the importance of the language used in his tasks;
2   children may have had difficulty in making sense of the questions being asked of them and the questioner's intended meaning;
3   the tasks set may be artificial ones, which children could not understand.

(Adapted from Wood 1998)

Looking at the first of these, Wood (1998) suggests that young children may not understand the adults' use of vocabulary sufficiently to allow them to understand the task, for example, use of an expression like 'as much as'. Wood asks: 'Do children actually *understand* these words and expressions in the way the adult intends?' (1998:60, emphasis in original). They may have similar confusion with regard to the questions put to them, as suggested in the second of Wood's points. Even where they comprehend the wording of the question, children may feel unsure of the questioner's intended meaning. For example, in Piaget's test situations, children were often asked a similar question at least twice, as part of the experimental procedure. In many contexts, this may be a signal that the first answer was wrong. Thus, children may find themselves working very hard trying to infer some alternative meaning to the question, when none is intended. Hughes and Grieve (1988) recount young children desperately trying to make sense of nonsense questions put to them (deliberately) by adults, assuming that there is some meaning to be gleaned. Donaldson (1978) demonstrates how even slight variation in the wording of a question can have a considerable impact on children's understanding of the question, and, as a result, their performance in a task.

The final point Wood makes may be the most important one for young children's understanding. Piaget's tests on children were carried out in experimental situations, disembedded from meaningful contexts, as in the three mountains test described earlier. Hughes (cited in Donaldson 1978) reframed this perspective-taking test, embedding it in a more familiar and meaningful context for children. In so doing, children aged $3\frac{1}{2}$ had a 90 per cent success rate, much earlier and better than Piaget would suggest. Kate, in Box 2.1, clearly shows this ability to both literally and figuratively take on another's perspective and to understand how they might feel, at an earlier age than Piaget would have suggested. The meaningful context of everyday life may have had some bearing on her success.

In contexts which make human sense to children, they have been shown to demonstrate aspects such as object conservation (Smith *et al.* 2003) and the ability to draw inferences (Thornton 2002) and learn by analogy (Whitebread 2000a) at much younger ages than Piaget suggests. Moreover, there is evidence to suggest that Piaget places unnecessary emphasis on logical thinking as a goal of development. Not only have young children demonstrated capability in logical thinking at an earlier age than expected by Piaget but a reasonable number of adults 'may not attain the holy grail of formal operations' (Cohen 2002:53). Good examples where adults make exactly the same kinds of errors as children are syllogistic and deductive reasoning, such as Whitebread illustrates:

> There are two kinds of aliens, Blobs and Blips.
> Blobs are blue.
> I meet an alien. It is blue.
> What kind of an alien is it?
> (Whitebread 2000a:146)

Whitebread points out that both adults and children will confidently say it is a Blob, because we have been told that Blobs are blue and thus infer that it must be a Blob, not a Blip. But a Blip could be blue as well; we just have not been told this.

Piaget has also been criticized on methodological grounds. He seldom reported quantitative information on numbers of children tested and percentages who passed, and his interview technique is difficult to replicate (Smith *et al.* 2003). He also based much of his study on his own children and those of other university professors, and it may be important to ask how representative such a sample is.

To conclude this section on Piaget and his critics, Box 2.2 illustrates the possibility of multiple interpretations of the same event, drawing particularly on the perspectives of both Piaget and Donaldson (1978).

Box 2.1 Kate, aged 4 years 5 months, in the nursery

Kate is 1 of 4 children seated at a table with their teacher, playing with playdough. Emma (3 years 3 months), new to the nursery, approaches the teacher, and points to the nearby easel.

EMMA: Me want do painting.

TEACHER: You would like to paint? Well, there's space at the easel, so that's fine. Remember that you'll need to wear an apron.

Emma walks past Kate, to where aprons are hanging, takes one from the hook and attempts to put it on. She experiences some difficulty. Kate gets out of her seat and walks towards Emma.

KATE: Do you want me to help you?

Emma holds out the apron and Kate takes it and holds it in a position that allows Emma to step into it.

KATE: Now this bit goes over your head. I know how to do it because I'm four. Do you know where to get the paper?

EMMA: Over there (pointing to paper store).

KATE: That's right. If you can't peg it up, I can help you.

Kate returns to her seat.

TEACHER: That was very kind of you to help Emma.

Kate smiles broadly: I'm four, so I can do lots of things now.

According to Piaget, at the age of four, Kate is right in the middle of the preoperational stage. Piaget argues that, because of a child's essential egocentricity, under the age of seven there is an inability to view a situation from another's perspective. Throughout the entire episode there are very clear examples of Kate's ability to see a perspective other than her own. She was in no way personally affected by any of Emma's actions, so her only motivation must have been desire to help. There is clear consideration of Emma's wishes, as she does not simply tell her what she is going to do, but rather enquires if she wants any help. It is also evident when she anticipates the possibility that Emma may have difficulty in pegging the paper to the easel. It would have been several months since she herself had experienced the same difficulty. Even if she can recall herself being in that situation, this is a clear indication of her capacity to decentre. She also shows that she is able to perceive Emma's physical perspective, by positioning the apron so that Emma is able to step into it.

Reproduced with permission of Yvonne Hutton

Some implications for practice of Piaget's theories

- 'The aim of education is to encourage the child to ask questions, try out experiments and speculate, rather than accept information unthinkingly' (Smith *et al.* 2003:413).
- Attention to children's different ways of thinking at different ages will need to be considered in making decisions about how they are best educated (Siegler *et al.* 2003). Children need to be 'ready' in order to learn.

- Learning is a process of active involvement: children learn by doing.
- Learning is an individual process of the construction of knowledge by the child, with the process being emphasized over product.
- Emphasis is on child-initiated activity, with the child setting the pace of learning, exploring the world and testing out ideas without external pressure.
- The most important source of motivation is the child, who is intrinsically motivated to engage in activities.
- The environment is organized to support open-ended self-discovery learning by children.
- The role of the adult is to observe and facilitate children's learning, rather than to engage in direct teaching:

> Piaget believed that educators should create the right environment for learning but then allow the child to problem solve and to learn through their own active discovery. The adult attends to the unfolding of these structures and provides social and physical environments that encourage a child's normal development.
>
> (MacNaughton 2003:44)

Box 2.2 Charlie, aged 3 years 8 months, at the writing table in the nursery

---

Charlie chooses a stapler to use:

ADULT: Oh Charlie, that stapler's empty, there's no staples in it.

Charlie chooses a piece of paper and puts it in the stapler's jaws.

ADULT: Charlie, there's no staples in that.

Charlie is staring hard at the stapler and the paper, using both hands and all his concentration. He works the stapler several times but nothing happens.

CHARLIE: Oh! John! There's no staples in it!

There is absolutely nothing wrong with Charlie's hearing, so what is the explanation for the above? Piaget might explain it in terms of egocentricity, an inability to decentre and see an immediate situation from another point of view. Donaldson's (1978) interpretation of this would be that Charlie has yet to develop the skill of focussing in on the shared meanings inherent in dialogue.

Reproduced with permission of John Griffiths

Information processing

As the name suggests, information processing models of cognitive development are concerned with the actual process of cognition and the impact of information on this process. They share with Piaget the view that perception, memory, knowledge and understanding are closely related, and change with development (Wood 1998). Unlike Piaget, they are not so concerned with stages of development.

The origins of information processing models lie in computer science and cognitive psychology, and it is easy to see how analogies with computers are used here to try to make sense of the development of thinking in humans. Thus, a common metaphor is that which compares the structural characteristics of cognition (aspects such as the three memory stores of sensory register, working memory and long-term memory, discussed in Chapter 1) to the 'hardware' of a computer and the processes (the specification of what processes should be carried out when for a particular task) as 'software'. One of the first models of information processing was formulated by Atkinson and Shiffrin (1968, cited in Smith *et al.* 2003). They describe cognitive processing in terms of the three memory stores and the control processes that operate between them. Short-term memory, in Atkinson and Shiffrin's model, is limited in its capacity to retain units of information. More recently, there has been greater emphasis on the idea of short-term memory as 'the conscious part of information processing, which is constrained by the number and the processes being carried out at the same time' (Smith *et al.* 2003:422). Some things we do may be relatively automatic, requiring little active thought and short-term processing. Other, less practised, activities, may make much greater demands on capacity. This emphasis on processing capacity has led to use of the term 'working memory' often instead of short-term memory, although as we noted in Chapter 1 Baddeley (cited in Cohen 2002) draws a distinction between the two.

Information then passes into long-term memory as a result of processes in short-term or working memory. The processes by which these memories are both transferred and retrieved are the fundamental elements of information processing theories. They include strategies such as planning, reasoning and the kinds of memory strategies touched on in Chapter 1. These are looked at in more detail later in the chapter. Before doing so, however, it is useful to set the scene by briefly summarizing some of the assumptions basic to the variety of information processing models.

Common assumptions of information processing models

All information processing models share some basic assumptions:

*   thinking is information processing – rather than focusing on stages of development, the emphasis is on the information that children represent, the processes they apply to the information, and the memory limits that constrain the amount of information they can represent and process;
*   the precise analysis of change mechanisms is emphasized – in particular, what are the change mechanisms that contribute most to development, and how do they work together to produce cognitive growth?;
*   change is produced by a process of continuous self-modification – the outcomes generated by the child's own activities change the way the child will think in the future, in particular, the strategies that children devise to surmount the challenges posed by the environment and by their own limited processing capacity and knowledge.

(Adapted from Siegler 1998:64)

Thus, as Meadows (1993:212) suggests, there is an emphasis on cognition as 'largely a matter of handling information in order to solve problems', with a focus on what mental processes are used to deal with information, how they are organized and how they change during learning or development.

Memory

Memory has a central role in information processing theories. In Chapter 1, a number of memory strategies were described. These, chiefly, involve encoding and recall. Smith *et al.* (2003) suggest that use of encoding strategies such as rehearsal (mentally repeating information to yourself in order to remember it) and organization (grouping information together) become increasingly sophisticated as children get older. A third encoding strategy, elaboration, concerns the ways in which we make associations between items in order to help recall them better. Smith *et al.* (2003) note an interesting difference between the ways in which children used this strategy, drawing on the work of Buckhalt, Mahoney and Paris (cited in Smith *et al.* 2003). Younger children tended to use 'static' elaborations, like 'the lady has a broom', whereas older children's elaborations tended to be more 'active', such as 'the lady flew on her broom to Hallowe'en' (Smith *et al.* 2003:435). They speculate that the benefit of this may be the creation of more memorable images. Whereas children younger than about 5 years seem not to spontaneously use strategies for recall (Thornton 2002) there is evidence that they can be helped to do so (Kuhn 2000) and that enhanced knowledge will be an important factor in the growth of strategy use (Smith *et al.* 2003).

Processing information: can we get better at it? Do we get better at it?

In information processing terms, the three memory stores outlined earlier provide a structure for memory, with a range of processes and strategies operating on the information in those stores. The problem is that both adults and children alike are limited in their capacity to handle information, certainly when it is in a random or unstructured form. Information theorists describe this as having 'limited and relatively fixed channel capacity' (Wood 1998:34). For example, the largest number of random items that adults can usually hold in working memory is about seven (Meadows 1993). If presented with, say, a string of random digits, most adults can usually transmit correct information on about seven before they start making errors and forgetting. However, information processing theorists suggest that with training and experience our accuracy and skill increases considerably. It is suggested that this is because we are able to organize our memory and to impose structures on our knowledge. Meadows (1993) gives the example of a student who, after daily practice for a year, was able to remember strings of 75 digits. This student did so by organizing the information into 'chunks' which had some meaning for him – for example, encoding '3492' into a race time of 3 minutes 49.2 seconds. This had meaning for him as he was an experienced cross-country runner. Thus, information processing theorists suggest that the development of thinking is related to our ability to impose meaningful structures on the information we receive and the ways in which we move that information within our memory systems.

This seems to suggest that the answer to the first part of the question above is yes, we can get better at processing information. What of the second part? Do we also, over time, get better as part of maturation? Do young children have even less channel capacity than older children and adults? Taking the example of the random string of digits, Wood (1988) records that 3-year-olds begin to falter after 3 items, and 5-year-olds after 5. It is not until about the age of 8 that mature levels of performance, that is, remembering about seven items, is achieved. He suggests that, because young children are relatively inexperienced, there are bound to be differences between adults and children in their competence in processing information. In essence, children do not have the same amount of experience and the same levels of expertise to draw upon which might help them to organize and structure their thinking in the ways that adults do. This idea of expertise may be important, and we shall return to it at several points throughout the book. Wood (1998) suggests that the benefit of using a word like expertise is that it combines both knowledge and action and draws attention to them both as two parts of the same process.

Does this combination of action and knowledge, as expertise, have an impact on other aspects of information processing? Siegler *et al.* (2003) suggest that a basic assumption of information processing is that young children are problem-solvers. Problem-solving, and ways in which it may be supported are discussed in Chapter 10. Here, it is worth looking at two key cognitive processes identified by Siegler *et al.* (2003) which link problem-solving and information processing.

Planning, reasoning and expertise

Among the mental processes that information processing theories suggest as important are ones concerned with planning and reasoning. Children begin to make simple plans before they are a year old (Karmiloff-Smith 1994), a process which requires them to be able to think ahead, and to organize and order their actions, on the basis of the available information. As they grow older, their plans become more elaborate and complex, enabling them to solve more of the problems they encounter (how to get to the biscuit tin, how to climb out of your cot, how to put your shoe on). However, despite the benefits of planning, many children fail to do so in situations where it would be helpful (Siegler *et al.* 2003). Why should this be? Siegler *et al.* (2003) suggest that analysis of the information processing requirements of planning shows that it involves making a sacrifice of immediate attempts to solve the problem in favour of trying to think through which

Box 2.3 Children aged between 3 years 1 month and 3 years 11 months, playing on a chalk-drawn road circuit in the outdoor area of the nursery

Five children have been engaged in road play, with bikes and scooters, for some time. Two sets of zebra crossing markings are drawn across the road and the word STOP is written on both sides of the crossing. The children drive round the circuit, and abide by the road markings. Those on bikes and scooters stop when they see two children standing at the crossing.

TOM TO ALL: We can see your bikes coming so we can go (chants, and uses exaggerated actions). Look left and right and left again.

The driving and safe crossing of the road continues, with all the children joining in the chanting of 'look left and right and left again'.

Tom extends his learning and helps the children to remember a three term sequence 'chunking' for safely crossing the road by chanting, which all of the children spontaneously adopt. According to Meadows (1993) the strategy of using verbal rehearsal helps to keep sensory information in the short term working memory long enough to be transferred permanently to long term memory.

Reproduced with permission of Meg Roberts

particular strategy might be most effective. Young children often fail to do this for a number of reasons. First, they find it difficult to resist the desire to act immediately. Second, they tend to be overoptimistic about what they can achieve without planning, whereas older children are more realistic about assessing what they can do. Finally, the fact that the plans they make often fail (they still can't get to the biscuit tin) contributes to making planning seem less attractive as an option. Siegler *et al.* (2003) suggest that a combination of brain maturation, along with experiences that demonstrate the value of planning to children, serve to increase the frequency and quality of planning. However, it is knowledge and expertise which are key here, not age. Given appropriate information, younger children can make use of planning strategies as successfully as older children and adults (Thornton 2002). In addition, adults may often not use planning strategies where they would be useful (Siegler *et al.* 2003).

The ability to use reasoning, particularly the kind of analogical reasoning which helps us to understand new situations and problems in relation to familiar ones, also appears by the time children are about a year old. Initially, and for much of early childhood, children's use of analogical reasoning will depend on how closely the two situations resemble one another. Again, as with planning, expertise is key to helping children to progressively see deeper, less superficial similarities between situations and problems, which support the making of analogies between them (Siegler *et al.* 2003).

Neural networks and overlapping waves

At the beginning of this section I emphasized the plurality of approaches which come under the heading of 'information processing'. Two of the best known, which are worth looking at briefly, are the neural network approach and the overlapping waves model.

Traditional information processing approaches emphasize the sequential nature of processing where thoughts follow one after the other. The neural network or connectionist approach, on the other hand, emphasizes a model of processing in which different types of cognitive activity occur simultaneously, in parallel. In this model, information is not stored in any one place but exists as a result of stimulation and inhibition: 'thus instead of there being a slot in memory in which information about Piaget is stored, the system has information about Piaget only when particular sets of units are active and stimulating or inhibiting each other in particular connection patterns' (Meadows 1993:234). *Siegler et al.* (2003) suggest that the neural network approach may be valuable as a good model for how thinking is achieved in the brain. In addition, while conventional information processing models work well for activities where conscious and strategic effort are required (playing chess, solving a mathematical puzzle or assembling a construction model), connectionist approaches provide a better account for activities performed without such strategic or conscious effort, such as recognizing something in the environment (Meadows 1993).

The overlapping waves model of information processing, developed by Siegler (1998, 2000) suggests that thinking is much more variable than both Piaget's theory and traditional information processing models imply (Siegler *et al.* 2003). Three premises underpin Siegler's theory. First, that children typically use a variety of ways of thinking, not just one, in tackling an activity or a problem; second, that these diverse strategies and approaches coexist over long periods of time and third, that experience results in changes in children's reliance on current strategies as well as introduction of new, more advanced strategies (Siegler 2000). The model suggests that, at any given time, children may use a number of different strategies for tackling the same activity. Over time, as a result of learning from both successes and failures, they gradually come to rely more upon those that prove most successful for them (Siegler 2000). Thornton (2002) suggests that the overlapping waves model may be particularly helpful in thinking about children's approaches to problem-solving.

Some implications for practice from information processing models

- Children are seen as active learners and problem-solvers.
- Both adults and children share the same ways of reasoning, but 'what children can think about changes with age as the capacity to construct increasingly complex mental models develops' (Wood 1998:200).
- The emphasis on task analysis in information processing accounts can be used by adults as a diagnostic tool for identifying and supporting individual children's needs (Siegler *et al.* 2003).
- 'Asking children to explain both why correct answers are correct and why incorrect answers are incorrect produces greater learning than only asking them to explain why correct answers are correct' (Siegler 2000:33) and can lead to the adoption of new strategies.
- Children can be helped to develop useful memory strategies, with a positive impact on their cognitive activity.
- Children's developing knowledge and expertise supports their use of strategies for planning and reasoning.

Lev Vygotsky

Born in Russia, in 1896, the same year as Piaget, Vygotsky's work was little known either inside or outside the country until the 1960s. The first translation of *Thought and Language*, with an introduction by Jerome Bruner (see later in the chapter) appeared in the West in 1961, and it was not until 1978 that *Mind in Society*, a collection of essays, was published. Like Piaget, it is important to look at Vygotsky within the contexts of time and place. A brilliant scholar, he was invited to join the Institute of Psychology in Moscow in 1924. Along with other psychologists in post-revolutionary Russia at that time, he saw human beings as inherently social animals, who could only be understood in the context of their society. His ideas were, however, not well received under Stalin, and much of his work was either suppressed or hidden by his colleagues. It was not until the 1950s that, even in Russia, his work began to be more widely available.

Vygotsky died of tuberculosis in 1934, and in the last years of his life worked intensively, producing fragments of writing, half-completed experiments and essays, not all of which are even now in the public domain. His early death, coupled with the fact that the vast majority of us are reading his work in translation means that we cannot know how he might have developed his ideas. However, his influence has been widespread, and is felt across the world. His ideas underpin those of the sociocultural theorists looked at in Chapter 3 as well as Bruner (see later in the chapter).

Vygotsky differs fundamentally from both Piaget and the majority of approaches in the information processing models looked at earlier in his emphasis on the social nature of learning. Like Piaget, he views children as actively constructing their understanding as a result of their experiences and in that sense his ideas can be described as constructivist. However, crucially, for Vygotsky, this construction occurs in the context of children's interactions with those around them. As a result, Vyogtsky's position is often described as social constructivist. As we saw in Chapter 1, Vygotsky and Piaget differ in their views on the relationship of learning to development. In Chapter 7 the area over which they fundamentally disagree, that of the relationship between language and thought, is explored.

Social constructivism

Whereas Piaget emphasizes the role of individual discovery in development, Vygotsky places instruction at the heart of learning and he argues that the capacity to learn through instruction is an essential feature of intelligence (Wood 1998). For Vygotsky, however, the relationship between instruction and internal learning is highly complex, and this is not a simple transmission model of 'teaching' whereby an adult instructs and a child listens. Instead it is a term which covers a wide range of strategies, including demonstration and discussion. The vehicles for this instruction are principally language and communication. In this, he has more in common with the ideas of Jerome Bruner, and Bruner was one of the people responsible for making Vygotsky's work more widely known in the West.

Thus, for Vygotsky, the social context in which learning takes place is as important as any specific activity the child undertakes: 'a child becomes himself through others' (Sutherland 1992:46). This is well illustrated in Box 2.4. Such a view highlights the different

Box 2.4 Daniel, aged 1 year 10 months, in his pushchair

Daniel was sitting strapped in his pushchair holding a small toy car in each hand. He gently attempted to balance each car on the flat metal frame at the end of his eat. Both cars tumbled to the ground. He reached for them but because his safety straps restrained him he could not retrieve them. His childminder, seeing his predicament, picked up and returned the cars to him. This happened several times, and, with Daniel's persistence, both cars eventually balanced. Carefully, so as not to jog the buggy, he arched his head forward and tilted it sideways so that he was looking towards the underside of the car on his left. He then turned and in the same way looked at the underside of the car on his right. A smile broke out on his face as he shook his legs and watched both cars fall to the ground. His smile widened and he looked to his childminder. She returned his smile.

Throughout the observation Daniel is supported by the actions of his carer. I believe she supported his play by returning his cars and by reciprocating a smile. These seemingly insignificant acts are of great importance to social constructivist theory. Vygotsky suggests that 'object orientated movement (Daniel reaching for his cars) becomes movement aimed at another person; a means of establishing relations' (1978:56). The fundamental proposition of social constructivist theory is that the child's potential for learning is primarily fostered by social interactions, language eventually being the key. In the early pre-language years it is the parent/carer's sensitive responses to the child that get internalized. Without the interaction of his carer I believe Daniel would not have had this opportunity to develop a reciprocal and trusting relationship within a cultural context.

Reproduced with permission of Jo Dabir-Alai

starting points of Piaget and Vygotsky. While both were interested in trying to reconcile psychology and biology in outlining cognition and development (Gopnik *et al.* 1999), Piaget, as we have seen, starts from a biological model of development. Vygotsky's 'primary concern lay in understanding the nature, evolution and transmission of human culture' (Wood 1998:11) where 'culture' is used to mean the customs of a particular people at a particular time and their collective achievements over historical time. This is where language and communication are so important for Vygotsky: language is both the medium through which culture can be transmitted, and it is also a tool of thought.

What are the processes by which this happens? For Vygotsky, learning is the key to development. He reverses Piaget's idea that development leads learning, and suggests instead that it is learning which fuels development. In Vygotsky's model we first come into contact with knowledge and ideas through experience of how others make sense of things in our interactions with them. He calls this the interpersonal plane. We gradually come to make this knowledge our own on the intrapersonal plane. (These two are also sometimes referred to as the intermental and intramental planes.) In the process, the knowledge practices and psychological tools of a culture are passed on to children. The idea of cultural tools is an important part of understanding Vygotsky's thinking. Interacting with cultural (or psychological) tools of all kinds (ranging from physical objects to representational devices such as books and maps, mnemonic devices, and ways of knowing about the world such as science and maths) helps children to better understand the social and physical world. Children's encounters with all of these cultural tools shape the ways in which they think about things. Language is one of the most important tools, allowing high level cognitive functioning. Meadows describes the role of tools in the following way:

> Individuals 'appropriate' psychological tools from their social and cultural milieu. They do not inherit them as instincts or reflexes, they do not normally reinvent them from scratch, they do not discover them in their independent interactions with the natural world. In particular they learn to use tools through their face to face communication and social interaction with other people who are also using psychological tools. Thus the tools have communication among their functions.
>
> (Meadows 1993:245)

The process as a whole is referred to as internalization. Trevarthen's (1995) work with babies suggests that this process begins from the very earliest moments of life. Vygotsky describes internalization as 'a series of transformations' (1978:56) between external social processes and internal psychological ones:

1   'An operation that initially represents an external activity is reconstructed and begins to occur internally': this involves assistance from more capable others, either adult or peer.
2   'An interpersonal process is transformed into an intrapersonal one': the child now provides his own assistance, through talking aloud, or through inner speech.
3   'The transformation of an interpersonal process into an intrapersonal one is the result of a long series of developmental events': internalization of knowledge, ideas and concepts is a prolonged developmental process.

(Adapted from Vygotsky 1978:56–7)

Internalization supports the development of 'higher mental processes' (Vygotsky 1978:57) and leads to more complex understanding through increased control of external, cultural processes. Although this may ultimately be for the better, initially it may seem to result in change for the worse: 'The small girl trying hard to learn to be "a ballerina" may move more awkwardly in her ballet class than she does normally' (Meadows 1993:241).

Vygotsky (1978) suggests that for young children play, particularly role-play, is a leading factor in development and a means of developing abstract thought. By providing children with opportunities to try out culturally defined roles, using culturally defined artefacts such as toys, play 'acts as a kind of mental support system which allows children to represent their everyday social reality' (Penn 2005:42). Vygotsky suggests that making one thing stand for another in play, for example, a stick for a horse, creates a 'pivot' (Vygotsky 1978) which detaches meaning from the real object. Increasingly, these representations become more symbolic, supporting the development of more abstract, symbolic ways of thinking. He suggests that imaginative play supports children in thinking in more mature ways than they are able to do outside of play, an idea expressed in his assertion that 'In play a child always behaves beyond his average age, above his daily behavior; [sic] in play it is as though he were a head taller than himself' (1978:102). In support of this idea, Moyles (1989) points to research which suggests that children engaged in fantasy play produce more varied and imaginative uses for objects than children who do not have such opportunities.

The zone of proximal development

The concept of Vygotsky's which has had the most circulation, particularly in relation to educational practice, is the idea of the zone of proximal development or ZPD. This concept refers to the 'gap' that exists for any individual between what he can achieve alone (his level of actual development) and what he can do with the help of another more knowledgeable or skilled person (his level of potential development). The role of this more experienced other person is to guide a child to a more sophisticated solution to a task in order to support the move from regulation by others to self-regulation. This is very clearly a radically different position to that taken by Piaget, for whom such adult intervention represents the teaching of empty procedures to children. Vygotsky defines the ZPD in the following way:

> It is the distance between the actual developmental level as determined by independent problem solving and the level of potential development as determined through problem solving under adult guidance or in collaboration with more capable peers...The zone of proximal development defines those functions that have not yet matured but are in the process of maturation, functions that will mature tomorrow but are currently in an embryonic state...What a child can do with assistance today she will be able to do by herself tomorrow.
>
> (Vygotsky 1978:86–7)

This ZPD is not fixed, and will vary both over time, in different areas of experience, and from child to child. Thus, for Vygotsky, two children with similar levels of actual development may have very different zones of proximal development, that is, very different potentials for learning through appropriate instruction. The principal vehicle for actualizing the ZPD is verbal exchange, including mechanisms such as open-ended questioning and the provision of useful prompts, but demonstration, emotional and non-verbal exchanges (Chak 2001), and joint problem-solving (Wood and Attfield 2005) are also valuable. Siraj-Blatchford et al. (2002) feature examples of sustained shared thinking in activities where adults and children are mutually involved. Vygotsky (1978) suggests that play is particularly important as a source of development, and for creating a ZPD, in the early years.

Vygotsky's emphasis on the role of a 'more capable' (1978:87) other person emphasizes that this support, or 'scaffolding' (see below) can come from children, as well as adults, as in the example in Box 2.5. What is needed is more knowledge or skill in the particular domain. Thornton (2002) suggests that even quite young children can modify their talk and behaviour in order to support a younger or less experienced child but that the ability to do so develops over time. Parents may do this quite naturally (Cohen 2002, Siegler *et al.* 2003) in the course of everyday conversation and interactions at home (Tizard and Hughes 2002, Wells 1987). For Vygotsky, this co-operatively achieved success is at the heart of learning, supporting the development of reflection and self-regulation. He suggests that children need to learn in order to be motivated (in contrast to the often held view that motivation is a precondition of learning), and that the creation of a leading edge of development, through the ZPD, helps in this process of supporting motivation.

The influence of Vygotsky's theories continues to be strongly felt in recent years more than ever (Wood 1998). Bruner, and others such as Wells (1987) and Wood and Wood (1996) have further developed the idea of the ZPD, and, as we see in Chapter 3, his ideas are

Box 2.5 A group of children aged between 3 years 9 months and 4 years 4 months, in the nursery

The previous day the children were spinning saucepan lids on the floor in the home area. In order to follow this interest, a range of spinning artefacts have been planned for. The children have been playing for some time.

CARL: (using a push down/pull up spinning top) Look I pushed it.

He glances at Amber, who has spent some time attempting to use a dynamo powered spinning top. He takes the toy and speaks to her:

CARL: I'll show you.

Amber allows Carl to demonstrate the workings of the toy, watching his actions closely. After a short while Carl returns the toy, and says to her:

CARL: See, like that.

Amber restarts her attempts at making the toy work. Eventually she manages to make the connection and the top spins for a short time on the table. She looks up at Carl and says to him:

AMBER: See, I doin'it like dis.

When Carl uses eye gaze (Pellicano and Rhodes 2003) to 'observe' Amber it could be suggested that he was aware of her zone of proximal development, which would imply that Carl displayed second-order intentionality (Bailey 2002). Therefore, it could be argued that Carl was able to use this understanding to scaffold Amber's thinking and understanding.

Reproduced with permission of Lynn Bartlett

fundamental to the thinking of sociocultural theorists such as Rogoff (1990, 2003). Rinaldi, commenting on practice in Reggio Emilia explicitly acknowledges the influence of Vygotsky on their practitioners' thinking, when she says: 'It is our belief that all knowledge emerges in the process of self and social construction' (1998:115).

Critiques of Vygotsky's theories

An inevitable difficulty in interpreting and analysing Vygotsky's work arises as a result of his early death. In his desire to record as much of his thinking as possible, much is only in out-line, and incomplete, with 'brilliant sketches' (Cohen 2002:59) rather than fully developed research. Wood (1998) suggests that his work is often speculative and self-contradictory. In addition, Cohen (2002) suggests that, methodologically, his studies would not nowadays be seen as models of good empirical practice. In his defence, Cole and Scribner (1978), writing in the Introduction to *Mind in Society*, emphasize both the implications of his early death, and the fact that many of the studies were pilots, never, they believe, intended for publication. They also caution against judging the experimental approaches of one culture by those of another – a fitting comment in the context of Vygotsky's emphasis on the role of culture in development.

Smith *et al.* (2003) suggest that there may be some drawbacks to Vygotsky's view of learning as situated in social context, pointing out that not all contexts are necessarily con-ducive to learning and that some may even inhibit it. In relation to the ZPD, Chak (2001) suggests that it serves more as a metaphor, and may be difficult to operationalize, particu-larly in the context of nurseries and schools, where one-to-one support and intervention is less likely than at home, for most children. Even where adults are able to do so, questions arise about how and when to intervene in order to provide appropriate scaffolding. MacNaughton and Williams suggest that settings in Reggio Emilia, while committed to working with Vygotsky's ideas, have also modified them in light of experience. They point to an important dilemma: 'The idea that an adult can help a child gain competence when the child is not yet competent is seen as problematic and the idea that there is just the right moment to offer help is also seen as problematic' (2004:366).

Some implications for practice of Vygotsky's theories

- Learning is seen as a social process, and collaborative learning with others is prioritized.
- 'Children's learning is maximised when they are regularly working at the upper levels of their competence' (MacNaughton and Williams 2004:335).
- Instruction is an essential part of learning.
- Imaginative play is important in building young children's intellectual and social competencies (MacNaughton and Williams 2004).
- Language is important both as a way in which children develop their thinking and understanding and as a means for sharing thoughts and understandings with others.
- Practitioners form a community of learners with children and parents (MacNaughton and Williams 2004).
- The role of the adult is interventionist, to extend and challenge children to go beyond where they would otherwise have been (Sutherland 1992).
- Adult support is contingent upon children's behaviour: more help is given when children experience difficulty, with this being gradually withdrawn as children succeed in an

activity (Wood and Wood 1996). In the early stages the help provided is more elaborate and explicit; later it is less explicit and less frequent, focusing on hints rather than instructions (Meadows 1993).

- Continuous assessment of children's levels within the ZPD, using verbal and non-verbal cues as indicators, is important, as levels are constantly changing (Chak 2001).
- Children can learn from each other as well as from adults, provided that one is more knowledgeable about the activity than the other. The gap between their understandings need not be great, however, as then the 'expert' is more likely to understand the problems the 'novice' faces (Smith *et al.* 2003).
- 'The environment needs to be richly stimulating with problems to solve and a wide range of individual, small group, and whole group opportunities' (Raban *et al.* 2003:72).
- The resources (physical tools) which children use in their play are important supports for their intellectual development (Broadhead 2004).

Jerome Bruner

Jerome Bruner was, as we have already noted, influential in promoting Vygotsky's ideas in the West. In many ways he sits between Piaget and Vygotsky in his ideas on children's development. Like Piaget, he emphasizes action and problem-solving in children's learning, but, like Vygotsky, he stresses the importance of social interaction, language and instruction in the development of thinking. Wood (1998) suggests that Bruner's thinking owes much to information processing theory. He also suggests that Bruner's early work involving the study of adult reasoning had an important impact on his ideas about the development of thinking in young children, emphasizing culture and growth as central factors. Bruner, like both Piaget and Vygotsky, sees play as an important aspect of young children's development. For Bruner 'play provides an excellent opportunity to try combinations of behaviour that would, under functional pressure, never be tried' (Bruner cited in MacNaughton 2003:43). It serves, in his view, both as practice in mastering skills, and as a way of trying out novel ways of thinking and acting in a safe context.

The main focus of disagreement between Piaget and Bruner is over the former's theory of stages of development. Piaget sets out a stage theory based on a gradual move towards more abstract forms of thought. Bruner argues that logical thinking is not the ultimate destination, rather it is one of several special ways of thinking. He is particularly concerned to look at the ways in which young children represent their experiences and their growing understanding of the world. He suggests (1966) three categories of such representation:

- enactive representation: when children represent through their actions;
- iconic representation: when children represent through looking at or making pictures or images of things;
- symbolic representation: when children use symbolic systems such as written language or mathematical symbols to represent their thinking.

These three categories embody an idea of a developing abstraction: clearly, symbolic representation, the ability to represent your thinking in ways which have no perceptual resemblance to the actual event, is a more abstract way of thinking than enacting an event. However, Bruner, unlike Piaget, believes that all three ways of representing are available to young children at any one time, with the adult's role, in scaffolding this process, being vital.

In Bruner's view, children return time and again to ideas and concepts, representing them in these different ways and deepening their understanding as a result. He characterizes this as a spiral curriculum (Bruner 1960) in which learning is both recursive, that is, repeated in different contexts, and incremental, embodying developing expertise. Children themselves do this without support, for example, the uses to which a baby might put building bricks would be different to the way that same child might use them at the age of 2 or 5. However, Bruner suggests that this principle can also be used by adults to support the development of children's thinking and understanding, as exemplified by his assertion that 'any subject can be taught in some intellectually honest form to any child at any stage of development' (Bruner 1960:33).

Scaffolding

The idea of Bruner's which has received most attention is the metaphor of scaffolding, a term coined in 1976 by Wood, Bruner and Ross to describe the kinds of support children need in order to reach their ZPD. The idea of scaffolding has been progressively elaborated and developed since then, and is particularly important to the sociocultural theories outlined in Chapter 3, although Rogoff (1990, 2003) favours the term 'guided participation' as a more inclusive concept than scaffolding.

For Bruner, scaffolding provides the solution to the 'puzzle' of Vygotsky's statement about the ZPD that 'the only "good" learning is that which is in advance of development' (Vygotsky 1978:89). As Bruner asks: 'how could "good learning" be that which is in advance of development and, as it were, bound initially to be unconscious since unmastered?' (Bruner 1988:89). He outlines his understanding of this seemingly contradictory idea:

> the tutor or the aiding peer serves the learner as a vicarious form of consciousness until such a time as the learner is able to master his own actions through his own consciousness and control. When the child achieves that conscious control over a new function or conceptual system, it is then that he is able to use it as a tool. Up to that point, the tutor in effect performs the critical function of 'scaffolding' the learning task to make it possible for the child, in Vygotsky's word, to internalise external knowledge and convert it into a tool for conscious control.
>
> (Bruner 1988:89)

What are the crucial features of this process of scaffolding, and how do adults provide support for children? Their first task is to engage the child's interest and encourage their involvement. Meadows neatly outlines the adult's role during the activity, once the child is engaged, which she suggests includes the need to:

> highlight critical features and information, buffer the learner's attention against distractions, channel the learner's activities so that there is freedom to succeed and not too much freedom to go wrong. Errors are turned into opportunities to learn, procedures are commented on and explained, efforts are praised, and responsibility for doing the task is gradually transferred to the learner, contingent on his or her having demonstrated an ability to succeed.
>
> (Meadows 1993:314)

Wood (1998) suggests that, within this general set of practices, some strategies may be more useful than others. Less likely to be successful is the strategy of first showing the child what to do before allowing them to have a go. This may lead both to overloading the child's powers of concentration, and to complaints that they are not able to take a turn themselves. Equally, over-reliance on verbal instructions as a strategy may also be problematic, as children may not understand them without first being shown the action in practice.

The most effective help may involve what has been termed contingent instruction (Wood and Wood 1996) because it involves changes in the levels of support and control by the adult, depending on the adult's assessment of the child's performance. This features two main ingredients. The first concerns circumstances where a child is in difficulty. Here, the adult immediately offers more specific help or instruction than previously, clarifying ideas, providing fuller explanation and demonstrating actions. The second ingredient is 'fading' or ensuring the minimal help needed to ensure success. For example, where initially a child had needed to be shown what to do, the adult will replace this with verbal hints, then with silence. Put succinctly: 'give more help when the learner gets into difficulty, and offer less help as they gain proficiency' (Wood and Wood 1996:7).

What remains unclear is the precise nature of what gets internalized during the course of such interactions. In addition, Chak (2001) questions whether, within the restrictions of scaffolding, children's creativity in identifying their own goals and in using their own strategies for reaching that goal may perhaps be hindered.

Some implications for practice of Bruner's ideas

It is useful to look back at the implications suggested for Vygotsky, as a number of these, in particular those on the role of instruction and adult support and intervention, are also appropriate here. In addition:

- High-quality scaffolding involves joint problem-solving, intersubjectivity (shared understanding of each others' thoughts and feelings between adult and child or between child and child), warmth and responsiveness, keeping the child in the ZPD and the promotion of self-regulation (children's control of their own learning) (MacNaughton and Williams 2004).
- In scaffolding children's understanding adults need to decide on the focus of what support is to be offered, how specific that help should be and the timing of any intervention (Wood and Wood 1996).

Modularity and Howard Gardner

A number of theorists propose that the mind is organized as a collection of mental modules or organs, each pre-structured for processing different kinds of input, for example perception or language (Chomsky 1957 and Chapter 7, this book). For Pinker, the rationale for such a view is that 'the mind has to be built out of specialized parts because it has to solve specialized problems' (1997:30). Some advocates of modularity suggest that every domain of knowledge is processed by a separate module. Of these, one of the best known whose work has had an impact on early childhood thinking is Howard Gardner.

Howard Gardner and multiple intelligences

Gardner suggests that 'the mind is organized into relatively independent realms of functioning' (1993:120). He believes that those who suggest a single form of intelligence look increasingly isolated, particularly in light of recent developments in understanding about the physiological make-up of the brain (see Chapter 4) (1998, 1999). In his view, we all possess a number of intelligences (multiple intelligences or MIs), and in every individual the relative strengths of each combine to give a unique overall profile of intelligences (1998).

Gardner defines intelligence as 'the ability to solve problems, or to fashion products, that are valued in one or more cultural or community settings' (1993:7), a definition that has elements in common with the ideas of both Piaget and Vygotsky. Concerned about what he saw as a narrow conception of intelligence, generally centred on linguistic and logico-mathematical understanding, Gardner originally identified 7 intelligences or types of thinking in 1983:

1   linguistic – relating to language and words;
2   logical–mathematical – abstractions and numbers;
3   musical – rhythm and sound;
4   spatial – patterning and imagery, knowing the environment;
5   bodily-kinesthetic – physical skills, reflexes and timing;
6   interpersonal – sensitivity to others' emotions and mental states;
7   intrapersonal – self-knowledge and inner-focusing.

In 1995 he added a further one:

8   Naturalist – categorization of natural objects.

He has since suggested the existence of a further 'half', which he calls existential intelligence, or 'the proclivity to pose (and ponder) questions about life, death and ultimate realities' (1999:72). Much conventional practice, Gardner suggests, focuses on a few of these forms of thinking, often at the expense of the development of the others.

In practice, just about every possible aspect of human activity may involve a blend of Gardner's different intelligences. A child digging in the garden will draw upon naturalist intelligence, as well as using physical intelligence to dig, spatial intelligence to understand the environment, interpersonal intelligence to negotiate a space alongside others, linguistic intelligence to talk about what is happening and existential intelligence in her awe and wonder about the natural world!

For Gardner, one important implication of his ideas is that, in practice, one of these intelligences will probably act as an entry point to engage others and that strength in one area may facilitate performance in another (1993). He describes what this looks like, drawing on examples from pre-school classrooms in the United States using a MI approach:

> A child who exhibited outstanding ability in story-telling, yet remained motionless in the creative movement sessions, moved with uncharacteristic expressiveness when storyboard props were used as a catalyst in one of the exercises. She also transformed tasks in visual arts, social analysis and mathematics into occasions for further storytelling. Her drawings often served to illustrate accompanying narratives. Her mother reported that she often made puppets and dolls at home, modelling them on characters from the books she was 'reading'. She also used the classroom model as a reality-based storyboard, creating vignettes with the figures of her classmates.
>
> (Howard Gardner 1993:95–6)

Gardner (1999) suggests that the MIs perspective can enhance children's understanding in three important ways: first, as a result of the ways in which MIs provide powerful entry points to a topic; second, by offering analogies that help connect the new to the better known and understood and third by providing multiple representations of the core ideas of a topic. He believes that these three elements imply a distinct order for adults working with children. First, begin with entry points, then offer analogies and finally converge on multiple representations of the same idea. In interview he describes their importance as follows:

> 'Multiple intelligences' do not just provide various entry points to a topic; they offer the opportunity to draw comparisons or analogies from many different domains and to capture the key ideas of a topic in a number of different symbol systems (for example, ordinary language, poetry, static graphs, dynamic flow charts, and so on).
>
> (Gardner in Scherer 1999:14)

Gardner stresses that his approach is supported by empirical evidence and the rigorous application of a set of criteria for the inclusion of each intelligence. These criteria are drawn from psychology, anthropology, biological sciences, cultural studies and case studies of learners. Briefly, they are:

- the potential isolation of the area by brain damage;
- the existence in it of prodigies, savants and other exceptional individuals;
- an identifiable core operation or set of operations;
- a distinctive developmental history within an individual, along with a definable nature of expert performance;
- an evolutionary history and evolutionary plausibility;
- support from tests in experimental psychology;
- support from psychometric findings;
- susceptibility to encoding in a symbol system.

(Adapted from Gardner 1983)

Gardner's ideas have been influential worldwide, spawning MI programmes, schools, tests, and even board games (Gold 2002). He maintains that this was never his intention, and that, ultimately, he developed his theories as a psychologist for other psychologists. There are, however, a number of ways in which his ideas link directly with others in early childhood. The emphasis on children's opportunities to represent their ideas in a wide range of different symbol systems– spoken and written language of all kinds, dynamically, enactively, graphically – links with the work of Chris Athey discussed in Chapters 6 and 9. In recent years he has worked closely with settings in Reggio Emilia, including on the *Making Thinking Visible* project (Project Zero and Reggio Children 2001), which is looked at in more detail in Chapters 6 and 9.

Critiques of Gardner's ideas

White (2002) provides the most trenchant criticism of Gardner's ideas, asserting that Gardner's criteria for selection, listed earlier, are open to serious criticism. Fundamentally, he suggests that Gardner provides no justification for the particular criteria he includes and asserts that at least two depend not on empirical evidence, as Gardner stresses, but on 'psychological or philosophical theories whose credentials rest on shaky foundations' (2002:94).

In addition, he questions whether all, or only a number, of the criteria must be fulfilled, saying that Gardner himself has provided contradictory commentary on this point.

Gardner acknowledges that some of his ideas have proved controversial, for example, the use of the word 'intelligence' to describe some of the abilities. He is emphatic in his insistence that either all or none of them should be called intelligences and that to do otherwise devalues aspects such as musical or bodily-kinaesthetic intelligence (1999). He has also been criticized for the basis of his selection with the suggestion that it overemphasizes the arts and undervalues practical intelligence (Gold 2002). For White, the eight look 'too close to familiar curricular areas for comfort' (2002:95). In response to criticism that there is no hard psychological evidence that the different intelligences exist, Gardner says that the work to do so would be considerable, and, while it is worth doing, that he does not want to spend his time doing it (Gold 2002).

Some implications for practice of Gardner's ideas

- An emphasis on the importance of ensuring opportunity for young children.
- A holistic approach that gives children the chance to discover interests and aptitudes.
- The importance of presenting ideas and activities to children that may pick up on their preferred ways of thinking ('entry points'), for example, telling stories to support linguistic understanding, physically active, hands-on activities that support kinaesthetic understanding and role play and discussion that support interpersonal understanding.
- The need for resources which evoke the use of a range of intelligences. Materials are not specifically labelled 'mathematical' or 'visual and spatial', for example, but may be used either by themselves, or in combinations, which might support various intelligences.
- The starting point is children's strengths, rather than weaknesses, which involves using what they are good at to support the development of areas of intelligence which are less developed, and presenting material in ways which tap into different children's strengths, to support their understanding of new ideas and concepts.

(Derived from Gardner 1993, 1999)

What conclusions can we draw?

The preceding models suggest a number of often very different processes and competences in young children's thinking and understanding. Is it possible to draw some useful conclusions from the current understandings? Whitebread suggests some key areas in which there is clear development in childhood:

- More exhaustive information processing: as children grow older they become less impulsive and more reflective, more likely to consider relevant information before acting.
- The ability to comprehend relations of successively higher orders: a progression from only being able to consider the task or object at hand towards being able to consider issues at a more abstract level, and to more easily see relationships between things.
- Flexibility in the use of strategy or information and the development of more sophisticated control strategies: a process of an increasing ability to monitor and evaluate cognitive processes, the building up of metacognitive knowledge (see Chapter 5) about tasks and our own intellectual processes, and increasing ability to construct and select ever more appropriate strategies.

(Adapted from Whitebread 2000a:147–51)

A note about other approaches to learning

There are, of course, other models of cognition. One of the most common models, not discussed here, is the 'Behaviourist' approach, also known as operant conditioning. Chiefly, I have not discussed this theory because it is a theory for learning rather than a theory of thinking. It casts the learner in a relatively passive role, placing responsibility for the selection and pacing of learning with the teacher. It stems very much from the work of Skinner, and, before him, of Pavlov, and is characterized by the ideas of stimulus, response and consequence (often referred to as S–R approaches). The influence of behaviourist theory is clearly evident in, for example, the use of positive reinforcement of effort and achievement, and negative sanctions to modify behaviour. The ideas behind these practices are complex and deserve careful consideration. However, when looking at the development of children's thinking and understanding they may have a more limited role. As Pinker (1997) suggests, we bring our thoughts to bear on a situation; we do not act merely in response to a behavioural trigger. In response to seeing a burning building people do not always act on this danger signal by running away. They may, indeed, react in a number of different ways. They may attempt to save someone they can see trapped, they may stand and watch, they may even, if they are suicidal, or motivated by seeking publicity for a cause, run into the flames. All of these alternatives are governed, Pinker (1997) suggests, by thought processes such as belief and desire. While this is a rather crude interpretation of behaviourist theory, it nevertheless draws attention to the complexity of the thought processes which guide people's actions.

Further reflection

1   For all of the models of cognition discussed here – constructivism, information processing, social constructivism, modular theory – now try to complete the following sentences:
    The image of a learner is_____
    The image of thinking is_____
    Characteristic child activity might be_____
    The potential advantages of this theory are_____
    The potential drawbacks of this theory are_____

2   Try to think about your own educational experiences: can you trace any particular models in the ways you were taught?

3   Do you agree with Penn's assertion that 'Piaget now belongs to history' (2005:40)?

4   How would you define scaffolding?

Further reading

Piaget

Cohen, D. (2002) chapter 2
Donaldson, M. (1978)
Duckworth, E. (1987)

Meadows, S. (1993) pp. 198–212
Piaget, J. (1950, 1959 and 1962)
Siegler, R. *et al.* (2003) chapter 4
Smith, P. *et al.* (2003) chapter 12
Thornton, S. (2002) chapters 3, 5 and 7

Information processing

Meadows, S. (1993) pp. 212–35
Siegler, R. *et al.* (2003) chapter 4
Thornton, S. (2002) pp. 112–15
Wood, D. (1998) pp. 12–14, 31–7 and 44–5

Vygotsky

Bruner, J. (1988)
Chak, A. (2001)
Meadows, S. (1993) pp. 235–51
Thornton, S. (2002) chapter 7
Vygotsky, L. (1978, 1986)
Wood, D. (1998) Introduction and chapters 1, 2 and 4
Wood, D. and Wood, H. (1996)
Wood, E. and Attfield, J. (2005) chapter 4

Bruner

Bruner, J. (1960, 1986, 1988)
Wood, D. (1988, 1998) Introduction and chapters 1, 4 and 8
Wood, D. and Wood, H. (1996)

Gardner

Gardner, H. (1983, 1993, 1999)
Project Zero and Reggio Children (2001)
Scherer, M. (1999)

Chapter 3

The social, cultural and emotional contexts of thinking and understanding

It is this chapter, perhaps more than any other in the book, which demonstrates the interrelationship of thinking and understanding to all aspects of children's experience. Children's thinking and understanding occurs in, and is conditioned by, the social and cultural contexts in which it takes place. Those contexts embody particular constructs of childhood and what are seen as appropriate ways of inducting children into a culture and 'bringing them up'. In addition, the ways in which children see themselves as thinkers and learners is dependent upon their self-image, self-esteem and view of themselves as part of their surrounding social world. It is a reciprocal process in which the socio-affective domain impacts upon children's cognitive development and vice versa. Meadows suggests that there is 'good reason to believe that the social and interpersonal context is particularly important in the development of complex cognitive skills' (1993:367). The importance of this area is reflected in the emphasis placed upon it in policy documents, for example, DfEE (2000), Ministry of Education New Zealand (1996) and practitioner-focused books such as Dowling (2000) and Roberts (2002). Dunn (1993) outlines the growth of interest in this area:

> Cognitive development was formerly conceptualized chiefly in terms of an individual actively exploring and acting on his or her environment in an autonomous fashion. Now, however, the social interactions and relationships within which children grow up are widely accepted as important in their cognitive development, both in fundamental cognitive advances and influencing cognitive performance.
>
> (Dunn 1993:2)

In this chapter we shall look at perspectives that have developed since Lev Vygotsky and which have often been influenced by his work. The influence of children's social and cultural worlds, particularly those of family and friends, are considered, along with the vital part played by emotion in the development of young children's thinking and understanding.

Urie Bronfenbrenner

Urie Bronfenbrenner provides something of a bridge between the constructivist and social constructivist theories of development outlined in Chapter 2 and the sociocultural perspectives outlined later in this chapter. In Bronfenbrenner's ecological theory of development, layers of influence on a young child's development are identified as a series of concentric circles radiating out from the child 'like a set of Russian dolls' (Bronfenbrenner 1979:22) with progressively less direct influence as the circles widen out. The most immediate layer of influence is the microsystem of immediate experience: the home, family and friends. The next layer, the mesosystem, encompasses the relationships between the different microsystems with which a person is involved: neighbourhood, school and religious settings. After these comes a layer of exosystems, in which children do not directly participate, but which, in Bronfenbrenner's view, are very influential. These include the parent's workplace, local government and health systems, local industry and mass media. The outermost layer, the macrosystem, is the 'overarching patterns of ideology and organization of the social institutions common to a particular culture or subculture' (Bronfenbrenner 1979:8). Bronfenbrenner is particularly interested in the interconnectedness between these different systems. He suggests that development can be defined as 'the person's evolving conception of the ecological environment and his relation to it, as well as the person's growing capacity to discover, sustain, or alter its properties' (Bronfenbrenner 1979:9). The emphasis is less on traditional psychological processes such as perception and motivation and more on the ways in which a person's interactions with their environment and the content of that environment impact upon those psychological processes.

While acknowledging the contribution Bronfenbrenner makes to ideas about cultural aspects of human development, Rogoff suggests that his model of separated though mutually influential systems (the nested structures of the Russian doll model) serves to constrain 'ideas of the relations between individual and cultural processes' (Rogoff 2003:48). As Penn (2005) points out, however, Bronfenbrenner's model attempts to show how the wider political and policy environments of the macrosystem ultimately affect what happens to children at the micro level.

Sociocultural perspectives

Barbara Rogoff herself is one of a number of psychologists, including Michael Cole and Jean Lave, whose approach is described variously as sociocultural, sociohistorical, cultural-historical and even 'cultural–historical activity theory' (Cole 2005:1). Building on the ideas of Vygotsky (Rogoff 2003), what sociocultural theorists have in common is a view of the sociocultural context as 'the crucible *for* rather than influence *on* development' (Edwards 2003:259, emphasis in original). Informing their ideas are, in many instances, ethnographic study of a range of cultural perspectives; for example, the Kpelle of Liberia (Cole *et al.* 1971) and the Mayan community of Guatemala (Rogoff 2003). Rogoff defines the overarching concept of a sociocultural–historical process as 'Humans develop through their changing participation in the sociocultural activities of their communities, which also change' (2003:11). From this perspective, cognitive development is not merely the acquisition of knowledge or skills. As Rogoff sees it:

> Cognitive development consists of individuals changing their ways of understanding, perceiving, noticing, thinking, remembering, classifying, reflecting, problem setting and solving, planning, and so on – in shared endeavors [*sic*] with other people building on the cultural practices and traditions of communities.
>
> (Rogoff 2003:237)

Learning, she suggests, comes about through a process of guided participation, a term which includes a whole range of ways in which children learn as they participate in activities within their communities, in 'rich configurations of mutual involvement' (Rogoff 1990:97) with caregivers, friends, neighbours and teachers. It thus includes processes which are intended to be instructional, as well as ones which are incidental, for example, when children 'help' their parents or observe and participate in everyday activities. She suggests that there are some basic processes of guided participation:

Mutual Bridging of Meanings   mutual understanding occurs between people in interactions, as participants adjust to communicate their ideas and coordinate their efforts, the new perspectives gained involve greater understanding.

Mutual Structuring of Participation   'children and caregivers and other companions together structure the situations in which children are involved' (Rogoff 2003:287). The structuring occurs through the choice of which activities children observe and engage in, and through shared situations such as conversations, recounting, elaborating and listening to narratives, and in practice and play with routines and roles.

(Adapted from Rogoff 2003)

Sociocultural theorists suggest that this process of guided participation, and ideas such as situated learning (Lave and Wenger 1992) are cross-cultural. What changes across cultures is the content, as embodied in the values, skills, symbols systems, and artefacts of a society, and these shape children's thinking (Siegler *et al.* 2003). A useful example to bear in mind in working with young children may be the place of play across cultures. Fleer suggests that very different types of children's play occur across cultures. Moreover, the valuing of play as a tool for children's cognitive, social and emotional development may be particular to Western society and not characteristic of much of the world (Fleer 1996).

Cultural context

A necessary consequence of this view is that development will, to some extent at least, be determined by cultural context and will reflect what is valued and what is learned (and therefore thought about) in a particular social context. Children growing up on a farm, for example, may have a better understanding of life and death from a much earlier age than children growing up in the city. Smith *et al.* (2003) describe a range of studies which show cross-cultural differences in the development of prosocial behaviour, dependent upon the varying emphasis placed upon co-operation and mutual support across different cultural contexts. There are, then, major differences between societies, and within societies, in expectations about what children will know about, and be able to do, at a particular age. Thornton suggests that, given some characteristics of development which she sees as universal, 'by and large, children live up to whatever expectations their culture has of them' (2002:168).

This may have considerable implications for children's success in educational contexts. Heath (1983) describes in detail the experiences of a group of children coming from a small community who, when on starting school in the 'mainstream' community of the nearest town, were faced with language and discourse practices with which they were unfamiliar. For the children from Trackton in Heath's study this meant learning about very different uses for questioning, for example. In their home community questions served a range of purposes, important among which were questions as rhetorical devices to start oral stories: 'Do you remember Tiggy's dog? Well...'. On entering school they responded to questions as they had done at home, by settling back to hear the story they assumed was to follow. As a consequence, their teachers, when faced with the children's lack of response to common school-type questions (implicit directives, or ones which required answers that demonstrate knowledge, for example, 'what colour is this?') assumed a lack of knowledge and understanding on the part of the children. Success in this new context of school may, as Brooker (2002) suggests, be most likely for the children when the social and cultural capital of the family most closely matches that of the setting.

Heath's work points to the very localized nature of cultural context. It is inappropriate (and inaccurate!) to conceptualize culture on regional, national, or ethnic bases. Lave's use of the idea of 'communities of practice' (Lave and Wenger 1992), to describe the cultural practices of particular groups, may be more helpful. In addition, as Bronfenbrenner's (1979) ecological model suggests, children will be interacting with a variety of different groups all of whom may have particular cultural practices. At the same time, the cultural practices of a community are not static but evolve continually. The second half of the twentieth century saw a huge growth in popular culture, including distinctive types of children's popular culture, in the form of television, followed by personal computers and the internet. As Cohen says, 'the infant brain has never before been bombarded with so much information to assimilate' (2002:183). While it is not my intention to review the research on the impact of technology on children (Cohen provides a good summary of this himself), it is worth remembering that the impact is global. Thus, it could be argued that, to some extent, cultural difference is being eroded by globalization. At the same time, as Penn (2005) suggests, those in rich and poor countries alike can now know more about each other's experiences and opportunities or lack of them.

Social understanding

'Human beings', Thornton asserts, are 'supremely social creatures' (2002:159). Such an assertion is supported by the work of Trevarthen who believes that 'from their very earliest days, babies are highly motivated to learn, and are profoundly influenced in their learning by the interplay or "protoconversations" between themselves and their parents and carers' (Trevarthen 1995:5). These protoconversations are driven by babies' needs to live and learn in culture and to be a part of that culture by constructing meanings with others. Studies of mothers and babies in the first hours after birth reveal the beginnings of these protoconversations, for example, reciprocating the gesture of sticking out the tongue.

Karmiloff-Smith (1994) suggests that such acts mark the dawning of social cognition, or 'the process of thinking about emotions, feelings, and how people interact with one another in social and cultural contexts' (Wood and Attfield 2005:81). In order to reciprocate the adult's gesture, the baby must be able to see the adult as a separate person. A growing sense of self runs alongside this sense of others and supports children in making relationships with others. Eliot (1999) believes that, while such actions are imitative, they show that even newborns can recognize emotional displays in those around them and that such imitation is also important for the later development of empathy.

Dunn (1988) suggests that, in order to live in the social world, children need to develop the following understandings:

An understanding of the feelings of others   The development of empathy, and the ability to see things from another person's point of view, and to understand how they might feel.
An understanding of the goals of others   A realization that other people want things as well as us. In children this may come about through conflicts over toy ownership, or when

children are playing together, with a common goal – a board game, or shared construction for example.

An understanding of social rules   The generally unwritten rules and routines that all groups have, both at home and outside of it. For example, the understanding that you do not write on the wall, or that everyone sits down to have their snack.

An understanding of other minds   The ability to 'read' other people – is she in a bad mood? Is he worried?

(Adapted from Dunn 1988)

In so doing, she suggests, children develop prosocial behaviour behaving in ways which promote good social relationships. Box 3.1 shows evidence of all four aspects of Dunn's suggested list, mostly in Lizzie, aged 3, but also in Freddie, at the age of 1.

What develops?

As with other aspects of development, Piagetian theory was a strong influence on people's thinking about social development, and the ages and stages at which young children are able to understand the emotions, perceptions and intentions of other people. However, a wide range of research, in particular naturalistic observational studies, has resulted in much rethinking of views about young children's social understanding. As we saw earlier, Trevarthen suggests that the roots of intersubjectivity, that is, mutual understanding shared between people during communication, are in the earliest days of life (1995). Before they are a year old babies show capability in what is known as joint attention, that is, in sharing an intentional focus on something in their environment. At around the same time they engage in the related behaviour of social referencing or looking to others to gauge how they should themselves react to a situation (Harris 1989). The period from around 18 months onwards sees the emergence of a number of critical features including a child's sense of self, which supports them in their efforts to make sense of others (Smith *et al.* 2003). In addition, at around this time children show evidence of being able to differentiate between their own desires and those of others (Gopnik *et al.* 1999) and to talk about mental states, in particular about emotion, commenting on their own and other people's feelings, desires and perceptions (Dunn 1993). Around 18 months also sees the emergence of early prosocial behaviour.

By the age of 2 children's sympathy for others (and empathy with them) in the form of attempts to help others, to share and to provide comfort in difficulty or distress is well documented (Smith *et al.* 2003). Between the ages of 2 and 3 children talk about why people behave the way they do and are able to begin to manage conflict (Dunn 2005). Dunn suggests that this early focus on emotion and desires is significant in that the later understanding of, and ability to talk about, cognitive states such as thinking and believing arises out of children's earlier understanding of emotional states. It may be, though, that children continue to find it easier to talk about feelings than thoughts for some time after they are able to do both. In our research we asked practitioners working with children aged 3–5 years how they met the requirements of the English Curriculum guidance for the foundation stage (DfEE 2000). Reflecting on the statement that 'practitioners should give particular attention to . . . providing opportunities for children to communicate thoughts, ideas and feelings' (DfEE 2000:44) one practitioner said 'Expressing their ideas and their feeling – yes, but thoughts? . . . They (the children) can talk about their ideas, they talk a lot about their feelings, but its getting them to verbalize their thoughts in that way, you have to do a bit of delving, I think' (Robson and Hargreaves 2005:91).

Box 3.1 Lizzie, aged 3, and Freddie, aged 1, in the kitchen at home

Freddie is sitting in a high chair, being fed by his mother, who is chatting to a relative. He is watching his sister, Lizzie, while occasionally opening his mouth for food. Lizzie is sitting on the floor playing with a toy mobile telephone. She hits the buttons, which make different noises, and laughs at the sounds, often holding the toy out to her mother and brother. She then speaks into the toy:

LIZZIE: Ello? Mummy, it's for you! (She holds the toy out).
MOTHER: Tell them mummy's busy.
LIZZIE: Okay, mummy's busy. Freddie, it's for you.

Freddie's attention is drawn to Lizzie at the mention of his name. Lizzie gets up.

LIZZIE: I'll take it to you 'cos you can't come here. (She holds the toy to Freddie's ear and presses a button. The toy plays a tune and Freddie laughs. Lizzie giggles, presses another button, and Freddie laughs again. Then Lizzie walks back to her original spot. Freddie's face drops, and his expression shows frustration. He pushes his food away, begins to make unhappy noises, and wriggles in his chair, his hand out towards Lizzie. She sees this and pauses.)
LIZZIE: Oh okay Freddie, you can play. (She walks back to the table, then pauses.) But you're not meant to play when you eat! (She looks at her mother, deep in conversation, then at Freddie's food, and finally at Freddie, who is trying to grasp the toy.
LIZZIE: Oh okay Freddie, but don't tell mummy. (She whispers and hands him the toy which he cheerfully accepts. She leaves the room, leaving Freddie happily engaged.)

In her pretend play, described by Dunn as 'the beginnings of social understanding' (1988:8), Lizzie explores social roles and norms. She understands that it is normal to greet a caller, and has observed that the majority of calls to her home are for her parents. From early on she shows she wants her mother and brother to experience the joy of her toy, but understands that her mother is busy. She joins Freddie at his highchair, knowing he is not able to leave it, and even holds the toy to his ear. Lizzie understands that Freddie is enjoying the toy noises, and so repeats them to make him laugh more. The two are clearly responding to each other's playful moods.

Freddie shows an understanding that he must interact with Lizzie if he is to get back the phone. Lizzie, recognizing Freddie's unhappiness, shows that she has learnt to put others' needs before her own. She empathizes with his feelings, and returns the toy to him, understanding that this will comfort him. However, she recollects that playing at table is not allowed. She acknowledges the social rules that operate within her family, but, realizing that her mother is inattentive, breaks the norm. Her hesitancy suggests that she has considered the consequences of her actions, but her compassion for Freddie overrides this.

Abridged and reproduced with permission of Philippa Cooper

Dunn (2005) suggests that children's talk about emotions supports the idea that they develop a theory of mind at a younger age than was hitherto believed. This is looked at more fully in Chapter 5. There is ample evidence to suggest that children are well able to take on another's perspective and to see things how others might see them, by the age of 3, when set in contexts which have some meaning for them (Gopnik *et al.* 1999). By the same age they also make reference to social rules and the expectations of their wider social world (Dunn 1993).

The importance of relationships

What is it that supports the emergence and development of these social understandings? The key seems to lie in children's relationships with family and friends. It is within the arena of young children's relationships with parents and carers, siblings and friends that their understanding is both developed and revealed. These relationships are complex and varied and highly context bound. Children behave differently depending upon whom they are with, and also at different times with the same people, and these different kinds of relationships 'present very different challenges to children's sociocognitive sophistication' (Dunn 1993:13). Parents will also differ in their treatment of children within a family dependent upon factors such as first born or later sibling, older or younger parent and just with experience over time (Thornton 2002). This, of course, lends support to the views of Vygotsky (1978), Rogoff (2003) and others, discussed earlier, that development is culturally bound and that models of social development, like those for cognitive development, are subject to as much variation as commonality.

For young children the social world of the family in all of its forms is a central part of their experience, as the many illuminating transcripts of episodes of family life in the work of Dunn (1987, 1988), Tizard and Hughes (2002) and Wells (1987) demonstrate. Family conflict, in the form of disputes between themselves and parents or siblings, teasing and witnessing disputes between other family members, both demonstrates and develops children's understanding of their social world. Children as young as 14 months may perform acts which seem to reflect some understanding of what will annoy another family member (Dunn 1987). Family life also provides the earliest forum for observation of, and discussion about, feeling states, as outlined earlier. Other aspects of children's family lives are similarly important: conversations about family events, social rules and routines, stories and television, sharing jokes, and all types of play and collaborative activity, particularly shared pretence (Dunn 2004a) provide valuable opportunities for the development of social understanding. Joint problem-solving, for example, may be valuable not, as Piaget might suggest, because of the exposure to a potential conflict of views but because of the ways in which children compromise in their sharing of decision-making (Thornton 2002).

Significantly, younger siblings may display such understandings earlier in life than their older brothers or sisters (Dunn 1987, 1993) and develop a theory of mind at an earlier age than their older siblings (Gopnik *et al.* 1999). This implies an important role for older siblings in helping to develop younger children's social understanding. They speculate that this may be the result of a number of factors: parents may provide fewer opportunities to develop social understanding via conflict situations (though speaking as a parent I am not so sure about this!), older siblings may be particularly attractive to younger brothers and sisters and getting them to do what you want may require considerably more expertise than it does with a parent. However, it is not merely having a sibling that matters and Dunn (2004a) points to the importance of the quality of the sibling relationship for children's social understanding. Box 3.2 describes an everyday episode in family life which illustrates some aspects of

Box 3.2 Jack, aged 3 and Alice, aged 7, at home after school with their mother

Alice and Jack are playing in Jack's bedroom. Mother hears the children start to shout at one another. By the time she arrives, Alice is going into the bathroom, muttering. Mother asks Jack what has happened. He looks uncertain, and slightly anxious.

JACK: She hit me. (As he says this he looks away, embarrassed.)
MOTHER: Jack, are you certain?
JACK: Yes, very hard, in the tummy! (He starts to cry. Mother takes his hand and takes him into the bathroom. She asks Alice what happened.)
ALICE: He had my bouncy ball, and he wouldn't give it back when I asked him nicely, so I took it, and he started shouting.
MOTHER: He said that you hit him.
JACK: Yes, she did mummy, she hit me.

Alice becomes highly indignant, and starts to cry.

ALICE: I didn't mummy, I wouldn't hit him.

Jack observes Alice furtively. His body language indicates discomfort.

MOTHER: Did Alice hit you Jack?

Jack shifts uncomfortably, and looks down.

JACK: She did mummy, *really*.
MOTHER: Jack, this is very important. Alice is very upset, and is crying. She is upset because she says she didn't hit you. It is unfair to get Alice into trouble. You need to tell mummy what really happened.
Jack moves towards Alice, puts his head on her tummy.
JACK: I didn't really. I'm sorry. (He looks at his mother.) I wanted her ball, but she took it back. I'm sorry, mummy. (Jack takes Alice's hand and looks up at her) I didn't mean it Alice.

Alice smiles and puts her arm around him.

It is apparent through his body language that Jack is not telling the truth. Dunn suggests that 'often... acts of denial or blame are made in situations where it is transparently obvious that the child is in fact the culprit' (1988:30). We see this occur when Jack says 'she did mummy, really'. He insists again that Alice has hit him, because by this stage he realizes he will get into trouble for telling a lie. Dunn suggests that a child may use his 'growing understanding in his family relationships to get his way, to escape blame, to deflect punishment onto his sibling' (1988:26). Early on it appears that Jack recognizes he has done something wrong. Dunn suggests that a three year old has the capability to show an understanding in real life family dramas. This could, she claims, be 'linked to the emotional significance of those family encounters' (1988:81). Throughout the episode Jack is uncomfortable. He appears to recognize the stress he is causing Alice, displaying what Dunn calls 'moral intuition' (1988:27). In addition, Dunn highlights Jack's possibly deeper understanding of the social consequences of his behaviour, as a result of his birth order. By apologizing and admitting what happened, it appears that he understands why Alice is so cross and upset with him. He shows that he knows that he was directly involved in making his sister unhappy, and understands the social rituals involved in making amends.

Abridged and reproduced with permission of Kathryn Torres

sibling relationships through an emotionally charged episode involving a boy, his older sister and their mother.

Friendship

While the family provides a major context for these kinds of interactions, such interactions also occur between friends. Paley (1981) suggests that friendship, along with fairness and fantasy, are the three things that interest a young child most and that these are the themes which constantly come through in their play and in their conversations with her. Children take pleasure from their social effectiveness in negotiation, conflict and its resolution, sharing jokes and play (Dunn 1988) and it is with friends that this social effectiveness is often most needed. As the poet Robert Frost says: 'home is the place where, when you have to go there, they have to take you in' (1915). Families are usually there for life, whether we like it or not. Friendships, on the other hand, are chosen and friendship has to be worked at to support 'connectedness' of communication and to understand when and why friends feel as they do and what will comfort or amuse them (Dunn et al. 2002). Practitioners in Reggio Emilia ensure that they model conflict, and its resolution, in front of the children, discussing and negotiating ideas and practice. In so doing, not only are they demonstrating to the children that adults disagree too, but they are also helping children to develop strategies of their own for use in their own interactions with their friends and peers.

Dunn (2004a) emphasizes the importance of friendship as marking the beginnings of children's independence from their family. She cites evidence for the existence of friendship, as characterized by reciprocity and mutuality of affection, in children under the age of 2 years. At first, what may be most apparent is an interest in doing the same things together but between about 18 months and $2\frac{1}{2}$ years of age behaviours such as turn-taking, co-ordination of actions and co-operation in order to solve a problem, play a game or engage in shared pretence become much more evident. By 3 and 4 years, children's 'passion for playing with other children has taken off in an astonishing trajectory' (Dunn 2004a:31). She suggests a number of ways in which young children's friendships may be significant for both their understanding of others and the development of their thinking. First, she suggests that in the context of a close friendship children make more efforts to conciliate, negotiate and make compromises than they do in their relationships within the family because they care about their friend and want to maintain the relationship. Second, the kind of talk about thoughts, feelings and inner states that takes place both in conversation and in pretend play (see the following paragraphs), and which may be particularly significant for later socio-cognitive outcomes, is especially likely to happen between friends. Third, she suggests that friendship 'is a context in which moral understanding is demonstrated very early' (Dunn 2004a:157) and in which children display more evidence of having learned about relationships than in their interactions within the family. Underpinning all of this is the emotional power of young children's friendships. In her view, it is this combination of emotion and understanding which makes friendship such a source of potential influence on children's development.

Pretend play

A particularly valuable context for the development of young children's social understanding and social self-regulation and one shared often, though not exclusively, between friends, is shared pretend play. Dunn et al. suggest that 'the experiences of sharing and negotiating an imaginary world in pretend play provides a potent context for talking and learning about why other people behave the way they do, and the links between inner states and human action' (2002:631–2). In the context of the family, she points to longitudinal research which demonstrates the significance of shared pretend play with a friendly older sibling for the development of an understanding of feelings and other minds (Dunn 2004a). Play, particularly shared pretence, is discussed in other places here, notably in Chapters 5 and 7. Looked at in the context of young children's social understanding, it is worth noting Broadhead's conclusion that the more co-operative the children's play was in her research, the more likely it was that children would connect with and understand the knowledge and thinking of the other players (2004). Wood and Attfield are similarly positive in their suggestion that play is valuable for developing young children's social cognition: 'Play provides many different opportunities for children to learn about social and cultural norms: appropriate and inappropriate behaviours, society's rules and conventions, roles and relationships, and boundaries' (2005:82).

What all of these contexts have in common is their shared nature, and there seems good reason to conclude that shared experiences are a key part of children's development as thinkers. In Chapters 7 and 8 the role of talk in these experiences is considered. At this point it is important to stress the ways in which shared experiences, which can be referred to by the participants, and reflected upon later, can help a child to develop their thinking about the past and about the future.

Emotion and cognition

Along with the closer focus in recent years on social processes in support of children's thinking has come a similar emphasis on the relationship between emotion and cognition. Bell and Wolfe suggest that, while acknowledging that the processes are complex, the two are 'dynamically linked and work together to process information and execute action' (2004:366). In Dunn's view (cited in Wood 1998) children often display their most advanced reasoning in situations that have the most emotional significance for them.

The idea that emotion and cognition are connected, and that 'pleasure, desire and emotions are powerful motivators of learning and that they drive our actions and interactions with others' is not new (MacNaughton 2003:53). It stems, in part at least, from the psychodynamic theories of Sigmund Freud. In recent years, writers such as Goleman (1996) and Claxton (1999b) have stressed the need for us to understand the place of emotions in learning, and, on an individual level, develop the ability to contain, manage and tolerate them. This ability, Claxton suggests, 'is one of the core ingredients of emotional intelligence and nowhere is it more crucial than in the domain of learning' (1999b:41). Emotional intelligence as a term was first coined by American psychologists Salovey and Mayer in 1990 (Gibbs 1995). It came to international prominence with the publication in 1995 of Goleman's *Emotional Intelligence: Why It Can Matter More than IQ*. The idea of emotional intelligence is analogous to Gardner's interpersonal and intrapersonal intelligences outlined in Chapter 2.

What is meant by emotional intelligence (or emotional literacy as it is also sometimes known)? Goleman defines it as 'the capacity for recognizing our own feelings and those of others, for motivating ourselves, and for managing emotions well in ourselves and in our relationships' (1999:317). He suggests it comprises some basic social and emotional competences: self-awareness, self-regulation, motivation, empathy, and social skills, some of which are discussed here and elsewhere in this chapter and in Chapter 5.

In support of claims for the importance of emotional intelligence Goleman (1996) cites research which points to a physiological basis to the argument for the value of attending to emotion. Part of the brain consists of two almond-shaped structures called the amygdala. These act as 'gatekeeper of the emotional brain' (Eliot 1999:292) sending information to many other parts of the brain via extensive neural connections. It is this facility, Eliot suggests, which 'explains how emotion influences every aspect of thought' (1999:294). For Goleman, 'the workings of the amygdala and its interplay with the neocortex are at the heart of emotional intelligence' (1996:16). Claxton similarly emphasizes the importance of biology here:

> When we meet a hitch, when our knowledge and know-how let us down, or when our own goals and interests conflict, feeling afraid (or sad or angry or shocked or disgusted) is part and parcel of the way we are built to respond. Emotions accompany the 'ways of knowing' that evolution has designed to help us out in such situations.
>
> (Claxton 1999b:39)

The complex interplay between emotion and cognition begins, like most things, in babyhood. Miller (1999) suggests that a baby will need to begin to develop a sense of being separate from her carer as a first step on the road to independent thought:

> There is a lot of emotional work for a baby to do before he or she can reliably call to mind the mother who is not there. Quite a risk is involved. You have to tolerate the concept, no matter how fleeting, that you are alone, before you can conceive of the other person as not there, as not part of you. With this beginning of a sense of singularity comes the possibility of mental activity and symbolic thought. Being in touch with another person need no longer mean touching them with your body. Mental contact, memory, a space in the mind where things happen, a distinction between mind and body, all start from here.
>
> (Miller 1999:37)

As seen in Chapter 5, these are also crucial in the development of theory of mind. Eliot (1999) points to the importance of the kinds of experiences we have in supporting this development and outlines another physiological link here in that many of the brain structures which control emotion also play an important role in memory storage. Consequently, events and experiences which have a strong emotional impact upon us are more likely to be stored in our memories.

A number of aspects of the development of children's social understanding outlined earlier are also central to emotional development and the growth of emotional self-regulation. One obvious example is children's awareness of and discussion about mental states involving emotion (Dunn 1993) and it is useful to refer back to the earlier sections of this chapter. Dowling cites a number of research studies which suggest that this may have a gender dimension in that parents may talk about feelings more often with their daughters than with their sons and use more emotion words in stories and display a wider range of emotions in play with girls rather than boys (Dowling 2000).

Flavell *et al.* (2001) outline what they describe as a three-step developmental sequence in children's understanding of the connection between thought and feeling, with much overlap, particularly between the second and third stages. First, they suggest that objective situations and events cause feelings appropriate to those events: 'even young preschoolers are aware that sad external happenings cause sad feelings' (Flavell *et al.* 2001:432), a view which concurs with those cited earlier. The second stage is an understanding that a reminder of a previous sad or happy event can trigger a memory of that situation which, in turn, can trigger emotions about it. As they suggest, this is an important step because it involves recognition of a causal connection between thoughts and feelings. The third step is children's awareness that spontaneous thoughts can trigger, and accompany, feelings.

Similarly, children's ability to regulate their emotions develops considerably in early childhood. Meadows (1993) describes a familiar developmental course of adult responsibility for emotional self-regulation followed by adult scaffolding of the child's attempts, adult and child discussion and reflection, and finally child responsibility. In the earliest months, caregivers tend to try to soothe or distract a distressed or frustrated baby (with varying degrees of success!). However, by 6 months babies show that they can reduce their stress by averting their gaze and even self-soothe (Siegler *et al.* 2003). In the course of the first few years children acquire the ability to regulate their emotions by an increasing repertoire of means, adding talking to others in order to negotiate ways of meeting their needs and inhibiting behaviour, for example, slowing down when asked, to those already mentioned (Siegler *et al.* 2003). By the time they are around 5 years old children are increasingly able to rely on strategies based in cognition rather than behaviour in order to regulate their emotions. For example, they are able to focus their attention and thoughts away from a desired treat (Siegler *et al.* 2003). Box 3.3 may be an example of this process of emotional self-regulation.

Attachment

Miller's (1999) emphasis on the importance of children's early interactions with their caregivers for their later emotional and cognitive development is reflected in the ideas of attachment theory, first outlined by John Bowlby. Bowlby (1969) suggests that babies need a warm, continuous relationship with a mother figure. This emotional attachment provides them with a sense of safety and security and a secure base from which they can then go out and explore their worlds. Bowlby's theory is considerably more sophisticated than this brief outline implies and is best studied by going to his original work or to texts on developmental psychology. A major shift in thinking about attachment is the current view that suggests that attachment is not solely a function of a mother–child dyad, but can, and does, occur, between babies and a range of people of emotional significance to a child. What is important to consider here is the possible relationship of these ideas to young children's thinking. A good starting point is an understanding that attachment is not a one-off event but a developmental process, which occurs as a function of the developing relationships between babies and young children and their caregivers. Babies develop 'internalized working models' (Gopnik *et al.* 1999:49) of relationships, which change as a result of experience, and in light of new information they receive about how people relate to one another. Accordingly, it is possible to point to a very close relationship between thought and emotion in that the knowledge gained through these experiences guides emotion. Gopnik *et al.* suggest that it does so 'more than emotion distorts knowledge' (1999:48).

What other links and possible beneficial relationships have been suggested between secure attachment and cognition? Secure attachment at 12 months has been associated with curiosity and problem-solving skills at age 2, with empathy and independence at age 5 (Smith *et al.* 2003) and possibly even with higher grades and more attention and involvement in school at a later stage (Siegler *et al.* 2003). Research discussed by Meins (1997) points to the importance of secure attachment in supporting the development of self-efficacy,

Box 3.3 Ayesha, aged 3 years 8 months, arriving at nursery

Ayesha enters with her mum, finding it a little difficult to separate. A member of staff supports her for a short period. Ayesha walks slowly to the end of the classroom, her face displaying some of the sadness she is feeling, her shoulders slumped. She stops at the carpet area, watches the group for a moment before dropping to her knees and sitting back on her heels, still looking cheerless. Her gaze appears to focus on one of her peers (Shaun) who is cutting through a large sheet of paper. After a while she jumps up, and selects a large sheet of paper, taking it to a space on the carpet. She alternates her gaze between Shaun's face and the cutting action he is making. She selects a small piece of paper from the many on the carpet, and sticks it carefully in position with tape. She sits back and studies her paper, then says to Shaun:

AYESHA: It's the Handsome Prince from Snow White.
SHAUN: I doin' a dinosaur, Tyrannosaurus Rex.
AYESHA: He hasn't got a hat (pause) a crown. I have to do a crown.
SHAUN: Tyrannosaurus Rex doesn't got no crown.
AYESHA: No, the Handsome Prince hasn't got a crown.

Ayesha continues to work on her picture, using tape, paper and felt tip pens. She looks up and, noticing a practitioner, smiles and says:

AYESHA: He's the Handsome Prince from Snow White and he kisses her to wake her up cos the Wicked Queen gives her an apple and she dies.

It is possible that Ayesha may have been consciously or unconsciously aware that 'merely perceiving a reminder of a previous . . . happy situation can trigger a memory of that situation, and that this memory can then trigger a happy feeling' (Flavell et al. 2001:432). Consequently, Ayesha may have been using a past experience in order to alter her own emotions. The recollection of the Snow White story may have engendered feelings of emotional security with a significant other. Her purposeful jumping up would appear to signal a change in her thinking and feelings, her actions becoming purposeful as she self-initiates a task. Ayesha may have been cognitively able to alter her affective response (Harris 1989) without the need for intervention by others, demonstrating that through thought, understanding and memory recall she has been able to contain and manage her own emotions.

Abridged and reproduced with permission of Lynn Bartlett

discussed later in the text. To sum up, Meadows suggests that an insecurely attached child may be more at risk 'of building a cognitive model which is less coherent' (1993:360) than a securely attached child. Dunn (2004a) cites the experiences of children who had been kept in extreme deprivation in Romanian orphanages where close attachments to caregivers were never made. Subsequently adopted by British families, at the age of 4 they tended to engage in less pretend play, less interactive role-play and made fewer references to mental states.

Given the subject of this chapter, it is important to consider whether attachment as a construct is culturally specific. As a way of assessing the level of attachment between a child and her caregiver, Mary Ainsworth and colleagues developed the Strange Situation (Ainsworth *et al*. 1978). In this approach the reactions of children to their caregivers leaving, a stranger entering and then the caregiver re-entering the room are observed. Ainsworth classifies children's reactions as securely attached (child shows wariness and upset on separation, but is comforted on caregiver's return), as anxious/avoidant (child does not take much notice of either the stranger, or the caregiver when he/she returns), or anxious/resistant (child is very upset when caregiver leaves, but not easily comforted on return, and simultaneously seeks and resists being close). A fourth category of 'disorganized' attachment has been identified, to describe chaotic family circumstances in which 'so much has gone wrong that there is no coherent defensive posture' (Gerhardt 2004:27). Rogoff (2003) points to research which suggests that there may be cultural variation in the extent to which children conform to particular patterns and suggests that these may reflect cultural values and practices. For example, the anxious/resistant pattern has been more common in studies of Japanese children and may reflect childrearing practices which mean that children are relatively unfamiliar with being left with strangers. She contrasts this with African-American babies who may be used to being looked after by several caregivers and encouraged to be friendly to the many strangers they encounter (Rogoff 2003:115).

Children's conceptions of the self: positive and negative emotions

Discussion of the reciprocal relationship between emotion and cognition is often centred on what is overwhelmingly seen as the beneficial parts played by children's sense of personal agency, high self-esteem and high self-efficacy (how 'good' they believe they are at something). In Chapter 6 the value attached to the development of what have been termed 'learning dispositions' (Carr 2001), in particular aspects such as a sense of mastery (Dweck 2000), is considered in relation to their usefulness as observational tools. It is worth looking here at some of the possible connections between thought and feeling as expressed by children's views of themselves as learners. Siegler *et al*. suggest that 'how children think and feel about themselves plays a role in how they respond to their successes and failures' (2003:428), and along with involvement (see Chapter 6, this book) Pascal and Bertram use children's levels of well being as measures of effectiveness in assessing quality in early childhood settings (Pascal and Bertram 1997).

Dweck (2000) suggests that children's sense of self-competence and self-efficacy, what she calls mastery, begins to develop from an early age and can have a significant impact on their attitudes to learning. When faced with difficulty or potential failure Dweck suggests that children tend to react in one of two ways. Some children display a mastery-oriented pattern of motivation, characterized by increasing their efforts to succeed and not blaming themselves for not doing well. Other children seem to respond in a different way by feeling bad, blaming themselves personally and not persisting with a task. Dweck calls this a helpless pattern. What characteristics does Dweck record in children in these two responses to difficulty?

The mastery-oriented students tended to:

- not see themselves as failing;
- engage in self-motivating strategies;

- engage in self-instruction or self-monitoring;
- remain confident that they would succeed;
- have an attitude that they could learn from their failures;
- did not see failure as an indictment of themselves as people.

The helpless students tended to:

- quickly denigrate their abilities;
- lose faith in their ability to succeed;
- focus on their failures rather than on their successes;
- lose focus on the task at hand;
- abandon strategies they had previously used successfully;
- give up trying more quickly than the mastery-oriented students.

(Adapted from Dweck 2000:7–10)

In Dweck's view, these differences can be accounted for by children's different personal theories about intelligence and about how one succeeds. Mastery-oriented children, she suggests, attribute their possible failure to unstable factors such as they did not prepare enough or put in enough effort. Therefore, with more preparation or more effort, they believe they can succeed. She even suggests that, in challenging situations, the mastery-oriented children often seem even happier and look upon difficulty as something to 'embrace with relish' (Dweck 2000:10). Baumeister *et al.* (2005) support Dweck's view and suggest that high self-esteem improves persistence. Children who display an attitude of learned helplessness tend to see the situation as beyond their control, attributing their failure at a task to stable factors such as that they are not clever enough, or do not have a good memory and believe that there is nothing that they can do to change that. Dweck suggests that such a response 'impairs students' ability to use their mind effectively' (Dweck 2000:9). Drawing on Dweck's work, Claxton suggests that the group most vulnerable here may be girls who have been perceived as 'bright' and who may have the least experience of persisting in the face of difficulty. This is further compounded by the responses of their teachers. Claxton suggests that, in such situations, there may be a tendency for teachers to offer girls comfort or an alternative activity, whereas boys in similar situations are exhorted to 'stick with it' (Claxton 1998:216).

  Dweck suggests that even very young children exhibit the two types of response. Furthermore, she believes that young children also relate this to a personal sense of 'goodness', and 'badness'. In a study of kindergarten children in the USA, 60 per cent of the children who displayed a helpless pattern said that they felt that they were not 'good kids' (Dweck 2000:104), while less than 10 per cent of the mastery-oriented children said they felt not good or not nice in a role-play scenario where they were criticized about an activity. While she is at pains to stress that 'most young children go around feeling good about themselves' (Dweck 2000:106), the difference for what she describes as vulnerable and hardy children is in how contingent that sense of goodness is, or how much it is affected by events. Hardy children, she suggests, recognize that they are still worthy when things go wrong. Vulnerable young children, by contrast, lose a sense of themselves as worthy at such times. Claxton calls this sense of worthiness 'resilience', a quality that will be needed in order for children to tolerate uncertainty, and the feeling of 'not knowing', without feeling insecure. He says: Uncertainty invites an ambivalent response. On the one hand, learning promises greater insight and control. On the other, it might blow up in your face (Claxton 1999b:40).

When it comes to thinking, problem-solving and tackling challenge, such resilience and willingness to take risks may help us to respond positively to the anxiety, worry, or lack of sureness that we feel. Respond positively, with confidence, resilience and perseverance, and the result can be a benign cycle. Gopnik *et al.* (1999:163–4) describe the 'intense pleasure' of understanding, and the ways in which this feeds back into ever greater desire to keep developing that understanding.

Does all of this translate to performance? A recent review of literature in the area suggests, at least in relation to older children and adolescents, that self-esteem may only be weakly predictive of later achievement (Baumeister *et al.* 2005). Siegler *et al.* (2003) suggest that, while not conclusive, evidence tends to suggest that academic achievement has a stronger effect on children's self-esteem than vice versa. While in both cases the focus is on older children, it does suggest a need for further research in the area.

Goleman (1996) and Meadows (1993) both point to the impact of emotional distress on learning, suggesting that continued emotional distress, of whatever kind, can have a lasting impact on thinking and understanding. The possibly reciprocal nature of this, that cognitive experience can lead to emotional distress, may also be familiar to most of us. I only have to think of the term 'geometric progression' in order to feel anxiety and butterflies in the pit of my stomach just as I did in mathematics classes when I was 14. Broadhead (1997, 2004) provides a good contrast here, however, suggesting the potential long-term impact of positive emotional experience on children, with examples which show the sheer fun, and shared joy, of cooperative and collaborative experiences, like that shown in Box 3.4.

Some implications for practice

- Learning occurs as children participate in activities within their communities. Some of this learning will be instructional, and at other times learning will be incidental to everyday life (Rogoff 2003).
- The cultural context in which children live will be an important factor in determining what is seen as important to know 'about'.
- The social world of the family supports children in developing their thinking and understanding through their participation in family activities and routines.
- Young children's friendships are significant both for their understanding of other people and for the development of their thinking and understanding, in particular because of the emotional significance of friendship.
- Pretend play is a valuable context for the development of children's social understanding (Wood and Attfield 2005).
- Children may often display their most advanced reasoning in situations that have the most emotional significance for them (Dunn in Wood 1998).
- Children's sense of self-competence and self-efficacy can have a significant impact on their attitudes to learning (Dweck 2000).
- Developing young children's resilience and willingness to take risks may be important for children's persistence in the face of challenge (Claxton 1999b).

Box 3.4 Frank and Jamil, aged 4, in the nursery

Frank and Jamil both put dough in the mincer, and then put the mincer into a saucepan, cooking 'dinner' together.

They then move over to the sand and work together to fill a large cardboard box with all the sand toys. They cover the box in sand. They both laugh as everything falls out. They then work together again to fill it. This is done spontaneously without discussion. They then work together fill the bag with sand, and both try to lift it together. They both shriek with laughter as the bag breaks and sand falls out.

Further reflection

1 Try (with their permission!) to observe children in group play of some kind. In what ways do they show social understanding?

2 Think about your own friendships and family relationships. How diverse are they? What makes them 'work', where they do, and what makes them unsuccessful, if any of them are?

3 Below are some possible implications for practice in relation to links between emotion and cognition. Do you agree with them? What others might you add?

 i The need to create and support an environment in which children feel free to take risks with their thinking, and able to tolerate the anxiety of 'not knowing';

 ii The need to make space for feelings (including adult modelling), and to help children develop *metamood* or *self-awareness* (Goleman);

 iii Adult sensitivity to the rise and fall of children's self-esteem and confidence.

Further reading

Culture and sociocultural theories

Bronfenbrenner, U. (1979)
Rogoff, B. (1990)
Rogoff, B. (2003)
Siegler, R. *et al.* (2003) chapter 9

Social understanding

Dunn, J. (1988, 1993, 2004a)
Gopnik, A. *et al.* (1999) chapter 2
Thornton, S. (2002) pp.158–69, 194–5, 215–16
Trevarthen, C. (1995)

Emotion and cognition

Claxton, G. (1999b) chapter 2
Dweck, C. (2000)
Goleman, D. (1996)
Gopnik, A. *et al.* (1999) chapter 2
Meadows, S. (1993) pp. 125–9, 356–60
Siegler, R. *et al.* (2003) chapter 10

Chapter 4

The developing brain

The focus of this chapter is on the physiological development of the brain and nervous system and their relationship to the development of thinking and understanding in young children. As Catherwood points out, all of our 'humanity' is bound up in the workings of the brain: 'our hopes, dreams, thoughts, feelings, memories, plans, problems, our very personality and sense of identity' (1999:29). For LeDoux (2003) the brain systems underlying the 'mental trilogy' of thinking, emotion and motivation interact with, and influence, one another to make us who we are.

In July 1989 the then President of the United States, George Bush Senior, pronounced the 1990s the 'Decade of the Brain'. In so doing, he was highlighting a field of study which was already of considerable scientific and public interest, and the work of neuroscientists, studying nerve systems in the brain, has had an increasing influence on views about child development and the growth of thinking and understanding in early childhood. For some people, both within the early childhood field and outside of it, the attraction seems to be the promise of some kind of certainty. For many years developmental psychology held a prominent position in early childhood theory and practice. The growth of theoretical positions which placed more emphasis on children's social and cultural experiences (Bronfenbrenner 1979, Cole *et al.* 1971, Rogoff 1990) led to a decline in the prominence of developmental psychology and its seeming certainties about patterns of child development. It may be that, for some people, neuroscience offers the promise of a new type of reliability, that of scientific method (Penn 2005).

This makes it even more important that those with an interest in early childhood and young children's development examine the research and claims being made as a result of it, very carefully: 'If educators do not develop a functional understanding of the brain and its processes, we will be vulnerable to pseudoscientific fads, inappropriate generalizations, and dubious programs' (Wolfe and Brandt 1998:10). Blakemore and Frith (2000) suggest that we need to develop an interdisciplinary 'learning science', which could bring together neuroscientists, educators and cognitive psychologists in order to address the relationship between the brain and thinking and learning. They believe that 'one of the major contributions neuroscience is capable of making is illuminating the nature of learning itself' (Blakemore and Frith 2005:2). This chapter, then, looks at some of the current understandings of how the brain develops, particularly in early childhood, and explores some of the possible implications of neuroscientific research for early childhood practice and provision.

Studying the brain

A major problem in studying the human brain is that of access. Until quite recently, the chief sources of information were animal studies, autopsies utilizing brain tissues of the dead and neuropsychological studies of brain-damaged patients. All three can be seen to have limitations, certainly in being able to infer more general human brain development and activity. Recent advances in medical and experimental technology have enabled neuroscientists to significantly take forward our knowledge of the brain and the mind. Underpinning these new techniques is the principle of recording metabolic change within the brain as a result of thought and action.

Functional neuroimaging techniques such as Positron Emission Tomography (PET) scans and functional Magnetic Resonance Imaging (fMRI) are brain imaging techniques which detect changes in blood flow during an activity and are used both in the diagnosis of specific problems in the brain and in charting changes in brain functioning. However, both have considerable practical, and more importantly, ethical, drawbacks, where their use with children is concerned (Thornton 2002). This is because they are either invasive, as in the case of PET scans, where a radioactive substance is injected into the person's bloodstream, or involve procedures which are unpleasant, and possibly damaging in themselves, as in the case of fMRI, where subjects need to be able to tolerate the noise and close confinement of an MRI machine. Consequently, the data derived from both techniques tends to come from children whose brains are being scanned for diagnostic purposes or children who are 6-years-old and above (Siegler *et al.* 2003). Blakemore and Frith (2000) suggest that fMRI offers considerable advantages over PET as a technique for use with young children.

Non-invasive approaches to monitoring brain activity use electroencephalographic (EEG) and magnetoencephalographic (MEG) recordings which measure electrical and magnetic (respectively) activity in the brain, obtained by placing electrodes on a child's, and even a very young baby's, skull. One particular EEG approach, the recording of event related potentials (ERP), measures changes in the brain's electrical activity that may occur in response to presentation of a particular stimulus. Thornton suggests that this approach, in particular, offers 'a new way into understanding what the infant mind is like and how it changes through development' (2002:23) with considerable potential for the future.

The development of the brain

The human brain, like that of other vertebrates, begins to develop very early in pregnancy and its prenatal growth and development closely resembles that of other primates. We are only now beginning to find out just how much babies learn while in the womb, and the ways in which they do so, but we do know that foetuses respond to different voices, can distinguish 'happy talk' from other kinds of speech and may even have developed a preference for particular smells and tastes even though they cannot directly experience them in the womb (Thornton 2002). At birth, however, brain development, especially that of the cerebral cortex, still has a long way to go, and the first year of life will see considerable maturation (Eliot 1999). In the earliest days of life, a baby's responses are mainly reflex. The part of the brain which controls these reflex actions is the subcortex, the most primitive part of the brain. With experience, the cortex becomes more dominant, and this is the part of the brain which allows for voluntary action, and, crucially, the development of language and thought.

Over the first year of life, the baby's brain will triple in volume, growing to three quarters of its adult size by the age of one. At birth the brain already has almost all of the (approximately) 100 billion nerve cells, or neurons, that it will need throughout its life, although few of them are, at that point, fixed in their specialist functions. Only in two areas of the brain, the hippocampus and the cerebellum, do brain cells increase after birth (Blakemore and Frith 2005). These neurons are responsible for sending and receiving electrical messages both within the brain and between the brain and the body. Although they

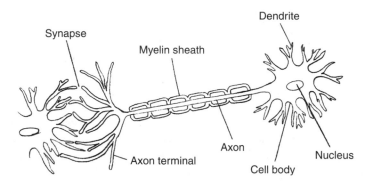

Figure 4.1 The neuron.

vary considerably in shape, size and function (for example, sensory neurons transmit information from sensory receptors that detect stimuli in the environment, or within the body, and motor neurons transmit information between the brain and muscles and glands), they all have three main components, as seen in Figure 4.1. At the centre, a cell body contains the nucleus and oversees the basic functioning of the neuron. Dendrites then receive input from other cells and conduct this, in the form of electrical impulses, towards the cell body. An axon then conducts electrical signals away from the cell body, relaying information to other neurons. When a neuron is activated it sends a brief electrical impulse called an action potential. This leads to the release of chemicals (neurotransmitters) from the axon terminal. These chemicals then cross the microscopic gap between the axon terminal of the original neuron and the dendrites of another.

These microscopic gaps are called synapses, and their total number is 'staggering' (Siegler *et al.* 2003:101), with some neurons having up to 15,000 synaptic connections with other neurons. The process of synapse formation, called synaptogenesis, begins prenatally and continues very rapidly both before and after birth. It provides for an 'exuberant explosion' of neuronal connections. (Siegler *et al.* 2003:107). Eliot suggests that 'the real business of brain development is in synapse formation' (1999:26). LeDoux (2003) believes that synapses are key to the operations of both 'nature' and 'nurture', with both contributing to the wiring of synapses in the brain.

As well as neurons, the brain contains other types of cells, notably glial cells, which provide vital support for the neurons. In particular, they are responsible for the formation of a myelin sheath around certain axons, which has the effect of insulating the axon and increasing the speed and efficiency of information transmission.

This 'exuberant explosion' of neuronal connections is an important feature of infancy and early childhood, entailing considerable overproduction of synapses. In normal patterns of development the synapses develop in response to stimulation, that is, as a result of the baby's experiences. At the same time, they are also selectively pruned, as the brain selects and preserves those most useful to the baby's development and eliminates others. 'Useful', in this context, is defined as level of electrical activity that essentially stabilizes the synapse in place, cementing the neural pathways which are most useful for that child in a given environment (Eliot 1999). Level of activity is, itself, a function of experience: a case of 'use it or lose it' (Eliot 1999:27), where the process is as follows: the more frequently the synapse is activated, the more likely it is to be preserved, and thus the greater the strength of connection between the neurons involved. A good example of this is the development of speech. At birth, babies are born with the potential to learn any language and the capability to make the speech sounds present in any language, but only those that babies hear around them in their particular environment will be strengthened. It is often suggested that this leads quite early on in childhood to an inability to vocalize the speech sounds of unfamiliar languages. What may happen, however, is not that the brain loses the ability to detect subtle differences in speech sounds, but does lose the capacity to treat them as significant (Karmiloff-Smith cited in Blakemore and Frith 2005). This capacity of the brain to be affected by experience is known as plasticity, and is, as we shall see later, a key feature of the argument for the importance of brain research to early childhood provision and practice.

It is interesting to speculate why the brain engages in such a seemingly wasteful exercise of massively overproducing synapses only to destroy them – children lose about 20 billion synapses each day between childhood and adolescence (Eliot 1999). Siegler *et al.* (2003) suggest that economy may be a big factor in that less information initially needs to be encoded in the genes with experience helping to complete the job of developing the nervous system. This system of 'fine tuning' in relation to environmental experiences may allow for 'a highly ordered and appropriate pattern to emerge from a much less organised one' (Meadows 1993:279). Eliot (1999) views the process as a positive one in helping our mental processes to become more efficient, streamlined and coherent. A possible corollary of this is, as she points out, that our mental processes may become less flexible and less creative as we mature.

Before moving on, it may be worth pausing to reflect on the importance of these ideas about the brain's general development for early childhood. What is clear is the huge amount of physical development that occurs in this area, both before birth and in the first years of life, with experience playing a key role in that development. As we have seen, and will see, in other chapters of this book, experience also seems to be a central factor in children's cognitive development, pointing to the close relationship between the physiological and psychological development of mind and brain. At the same time, however, it is worth questioning the idea that there is a causal link between 'intelligence' and synaptic density as a result of experience. The clear implication is that 'more is better', but the relationship of synaptic density to intelligence is not yet (if it ever will be!) proven (Griffiths 2003), and neuroscientists such as Bruer (1998, 1999) urge us to exercise caution in the face of sometimes extravagant claims in this area.

More generally, the scale of neurological development in these early years has come to be seen as an important reason in itself for focusing on the early years. Blakemore quotes Hilary Clinton, wife of the then President of the United States, at a White House conference in 1996, citing brain development research: 'Experiences (between the ages of zero and three) can determine whether children will grow up to be peaceful or violent citizens, focused or undisciplined workers, attentive or detached parents' (Blakemore 2005:36). Such unequivocal statements may not, ultimately, serve us well, if they lead to a view that the early years are the only time during which children can develop the qualities needed to grow into rounded adults.

Individual difference

As yet little is really known about individual difference in the brain (Blakemore and Frith 2000). While such difference is not considered in detail here, it is worth noting that developmental disorders which arise from biological difference, for example, attention deficit/hyperactivity disorder (ADHD), autistic spectrum disorders, dyscalculia and dyslexia, occur in substantial numbers. Dyslexia, for example, affects about 5 per cent of the population (Blakemore and Frith 2005). The effects of such difference are felt in a range of areas related to children's thinking and understanding as for example, in relation to the development of theory of mind in children with autism (see Chapter 5).

This is an area of some controversy, and Blakemore and Frith (2005) point out that the idea that developmental disorders can be caused by subtle brain abnormality is not widely accepted. What does seem clear is that such differences, while they may have a biological basis, are not solely attributable to brain difference. Dyslexia, for example, is now often viewed as a developmental disorder with its basis in both brain and genes (it often runs in families) and impacted upon by environmental factors. Blakemore and Frith (2005) cite research which demonstrates reduced activity in the major elements of the reading and speech-processing system of the brain. In particular, dyslexic readers may have difficulties in processing the form and sounds of whole words. The highly irregular nature of the English language makes this crucial when reading English, but less problematic in the case of a much more regular language such as Italian. The evidence of some research suggests that it is possible to strengthen regions of the brain which process speech sounds, and, as a result, remediate some of the difficulties dyslexic children and adults face (Blakemore and Frith 2005). In general, much more remains to be done in exploring the interplay between biology and experience in relation to developmental disorders and individual differences between children.

Gender and the brain

This aspect of brain development remains contentious, and is of much current interest. See, for example, Pinker's (2002) discussion of feminism and gender. Cahill (2005) suggests that there is evidence for anatomical, chemical and functional differences between the brains of men and women in those areas which affect memory, emotion, vision, hearing and navigation. While it is accepted that there are differences between male and female brains, there is no general agreement on what these differences mean. Blakemore and Frith (2000) point to research which suggests that women often outperform men on verbal tasks, while men frequently seem to be better at spatial tasks than women. Such spatial understanding is often linked to performance in mathematics and used as evidence where boys do outperform girls in this subject. However, such broad generalizations may obscure differences at different ages and ignore the roles of social and cultural experiences. For example, as Hutt *et al.* (1989) demonstrate in relation to the children in their research, girls often seem to be drawn to activities where adults are present. In nurseries and schools these may often be seat-based activities, involving discussion and talk of all kinds. Boys, on the other hand, in Hutt *et al.*'s (1989) research, tended to be attracted to activities where adults were not always so evident. These may often be areas such as large block play, climbing and gross motor activities, which may support spatial and mathematical experience. Thus, not only do boys gain more experience of spatial activities but also a process of socialization results in the 'gendering' of these activities, such that they may become seen by the children themselves as activities for boys. This may then result in girls having even less motivation to engage with them. The situation may be further exacerbated by the responses that children receive from adults. Wood (1998) cites research by Dweck which suggested that the teachers in their study gave very different kinds of feedback to girls. In the context of mathematics, for example, negative feedback to boys tended to focus on unstable factors such as inattentiveness. Similar feedback to girls tended to reflect on their ability at maths. Positive feedback to boys tended to focus upon, and reinforce, a view that they were 'good' at maths. Nunes (2005) outlines research which suggests that this adult view of boys as inherently better at mathematics than girls can lead to the children themselves taking on this belief. Looked at in this way, differences in achievement may be at least as much to do with experience as biology.

Rogoff (2003) emphasizes that gender differences are based on both biological and cultural heritage. Children develop the distinctive gender roles of their communities as a result of the models they see around them and the encouragement they receive about gender-related activities. This process of gender role training is often largely taken for granted. She suggests that this factor may make changes in gender roles more difficult, because these unconsciously accepted patterns of behaviour are seen as preferable. Baron-Cohen (2004), while agreeing that both biology and culture are factors, suggests that there are important psychological differences related to gender, that arise more from biological than cultural causes. He contends that 'The female brain is predominantly hard-wired for empathy. The male brain is predominantly hard-wired for understanding and building systems' (Baron-Cohen 2004:1). In support of his view, Baron-Cohen points to differences between girls and boys in their play preferences and in their use of verbal or physical skills. He also suggests that girls may develop the ability to infer what other people might be thinking or intending (a central feature of theory of mind – see Chapter 5) earlier than boys. His research demonstrates one-day-old baby boys looking at a mechanical mobile for longer than they looked at a picture of a woman's face. In girls the results were opposite, and they looked for longer at the face. At the age of 12 months, boys showed more interest in watching a video of cars, while girls showed more preference for a silent video of a 'talking head' (Baron-Cohen 2004). It is interesting to look at Baron-Cohen's assertions in relation to the mapping activity discussed in Chapter 8 where the girls paid more attention to features related to people and the boys showed more interest in depicting functional features, such as the sewage and electricity systems. As with the examples about mathematics, disentangling the impact of experience from possible physiological difference is tremendously difficult.

Baron-Cohen (2004) is at pains to point out, however, that he is talking about statistical averages rather than suggesting that his ideas can be used to describe all men as 'systematizers', and all women as 'empathizers'. Perhaps the most important message, then, is that 'there are brain differences between genders, but even bigger differences between individuals' (Blakemore and Frith 2005:63) and that the things which make boys and girls similar far outweigh those which might make them different.

Emotion and the brain

In Chapter 3 I looked at some features of the relationship of emotion to cognition. While this relationship has often been downplayed in the past (LeDoux 1998), more emphasis is now placed upon the intimate connection between these two aspects of what makes us who we are. LeDoux believes that 'emotion and cognition are best thought of as separate but interacting mental functions mediated by separate but interacting brain systems' (1998:69). The power of emotional feelings, he suggests, is that they involve many more brain systems than 'mere thoughts' (1998:299). Emotions mobilize and synchronize brain activity, enhancing the opportunity for co-ordinated learning across brain systems. In the face of danger, for example, many different aspects of the brain's resources are focused on one goal in ways that they may not be in less emotional situations.

The biological processes which occur in the brain in relation to emotion and emotional processing are complex and can be read about in detail in LeDoux (1998, 2003). In brief, this activity is centred on the brain's emotional system, often referred to as the limbic system. LeDoux (2003), however, suggests that, while the limbic system remains the predominant explanation for how the brain makes emotions, it is a flawed and inadequate explanation of the specific brain circuits of emotion. For LeDoux, there may be not one emotional system in the brain, but many, all of which have evolved for different reasons. He suggests: 'The system we use to defend against danger is different from the one we use in procreation, and the feelings that result from activating these systems – fear and sexual pleasure – do not have a common origin' (1998:16). One particular structure does seem to play a central role in some important aspects of the brain's emotional workings. This is the amygdala, two small, almond-shaped structures situated deep inside the brain. In particular, the amygdala is concerned with the automatic processing of emotions, particularly ones associated with fear and distress (Blakemore and Frith 2005). As we saw in Chapter 3, Goleman (1996) places much emphasis on the role of the amygdala in the development of what he calls 'emotional intelligence'.

What happens in the brain when information from the environment (a car speeding towards you, or a warm hug from someone you care about, for example) is received and needs processing? In this context, LeDoux suggests that 'emotion can be defined as the process by which the brain determines or computes the value of a stimulus' (2003:206). As a consequence of this process, a number of things may follow. First, emotional reactions occur in response to the information. This is followed by feelings that are generated as we become aware of the emotional significance of the information. Finally, but not always, we may take some kind of action as a result.

The workings of the amygdala, 'the centrepiece of the defense system' (LeDoux 2003:207) illustrate this whole process well. Amygdala cells receive input from the sensory world constantly but ignore most of them. Once the amygdala does detect a threatening stimulus it activates a number of other brain networks with the result that these different systems are co-ordinated in their response to threat. These networks include sensory ones, others connected with thinking, and, importantly, with memory formation. In stressful situations, the amygdala triggers the release of a number of hormones, including the stress hormone cortisol, the job of which is to mobilize bodily resources to cope with the impact of stress. This is a short-term measure, enabling us to cope until physiological normality is restored. In the longer term, if stress persists, damage, including shrinkage of dendrites and cell death can occur (LeDoux 2003), and functions like explicit memory, impaired.

These are negative consequences for anyone, but Gerhardt (2004) suggests that the impact may be particularly important for babies. Very young children rely upon adults to manage their stress for them, through the ways in which they care for them, both physically and emotionally. Where adults do not respond appropriately to them, for example by neglecting them, or ignoring their needs, babies become stressed. One consequence of this may be high levels of cortisol production, particularly in the case of newborns (Eliot 1999). This may have a lasting impact on their development, including the development of parts of the brain concerned with reading social cues and adapting behaviour to social norms (Gerhardt 2004). Both Eliot (1999) and Gerhardt (2004) link babies' ability to modulate their stress systems to attachment, suggesting that securely attached babies show lower levels of stress hormone production in response to strange or fearful events.

The kind of fear conditioning of the amygdala looked at earlier is an implicit form of learning, which does not require conscious involvement. However, at the same time that an implicit memory of an emotional situation is being stored, more explicit memories about the situation are also being created. Let's look at an example of what this means. As a small child I once ran across the road narrowly missing a particular grey car speeding towards me. After that, any sight of a similar model and colour car revived an unconscious memory of the incident. At the same time, I also remembered how frightened I was, and often my heart began beating faster, reliving the conscious, explicit memory of the event. LeDoux (1998) suggests that these implicit and explicit systems function in parallel, and as with my own example both are likely to be reactivated, as part of one memory function.

While the amygdala is responsible for implicit memory, it is also involved in the formation of explicit memory along with another region of the brain known as the hippocampus. This idea of separate systems for implicit and explicit memory may be relevant as an explanation for the phenomenon known as infantile amnesia. Most people cannot remember early experiences, usually those that happen before the age of about three. The hippocampus is an area of the brain which has a relatively prolonged period of maturation, leading to the suggestion that we do not have explicit memories of early childhood because the systems needed for their formation are not yet ready (LeDoux 1998). However, children clearly learn and remember a great deal during this period, which must mean that there are other memory systems in operation, even if they do not have conscious memories of it later.

The examples I have drawn upon here have tended to be about negative emotional states such as fear. Partly, this is because this aspect of brain development has been more extensively researched. However, it is important to emphasize that similar processes govern positive emotional processing. I began this section by emphasizing how big a part is played by emotion in making us who we are. For LeDoux (2003), this is what makes it important for us to try to uncover as much as we can about the brain mechanisms of emotions. He points out that, while we are still in the early stages of this process, 'the future is bright' (2003:234).

Neuroscience and early childhood: the three 'big ideas'

Three 'big ideas' (Bruer 1998:14) from the research in neuroscience have come, in particular, to be associated with arguments around interventions in early childhood provision and practice:

- the importance of early synapse formation;
- the idea of critical or sensitive periods in development;
- the impact of enriched environments on brain development in the early years.

Early synapse formation – plasticity and neural connections

As we saw earlier, synapse formation (synaptogenesis) plays a central role in developing complex neural connections, and at no time does this happen more prolifically than in the early years of life. From this phenomenon, a conclusion has been drawn by some people to the effect that appropriate stimulation will facilitate the fixing of more of these synaptic connections, and 'with more connections to draw on, a child would be more intelligent' (Griffiths 2003:7). The plasticity, or adaptability, of the young brain allows, for example, for recovery from injury, in a way that 'would not ordinarily be possible in the later years' (Talay-Ongan 2000:29).

What, though, is the evidence for such a claim? Synaptogenesis was first demonstrated in 1975, following research on cats (Blakemore 2005). Further research on monkeys showed that synaptic densities peak 2–4 months after birth, after which pruning begins, reaching adult levels at around 3 years. Is this, though, the same in humans? Blakemore (2005) points to the much quicker development of monkeys by comparison to human beings and suggests that the period of most rapid brain development is likely to be longer in humans than in monkeys.

The timescale for brain development, then, varies between species. It is also true to say that the course of development for different areas in the same brain varies. Synapse generation is complete much earlier in the visual cortex than it is in the frontal cortex, the area of the brain involved in attention, short-term memory and planning (Bruer 1998). In the frontal cortex, neuronal development continues throughout adolescence, suggesting greater plasticity for a far longer period than the early childhood years, at least in some brain areas. In addition, whereas increases in synaptic density may be associated with the initial emergence of some skills and capabilities (for example, visual memory) these same skills continue to improve after synaptic density has begun to decline to adult levels and adults continue to be able to develop new skills. So, even if synaptogenesis is necessary for the initial emergence of some skills, it cannot account for their continued refinement (Blakemore and Frith 2000).

To conclude, Bruer asserts that 'neuroscience suggests that there is no simple, direct relationship between synaptic densities and intelligence' (Bruer 1998:15). Furthermore, very little is yet known about the ways in which particular forms of learning, for example, learning in nurseries and schools, affects the brain at synaptic level.

Developmental periods: critical or sensitive?

Extensive research in developmental neurobiology over the course of 30 years has demonstrated the need for the occurrence of particular kinds of experience at specific times, if some motor, sensory and language skills are to develop normally in human beings (Bruer 1999). For example, babies born with cataracts which are not removed before the age of 2 years may become cortically blind. The work of Hubel and Wiesel (cited in Blakemore 2005, Bruer 1998, 1999) demonstrated that kittens, who had one eye temporarily covered early in life, did not regain functional use of that eye when it was subsequently uncovered. Moreover, their research demonstrated considerable deterioration of the neuronal connections in the visual area of the brain connected to the covered eye. By comparison, in fully grown cats the same, or longer, periods of sight deprivation had no lasting effect, suggesting that there is a 'critical period', or 'window of opportunity' for sensory experiences such as sight to develop, outside of which achieving that function will be 'most difficult, and sometimes impossible' (Talay-Ongan 2000:29).

Hubel and Wiesel's work has been replicated and further developed, and the results used to suggest that a whole range of different learning experiences must occur by a certain age (notably during early childhood) or the brain will never develop properly, and achieve function in those areas. Talay-Ongan suggests that these critical periods are evident for 'most domains of development' (2000:29).

Such a suggestion needs to be examined in two principal ways:

- Are 'critical periods' as rigid as some writers suggest?
- Do such 'critical periods' exist for a wide range of aspects of development?

With regard to the first question, studies conducted since Hubel and Wiesel's original work have shown interesting results, suggesting that it is not the amount of stimulation which matters in developing the visual cortex, but the balance and relative timing of stimulation. Closing both eyes of an animal for six months during the critical period had no permanent ill-effect on their vision or brain structure, for example (Bruer 1999). In addition, subsequent research suggests that recovery of function may be possible, depending upon the period of deprivation, and the use of remedial stimulation and training afterwards (Blakemore 2005). Corrie goes further, in citing research which suggests that any such critical periods are more complex and much longer than has been suggested (Corrie 2000). In essence, the 'windows of opportunity' may be open for much longer, and may not even close as firmly as Talay-Ongan (2000) suggests. The role of critical periods may be to 'fine-tune' the neural circuitry and help it adapt to the particular environment, a role characterized as 'experience expectant brain plasticity' (Bruer 1998:16).

Blakemore and Frith (2005) suggest that the more common view of neuroscientists now is that we should conceptualize such periods as 'sensitive' rather than critical. These periods are neither rigid nor inflexible. Within these periods, sensory input from the environment does not need to be particularly special for functions to develop normally. They suggest the importance of visual and aural stimuli to look at, listen to, touch and manipulate, but conclude: 'what is particularly important in the case of human infants is interaction with other human beings, including language and communication' (2005:26).

Turning to the second question, research evidence is strongest for the existence of sensitive periods for species-wide, evolution-based behaviours. For example, while sensory functions such as vision and hearing, and learning phonology (learning to speak a language without a perceptible accent) may be subject to stimulation at quite specific times, very little is known about whether sensitive periods exist for culturally – or socially-transmitted knowledge systems such as mathematics, reading or music (Bruer 1998), or of human social and emotional functioning. Even within language acquisition, while there may be a sensitive period for the acquisition of phonemic representations (leading to the theory that humans have a predisposition to learn and generalize the rules of language, as suggested by Pinker 1994), acquisition of the semantics and vocabulary of a language can go on throughout life (Blakemore and Frith 2005). Thus, it is possible to conclude that early identification and treatment of sensory problems such as sight and hearing impairment may be very important and lead to normal (if belated) function. Whether there are sensitive periods for the acquisition of aspects of knowledge such as arithmetic, for example, is less clear. It may be that overemphasis of the idea of critical periods has led to more attention being paid to when learning occurs with too little emphasis on how it occurs (Griffiths 2003).

Enriched environments and synapse formation

The underpinning part played by experience is emphasized throughout this book. Data on the role of experience in children's neurological development rests, as often in this area, on experimental studies conducted on animals. Greenough (cited in Blakemore 2005, Blakemore and Frith 2000, 2005, Bruer 1998, 1999) has conducted a series of studies on rats, with the intention of examining the impact of different environments on brain structure. The results of his studies have often been cited as evidence for the importance of providing so-called enriched environments for young children. Typically, groups of rats were placed in two contrasting environments. One group was separated and rats were raised alone in laboratory cages with only food and water – the typical laboratory environment for a rat. The other group was raised together in large group cages that contained tunnels to run through, wheels to spin on, and other rats to play with. The rats raised in this enriched laboratory environment had up to 25 per cent more synapses per neuron in the visual areas of their brains, performed learning tasks better, and were quicker in navigating their way around mazes (Blakemore 2005:39). The conclusion reached was that rats living in 'enriched' environments developed better neuronal connections, stronger blood supplies and were cleverer than their counterparts in the isolated or 'deprived' environments. Therefore, provision of enriched environments could lead to similar gains in human beings.

There may, however, be some leaps too far in this. In the first instance, what works for rats may not work for human beings; we just do not know. More elementary, though, is some examination of the two environments. The so-called enriched environment of the socially raised rats is only enriched in laboratory terms. For most rats, living in sewers, running free on the London Underground system, negotiating woodpiles and dustbins and avoiding rat traps is not an enriched but a 'normal' environment, which provides all of the challenges of the laboratory-based enriched environment. By contrast, the laboratory rats living in isolated conditions with little stimulus could be said to be in a 'deprived' environment. Thus, the conclusion that especially enriched environments are advantageous begins to look a little less secure. Bruer (1998) suggests that we should replace the word 'enriched' with 'complex', a word which could reflect more realistically the conditions under which most rats (and children) live. Looked at in this way, it is possible to suggest that it may be deprivation which is disadvantageous for brain development and that what is important for brain development is some level of stimulus. For the vast majority of children, then, their 'normal' environments will provide appropriate conditions for normal brain development, and 'enriched' environments will not, of themselves, necessarily be better. It may even be that an environment can be overly rich, militating against a baby's effort to sustain attention without distraction from other sources (Catherwood 1999).

Research carried out on children kept in extreme deprivation in Romanian orphanages tends to support both the deleterious effects of such conditions and the possibility of remediation. Under President Ceauscescu, children were placed in orphanages at only a few weeks old. Studies of their progress after they were adopted by British families showed that, as a result of their poor nutrition, ill-health and lack of stimulation, they were likely to have delayed or impaired development in all areas – cognitively, socially, emotionally and physically – with a close association between length of deprivation and severity of impairment. What is remarkable is that 'most babies made a full recovery' (Blakemore 2005:39), suggesting that remedial stimulation and care can have an important impact. It is important to say, however, that the extent of the recovery of these children was related to the length of time they had spent in the orphanages and the age at which they were adopted. Those who had been adopted before the age of 6 months demonstrated levels of development comparable to the control group against whom they were being measured at the age of 6 years. Those adopted later than that tended to do progressively less well (Siegler *et al.* 2003).

The three big ideas: some issues of equity and social justice

While research in this area is proceeding at a very fast pace (one reason for early childhood professionals to at least retain healthy scepticism about current findings, which may be outdated by next year!), the three areas looked at earlier are not, themselves, new:

> Neuroscientists have known about all three big ideas for 20 to 30 years. What we need to be critical of is not the ideas themselves, but how they are interpreted for educators and parents.
>
> (Bruer 1998:14)

What has proved highly seductive, both to parents and early childhood professionals, is the idea that, by behaving in particular ways with children, we can have a positive impact on the physical growth of their brains, and, thus, on their learning and development. As a consequence, articles in the popular press and websites aimed at parents have captured the interest of parents and carers, and many early childhood educators have sought to incorporate findings from brain research into their thinking and practice. Well-known interventions include Accelerated Learning in Practice (ALPS), described as an approach which is concerned with 'brain-based methods for accelerating movement and achievement' in children (Smith 1998, Smith and Call 1999), and Brain Gym, designed 'to enhance students' experience of whole-brain (using both brain hemispheres simultaneously) learning' (Dennison and Dennison 1994:VII). However, as Bruer's quote implies, we need to look closely at what is being suggested here. Goswami points out that children doing something as simple and ordinary as counting on their fingers prior to counting in their heads are activating neural circuitry in the brain (2004). This suggests that special interventions may perhaps be effective in just making more systematic use of the kinds of things people do already. Research continues to challenge thinking, and new ideas and models are constantly being presented. What may seem to be 'fact' now can be rapidly overtaken by new developments. For example, it is now more generally accepted that the first 3 years are not as crucial a 'window of opportunity' as was previously thought. The Organization for Economic Cooperation and Development (OECD) concludes: 'Though many important achievements occur during early childhood, it would be a myth to say that everything is determined during this preschool period' (OECD 2001:27).

In outlining some of the research in the areas of plasticity and synapse formation, sensitive periods and enriched environments, I have looked at some of the methodological questions that arise from each of them. There are, though, other questions, which revolve around issues of equity and social justice for young children and families:

- On the one hand, the research evidence about 'enriched' environments can be used to support calls for greater resourcing and funding for early childhood services. On the other hand, it is vital to consider the values implicit in a term like 'enriched'. As Bruer suggests:

  > In the popular and education literature, enriched environments tend to be culturally preferred, middle-class environments. These environments tend to include things that the writers value – Mozart, piano lessons, playing chess – and to exclude things that they scorn – video games, MTV, shooting pool.
  >
  > (Bruer 1998:18)

The danger is, then, of returning to ideas of providing 'compensatory' care and education for the vast majorities of children who do not conform to this group, replacing their social, cultural and environmental experiences with 'enriched', acceptable ones (Corrie 2000).

- If claims about the vital importance of critical periods are closely adhered to, the potential is there for services, and policy makers, to give up on children beyond the early years, believing that it would be 'too late' to do anything more, as the critical periods have passed. This could be seen as a general danger for children, but, from the perspective of equity, may unfairly affect children from particular backgrounds. As Corrie (2000) suggests, this position is dangerously close to suggesting that some children may be irredeemable.

- Using the brain as a way of explaining a child's behaviour or achievement may lead to other possible factors, such as discrimination and disadvantage, being ignored or downplayed (MacNaughton 2003).

- Locating 'problems' as within a child's brain rather than as part of their whole experience can lead us to a view of the child as a passive receptor of stimuli rather than as an active constructor of meaning (Corrie 2000).

Some tentative implications for practice

Are there, then, some lessons that we can learn, in addition to those already discussed? Some suggestions from the literature include:

- Studies of children's brain weights at autopsy suggest that, from half way through gestation to about 2 years of age, brain development as defined by physical measurement depends on nutrition. Evidence suggests that low brain weight may be related to cognitive deficiency (Griffiths 2003).

- Maternal stress during pregnancy may contribute to reduced production of foetal neurons and glia, and lower levels of synaptogenesis (Griffiths 2003).

- Stressful environments can result in the production of cortisol, a hormone which can reduce brain cells and neural connections (Gerhardt 2004).

- Environments provided for young children should offer them contexts that support their early capacities for responding coherently to, and retaining faithful records of, their sensory world. This means providing appropriate, but not overwhelming, stimuli (physical and interpersonal). In addition, the aim should be to ensure that babies and young children have the opportunity to direct their own sensory exploration of the environment, according to their individual preferences (Catherwood 1999).

- 'Physical exercise may boost brain function, improve mood and increase learning' (Blakemore and Frith 2005:134).

- 'Experiences that support children in making connections amongst domains of knowledge ... are likely to impact on and enhance the richness of neural networks in the child's brain' (Catherwood 1999:33).

- The cultural contexts in which children develop may have a permanent impact on brain physiology. 'Thus, subtly different brains are built in different cultures, and different teaching methods may be optimal in different places' (Blakemore and Frith 2000:30).

- Children learn at very different rates, and new learning is heavily influenced by previous experience via stored biases in the neurons (Scoffham 2003).

- As with the adult brain, the sensory-cognitive networks of children's brains are not wholly separate from the affective, interpersonal or motivational networks (Catherwood 1999).

- Learning and memory are strongly influenced by emotion. 'The stronger the emotion connected with an experience, the stronger the memory associated with it' (Wolfe and

Brandt 1998:13), as chemicals in the brain send out messages about the importance of remembering something, whether it be associated with positive or negative emotions. However, memory and learning may be lessened where the emotion is too strongly negative (LeDoux 2003).

- Memories may be more easily retrieved where the emotional state of the memory matches the state at the time of retrieval; for example, we are more likely to remember happy events when we are feeling happy (LeDoux 2003).

Further reflection

1   Would you describe yourself as predominantly a 'synthesizer' or an 'empathizer'? (Baron-Cohen 2004). What qualities do you think you have which might lead you to your conclusion?

2   Do you feel that exercise, food and sleep have a positive impact on your own brain functioning?

3   What is your position on the arguments set out earlier in this chapter about the implications of brain science for early childhood practice and provision?

4   What impact do you think the environment has on young children's brain development?

Further reading

Baron-Cohen, S. (2004)
Blakemore, S.-J. (2005)
Blakemore, S.-J. and Frith, U. (2000, 2005)
Bruer, J. (1998, 1999)
Catherwood, D. (1999)
Cohen, D. (2002) chapter 1
Corrie, L. (2000)
Eliot, L. (1999)
Gerhardt, S. (2004)
Gopnik, A. *et al.* (1999) pp. 102–10 and chapter 6
Griffiths, J. (2003)
LeDoux, J. (1998, 2003)
Siegler, R. *et al.* (2003) chapter 3
Talay-Ongan, A. (2000)
Wolfe, P. and Brandt, R. (1998)

Chapter 5

Knowing about the mind

Theory of mind, cognitive self-regulation and metacognition

This chapter focuses on young children's growing awareness, and understanding, of their own and other people's minds. Many of the ideas introduced in earlier chapters have a fundamental relationship to this understanding. Cognitive self-regulation, for example, is part of a bigger picture which also includes social- and emotional self-regulation, looked at in Chapter 3. Children's understanding of other people's minds develops as part of their interactions with others in a social world. As Astington suggests:

> The understanding of minds that children acquire in the preschool years underlies their social interactions with family and friends and provides the foundation for their cognitive activities in school. School and family, cognition and affect, work and love – these remain of fundamental importance throughout our lives. It all begins with the child's discovery of the mind.
>
> (Astington 1994:190)

The importance of the ideas focused on here is reflected in the lively research interest in the area, particularly in relation to young children. Flavell (1977) suggests that the development of metacognition, for example, is 'one of the really central and significant cognitive-developmental hallmarks of the early childhood period' (1977:64). There is, though, much that we do not know. Thornton (2002) speculates on the relationship of theory of mind to general cognitive development, and the extent to which children's growing understanding of their own thinking is an individual or a social process. As she points out, we do not know.

Theory of mind

What is theory of mind?

Theory of mind (ToM) is a topic which has dominated cognitive developmental research for the past 15 years (Dunn 2004b). The term 'theory of mind' was coined by researchers looking at chimpanzee behaviour. Other writers have used the terms 'mindreading', 'mentalizing', 'adopting the intentional stance', 'social chess' (Bailey 2002:166) and 'empathizing' (Baron-Cohen 2004). All of them relate to a process which can be defined as 'the ability to infer mental states in ourselves and others' (Bailey 2002:163), which includes an understanding that other people's thoughts, beliefs, feelings and desires may differ from our own, and that our own can change over time. Wellman suggests that, along with language, theory of mind is 'a distinctively *human* core capacity' (2004:2, emphasis in original) that shapes human thought and learning. The capacity to think in this way is closely related to the development of metacognition and self-regulation (see later in this chapter), and social understanding (Chapter 3). Bailey suggests:

> the ability to infer mental states in ourselves and others lies at the very heart of social interaction, of communication, of co-operation and competition, indeed, of almost every feature of the social life of humans. If you were blind to mental states, what sense would you make of the mosaic of conversations that occur during an average day, some fleeting, others intimate, some involving numerous speakers, others referring to people not even present? What sense would you make of jokes, or innuendoes, or lies?
>
> (Bailey 2002:163)

Astington concurs with this, when she says that 'Social interaction is really an interaction of minds, of mental states, but we have to communicate those states to others. We have to let the other person know we want something, or that we want them to believe something' (1994:43). This implies that ideas (or 'mental states') such as desire and belief underpin the development of theory of mind – we act to fulfil our desires in the light of our beliefs about things and we infer these same states in the actions of others. She refers to these as 'core concepts' in the theory of mind (Figure 5.1):

BELIEF + DESIRE

ACTION

Figure 5.1 Core concepts within the theory of mind.
Source: Astington, J. (1994) *The Child's Discovery of the Mind*, London: Fontana, p. 74.

When do children develop a theory of mind, and what develops?

Precise definitions of what it means to have a theory of mind, and thus at what point children can be said to have such a theory, are contested. As Smith *et al.* ask: 'how much knowledge about the mind do you have to have for a theory of mind?' (2003:461). Observations of 18-month-olds recognizing and responding to signs of distress in others, for example, might suggest at least some understanding that others have feelings, but could also just be recognition of an unhappy facial expression, learned more mechanically from noticing an association on previous occasions (Thornton 2002). However, as Thornton (2002) suggests, it seems unlikely that children will have no understanding of mental states one day, and a good understanding the next, making it worthwhile trying to look at what develops, and at what aspects of children's behaviour seem to indicate development of their theory of mind.

The ability to infer mental states in others presupposes an awareness of other people. In Chapter 3 it was suggested that this awareness is present in newborn babies and can be demonstrated by the ways in which they reciprocate the gestures of carers. In the first year of life babies show that they have some understanding that people have intentions (Wellman 2004), albeit that they do not yet recognize that such goal-directed behaviour derives from a mental state (Thornton 2002). A number of aspects of young children's behaviour begin to appear at around the age of 18 months which do seem to reflect some understanding of the mind. By about this age children are beginning to engage in pretence, which requires them to have an intuitive understanding of the difference between what is real and what is not. Bailey (2002) believes that such play is a precondition for the development of 'mindreading' skills. At some time before their second birthday children begin to comment on feelings and desires (Bartsch and Wellman 1995), and to adapt their speech to suit their audience (Karmiloff-Smith 1994), much as Sean does to his younger sister in Box 7.5 (see Chapter 7). By the age of 2 they are talking about emotions in ways which suggest that they understand that these are mental states. They also show some understanding that what one person wants may be different to what someone else wants (Bartsch and Wellman 1995). Box 5.1 shows both this talk about, and understanding of, feeling states in a young boy of 30 months.

The clear focus in young children's talk on emotion may be highly significant. Bartsch and Wellman suggest that young children's talk about desires precedes talk about beliefs and thoughts, which does not appear until around the age of 3, as in Box 5.2. Dunn (2005)

Box 5.1 Evidence from Judy Dunn

The older brother Len is crying because his mother scolded him and refused to comport him after he had bitten his younger brother.
    Family J, Child 30 months. Sibling is crying, C attempts to comfort.

C TO SIB: Len. Don't – stop crying, mate. Stop it crying.
C TO MUM: Len crying Mummy! Len crying. Look. Me show you. Len crying.
C TO SIB: Look, Len. No go on crying (pats sib)...(Sib still sobs.) Ah Len (helps sib with Lego bag). I put it back for Lennie, hey?...(shows sib a car) There's this man in here. What's this, Len? What's this, Len? (Sib sobs.)
MUM TO SIB: Do you want me to smack you?
SIB TO MUM: No.
MUM: Then just stop it, please.
SIB TO MUM: I'm trying to (sobs)...
C TO SIB (STILL CRYING): Stop crying, Len. Smack your bottom.

(Dunn 1988:94–5)

Box 5.2 Adam

ADULT: What happened to Tom?
ADAM: I don't know.
ADULT: What happened to him?
ADAM: I don't know. He ran down the street?

(Bartsch and Wellman 1995:107)

---

suggests that Bartsch and Wellman's data demonstrates that young children's understanding of cognitive states such as thinking and believing arises out of their earlier understanding of emotional states. Her research shows a clear association between young children's opportunities to engage in family talk about things such as co-operation among siblings, and feelings, and their later emotional understanding and performance in false-belief tasks (see later in this text) (Dunn *et al.* 1991). In addition, the children's individual experiences of social pretend play with mothers and siblings at the same age (33 months) related to social understanding at 40 months (Dunn *et al.* 1991). As we saw in Chapter 3, the social world of family and friends may be highly significant here. Not only do younger siblings develop a theory of mind earlier than first-borns, but children with two or more older siblings may pass such tasks even earlier (Wood 1998). Astington (1994, 1998) speculates that this may be because of their exposure to more tricks, jokes and teasing or to more talk about intentions and feelings by parents trying to settle family disputes.

False belief

By the age of 3, then, children already know a lot about people. They may have an understanding of the difference between thoughts in the mind and things in the world (Astington 1994). For the majority of them, the following year and a half will be a period of considerable development, notably in their understanding that, just as they themselves have a mind, so do other people, and that the thoughts and feelings in our minds will be different. They will have developed a representational theory of mind: 'By age 4 or 5, children realize that people talk and act on the basis of the way they *think* the world is, even when their thoughts do not reflect reality.' (Astington 1998:47, emphasis in original.) What they have come to understand is that thoughts in the mind may not always be true, and that people can hold a false belief, that is, one which contradicts reality.

Investigation of false belief in young children has been one of the most popular research topics over the past few years. Psychologists have developed a battery of experiments designed to explore whether, and at what age, young children appreciate that other people can have false beliefs. Box 5.3 describes a typical false-belief task, the so-called Sally–Anne task. In a meta-analysis of false-belief experiments, Wellman *et al.* (2001) conclude that at the age of 3 the average performance of children in false-belief tasks is significantly wrong. By about $4\frac{1}{2}$ years, children's average performance is significantly correct. However, these

single tribe experiment.

Box 5.3 The Sally–Anne false-belief task

In the task, children are shown two dolls, Sally (who has a basket) and Anne (who has a box). Sally has a marble, which she puts in the basket, and then she leaves the room. While Sally is out of the room, Anne removes the marble from the basket and hides it in the box. The children are asked where Sally will look for the marble when she returns.

The typical result from this task is that three year olds say that Sally will look in the box, because that is where *they* know the marble is, and they assume that Sally's thoughts are the same as theirs. By the age of 4, children will typically now understand that, while they know where the marble is, Sally will not know that it has been moved.

statistics belie individual differences not just between the children, but also between both task demand and the type of language used to introduce the task, leading to correct per-formance at earlier ages in some tasks than in others (Cohen 2002, Smith *et al.* 2003). Young children's understanding of diverse desires (their own versus someone else's about the same object) in false-belief tasks may develop much earlier than, for example, their ability to judge how a person will feel, given a belief that is mistaken (Wellman and Liu 2004). The work of some psychologists, notably Judy Dunn (1999, 2004a) and Judy Dunn *et al.* (1991), also suggests that such experimental studies may not be the best way to find out about young children's theories of mind. She emphasizes the value of observation of children in their familiar contexts, in everyday encounters with family and friends, suggesting that, in these meaningful, emotionally charged encounters, children will tend to display an understanding of other minds earlier than they do in false-belief tasks. Foote and Holmes-Lonergan (2003) suggest a positive relationship between false-belief understanding and the use of argument in sibling conflicts, particularly of what they call 'other-oriented argument', such as 'I'll give you all of these . . . if you give me that one' (2003:58).

How universal is theory of mind development?

Opinion differs as to the universality of theory of mind across cultures. Wellman *et al.* (2001) suggest a similar developmental trajectory across different cultural groups, differing only in the ages at which children achieve false-belief understanding (although they do stress that false-belief tasks only measure a narrow aspect of social cognitive development). By contrast, Naito (2004) believes that different cultural practices may contribute to different developmen-tal paths for theory of mind understanding. Cutting and Dunn (1999) and Sperling *et al.* (2000) also suggest that social class may be a factor. We noted earlier (Chapter 3) that parents may talk about emotions more with girls than with boys. Dunn (2004a) also found that conversa-tions about feeling states were more common in girl friendships than in boys, which may be important for an understanding of other minds. She also cites research in which girls have performed more successfully on theory of mind and emotion understanding tasks (2004a).

Particular groups of children across all cultures seem to experience more difficulty in developing a theory of mind than their peers. Notable among these groups are children on the autistic spectrum, who are either autistic, or have Asperger's syndrome. Such children rarely develop theory of mind, and, where they do, it is severely delayed. Characteristic of people with autism are difficulties in social interaction (they may have difficulty relating to others, prefer playing with objects rather than people, and be unable to interpret emotions or feelings), social communication (they may have difficulties with language, both speaking and interpreting that of others, and make little physical or eye contact) and imagination (they may have difficulty appreciating other people's perspectives, and do not engage in pretend play) (Wall 2004). A number of these features seem to be significant for development of the-ory of mind. Astington (1994:148) suggests that autistic children are quite different from other children in their lack of awareness of the mind and their own and others' mental states. Charlotte Moore, writing about her own experiences as the mother of three boys, the first two of whom are autistic, says that she knew, from very early on, that her third son was not:

> I knew, for certain, that Jake wasn't autistic when he was about fifteen months old. He had just learned to walk. He had a biscuit in his hand, and he toddled off into the garden, round the corner, out of my sight. He came back, empty-handed, weeping. 'Want

bikkit,' he wailed. He guided me, pointing round the corner, to where the biscuit was, wedged in the spout of a watering-can. He knew he had to tell me where the biscuit was. He knew I didn't know.

(Moore 2004:74)

As she goes on to say, her other two sons would not have done this. While, as the mother of two autistic children, Charlotte Moore could reasonably be expected to be more 'tuned-in' to looking for cues in her son, it nevertheless suggests that it may be possible to see the development of theory of mind from a relatively early age.

The difficulties autistic children have with theory of mind have been explained in two ways. The first, nativist, neurobiological account suggests that autistic children are 'mind-blind', and that an innate module of the mind is impaired (Baron-Cohen 1995, Pinker 1997). Blakemore and Frith (2005) cite research which suggests that those regions of the brain associated with theory of mind, or mentalizing, are more weakly connected in people with Asperger's syndrome than in neurotypical people, and, as a result, are less active. The second explanation sees the growth of mental state understanding as a product of social and conversational interaction. Peterson suggests that this latter explanation may also account for the delayed development of theory of mind in children who are blind, and deaf children who have hearing parents, because 'the child's disability imposes upon the fluent sharing of mentalistic information with family members' (Peterson 2004:13). The unimpaired development of ToM by deaf children living with deaf parents, it is suggested, is a result of growing up with fluent signing conversational partners, who share a common means of communication and interaction. Further discussion of different attempts to explain autism can be found in Baron-Cohen (1995, 2004), among others.

Theories about theory of mind

A number of theoretical positions have been put forward to account for how theory of mind develops. As I described earlier, psychologists such as Pinker (1997) and Baron-Cohen (1995) suggest an innate, domain-specific modular mechanism, a 'ToMM', or 'Theory of Mind Module'. A second, domain-general account emphasizes the development of children's general cognitive processing power, which enables them to represent two versions of reality: their own, and another person's (Thornton 2002). A third account suggests that children come to understand that others have minds by a process of mental simulation, introspecting on their own subjective experience and then using this to imagine the thoughts and feelings of another person in a similar situation (Harris 1989). Wellman (2004) suggests that these different views reflect wider disputes about general cognitive development, and it is true to say that the relationship between theory of mind and more general cognitive development is an area of considerable current research interest. A generally widespread view is that theory of mind development involves both innate mechanisms and experience (Astington 1998, Bailey 2002, Hatano 2004, Thornton 2002).

A number of current theorists and psychologists suggest that study of the development of theory of mind needs to take greater account of the sociocultural nature of development. Dunn and Bruner, for example, 'argue for a social constructivist, or "apprenticeship", interpretation of the child's developing competence in theory of mind tasks' (Wood 1998:166), and draw on Vygotskian ideas on the importance of talk and narrative. Nelson (2004) believes that it is time to replace 'ToM' with 'CoM', or 'Communities of Minds', with a greater emphasis on the centrality of communication, language and the culture of a community.

Is having a theory of mind always beneficial?

Are there any negative implications to the development of theory of mind, in particular to its early emergence? Dunn (2004a) speculates that, while early sensitivity to others' thoughts and feelings could be advantageous to a child in making and keeping friends and explaining a point of view it might also be disadvantageous if it also leads to a similar sensitivity to other people's disparaging comments, including adult criticism. This could be potentially damaging to a child's sense of self, and their feelings of self-competence and self-worth. She suggests the value of further research in this area.

Language, narrative and pretend play as contexts for developing understanding of the mind

Language

The relationship between language and theory of mind is complex and multifaceted, and, as yet, still imperfectly understood. The extent to which language is viewed as crucial for the development of theory of mind may depend on which 'theory' of theory of mind one holds. As Astington and Baird (2004) suggest, an innate view of its development suggests a less developmental role for language. They, along with others such as Dunn, position language as much more central to the development of theory of mind.

What is the nature of this relationship? Cutting and Dunn (1999) speculate that it may be that language influences theory of mind development, that the opposite may be true or that, very much in keeping with Vygotsky's views set out in Chapter 7, the influence may be mutual. In addition, the relationship between the two may not be stable, with different aspects being more important at different times (Astington and Baird 2004). They point to the interdependence of the development of language, social communication and theory of mind, but also stress that, in their view, language plays a part that is independent of social interaction. Social interaction, they suggest, provides opportunities for experiencing mental-state concepts. Language provides for their symbolic encoding, allowing for 'a level of abstraction that can support concepts about unobservable mental states' (Astington and Baird 2004:8). Through language children are exposed to different points of view, as people talk about what they 'think', 'know' and 'want', for example. Cutting and Dunn (1999) cite evidence from the literature of links between general language ability and false-belief performance, and Dunn's own research (Dunn *et al.*1991), cited earlier, suggests the significance of family discussion for aspects such as social and emotion understanding, as well as false-belief performance.

Narrative

Are particular aspects of language more important than others for theory of mind development? While pointing out that research has, at different times, suggested just about all aspects, Cutting and Dunn (1999) illustrate a difference between the language abilities of boys and girls in their study. For boys, all aspects of language related to their false-belief understanding. For girls, narrative ability seemed particularly important. Szarkowicz (2000) suggests that narrative contexts may be particularly valuable for studying young children's understanding of the mind, for a number of reasons. First, narrative contexts are often more naturalistic than experimental ones, and so may feel more familiar to young children. Dunn, as we have seen, emphasizes the value of everyday contexts both for developing young children's understanding of mind and for eliciting a more accurate picture of their understanding. Second, narrative is fundamental to how young children make sense of the world (Wells 1987). Finally, narrative 'provides individuals with opportunities to be both in the realm of action and in the characters' minds simultaneously' (Szarkowicz 2000:73). As she suggests, given that research on ToM focuses on an understanding of the interplay between mentalizing and action, narrative may be particularly helpful in exploring this.

Bruner is a powerful advocate of the important role of narrative in the development of theory of mind: 'it is conceivable that our sensitivity to narrative provides the major link between our own sense of self and our sense of others in the world around us' (1987:94). In support of this, Dunn cites research (Lewis *et al.* cited in Dunn 2004a) which shows children demonstrating more success in their understanding of other minds when they were given the opportunity to link the events involved in a task situation into a coherent narrative. Children's own narratives, in the context of language and thinking, are looked at in Chapter 7, and in the discussion on pretend play in the following section.

Szarkowicz suggests the value of narrative in the form of children's literature for studying theory of mind. Stories in picture and story books are familiar to children in many (though not all) cultural contexts and form social events both within the family and in early childhood settings. They are often shared with significant people. Many stories are also multilayered, often with parallel narratives of picture and text, providing opportunities for ambiguity and speculation on appearance and reality, for example. Box 5.4 features just such a story, and the children's responses to the practitioner's false-belief questioning.

Szarcowicz's research shows children having a greater chance of demonstrating their understanding of false belief in the narrative activity of sharing a story than in a more traditional task (2000). She suggests that the format of stories, particularly the repetitive and cumulative nature of many texts, may give children better 'markers' of what is important to notice. There are, in her view, some important implications for practice. She emphasizes the role of more experienced others in helping to 'unpack' (2000:79) the text, particularly in providing support around understanding of mentality in the story. Reading stories will need to be seen as a social, interactive event, where thoughts are shared, and where all participants are able to express their thoughts and feelings about the story as it unfolds. The practitioner in Box 5.5 uses stories as the context for a wider discussion with the children, supporting explicit discussion about their knowledge and thinking.

Pretend play

Pretend play, especially shared pretence, may be particularly significant for the development of theory of mind. Bailey (2002) suggests it could even be a precondition for the acquisition of the kind of mindreading skills that underpin theory of mind. If this is so, it may be an important area to consider in looking at the failure of children with autism to develop a theory of mind. As I outlined earlier, children on the autistic spectrum rarely engage in pretend play, either alone or with others. For Paley, fantasy play is 'the glue that binds together all other pursuits, including the early teaching of reading and writing skills' (2004:8). As an

Yvonne, the practitioner, is reading *Handa's Surprise* (Browne 1994) with the children, in order to explore the development of theory of mind through narrative. Set in Ghana, the book tells the story of Handa, who decides to take a surprise to her friend Akeyo in the neighbouring village. She loads a basket with 7 kinds of fruit, and sets off with it on her head. On the way, unknown to her, a succession of animals each takes a piece of fruit, until the basket is empty. At this point, a goat, tethered to a tangerine tree, butts the tree as Handa walks past, and fills her basket with tangerines, a fruit not originally in the basket. When Handa arrives at Akeyo's village she hands the basket (a 'surprise') to Akeyo – but the biggest surprise is, of course, for Handa herself, and she says: 'Tangerines! That *is* a surprise!'

YVONNE: As we read this story, as well as using your ears, to listen to the words, you will have to use your eyes, to look at the pictures carefully. (She reads the story, posing the question 'can you tell me what is happening in this picture?' each time.)
JOE: The naughty monkey is taking the banana.
DYLAN: The ostrich is stealing her guava.
LILY: The elephant is reaching over, with his long trunk, to take Handa's mango.

As the different animals appear in the illustrations, taking fruit from Handa's basket, the children laugh, and appear excited. As I read the last page most of them are smiling broadly.

YVONNE: What did Handa have in her basket when she arrived in Akeyo's village?
CHILDREN: Tangerines.
YVONNE: What did Handa *think* she had in her basket?
CHILDREN: Tangerines.
YVONNE: Okay, listen carefully now. As Handa walked into Akeyo's village, and she had the basket on her head (gesturing to demonstrate) what did she *think* she had in the basket.

For a few seconds everyone is quiet and looking thoughtful.

ELLA: Lots of different fruit.

Some of the children look puzzled.

YVONNE: That's right, Ella. Handa *thought* she had lots of different fruit in her basket, didn't she? Why did she think that? (Again, several children look uncertain.)
ELLA: Because she didn't see the animals taking it.

The children's reactions (laughter and excitement) and their responses to the questions (use of the words 'naughty' and 'stealing') suggest that they understood what was happening in the illustrations. However, they had been prompted at the start to look carefully, and their attention throughout was directed towards the action in the pictures. I deliberately chose not to ask any questions concerning Handa's perspective, so as not to lead them in this area. It is worth considering whether some of the children were not able to answer the final questions because they had lost concentration and so were not sufficiently focused to respond. However, nobody appeared distracted and all of them, except Ella, seemed puzzled by the questions, suggesting lack of understanding rather than attention.

Reproduced with permission of Yvonne Hatton

Box 5.5 Story reading with children aged 3 and 4 years, in a nursery

The children, with their teacher, are reflecting on listening to different versions of a range of traditional tales. She has asked them how they know that the stories were different, and what they needed to do to talk about the differences:

MAX: You have to think in your head and in your brain.
HASSAN: You have to think hard.
SIOBHAN: You have to remember all of them.
SHAUNA: You just stop talking and then you think. If you don't remember you could look at the book and you could see it on the book and think about it.

Reproduced with permission of Pat Gura and Ann Bridges and the staff, children and parents of Vanessa Nursery School

activity that often has considerable importance for young children (children in our research often chose as 'their favourite place' areas such as dressing up, role-play and construction, all rich in their potential for pretence), pretend play may act both to reflect children's understanding, and promote it.

Several features of pretend play may be especially significant for the development of theory of mind. In pretend play, children step in and out of role, represent situations and transform objects, talk about mental states ('Okay, you be the mum, and you're really cross') and have to negotiate meanings and actions with others. They have to make the 'leap of imagination into someone else's head' (Baron-Cohen 2004:26), which characterizes empathy with another person. This act of sharing an imaginative world with friends or siblings, in particular siblings who like each other (Dunn 2004a), involves recognition of their intentions, shared perspectives and co-ordination of communications about the play, often termed intersubjectivity. This creates the potential for internalization of these perspectives, a process which Vygotsky (1978) suggests supports higher levels of understanding and the potential for abstract thought. Pretend play seems to embody a complexity of understanding that may not be apparent in other contexts, for example, even 2- and 3-year-olds know that they are pretending (Dunn 2004a). In pretend play children can reason and draw causal inferences (Dunn 2004a), and seem able to identify intention as the mental cause of action, and to read intentionality in others (so-called second-order intentionality), at a much earlier age than they can in non-pretend contexts (Bailey 2002, Dunn 2004a). In Box 5.6, Abby clearly shows this second-order intentionality in her comment to her friends, Michaela and Jordan.

A crucial feature of pretend play is its emotional and social significance for young children, as noted in Chapter 3. Dockett suggests that, through their exposure to different perspectives in pretend play, and involvement in negotiations to resolve the kinds of conflicts that arise as a result, 'children may be forced to evaluate and modify their own perspectives and representations of reality, and to realise that their views are not necessarily shared by others' (1998:112). Higher levels of social understanding are particularly related to experience of engagement in shared pretence, above other forms of shared play such as rough and tumble play or shared delight in rule-breaking (Dunn 2004a). The conversations

Box 5.6 Abby, Michaela and Jordan, aged 4 years, in the role play area

> The three girls have been playing for some time, including shared play with a doll and doll's bed.
>
> MICHAELA: I'm Cinderella.
> JORDAN: Yeah, we're Cinderella.
> ABBY: You can't be, you've got a baby.

that children share in their pretend play often include reference to thinking and mental states, and children experienced in such talk are more mature in their later ability to 'mind-read' (Dunn 2004a:59). The importance of children's talk in pretend play and their metaplay behaviours are looked at in more detail in Chapter 7.

Pretend play, then, may be particularly valuable for the development of theory of mind. However, as with other aspects of development, it cannot be a pre-requisite, or children in societies with little pretend play in childhood might not develop theory of mind. Even across societies where children do engage in pretence the play themes will differ across cultures and reflect activities important to particular cultures (Garvey 1977). Dunn (2004a) suggests that play themes may also vary with gender, with themes of nurturance and relationships more common in, but certainly not exclusive to, girls' same-gender play than boys. Baron-Cohen (2004) suggests that boys also may be more interested in solitary, rather than co-operative, pretend play where being empathetic towards co-players will clearly be less of a feature.

Cognitive self-regulation and metacognition – separate and together

The focus of the remainder of this chapter is on cognitive self-regulation and metacognition. It is useful to begin by looking at both separately, for what each might mean. However, the relationship between the two is complex and intertwined making it more appropriate to then consider together how both might develop and how this development might be facilitated. This close relationship is reflected in some of the research and literature in this area, which occasionally uses the terms interchangeably, including reference to 'metacognitive self-regulation' (Sperling *et al.* 2000), for example. My own feeling is that one possible difference between the two is that self-regulation may be essentially a more unstable concept: one can choose to regulate one's behaviour or not, in many circumstances. Metacognition, on the other hand, may be more stable: it is difficult to *not* know about and have strategies for thinking about one's thinking, once they have been acquired. For much of the time, it is possible, and probably useful, to look at them together.

Cognitive self-regulation

Self-regulation is a complex, multifaceted concept, which brings together children's emotional, social, physical and cognitive experiences. There is no single, or simple, definition of self-regulation, and, like theory of mind, it is often referred to in different ways, including as 'impulse control, self-control, self-management, self-direction, independence' (Bronson 2000a:3). Ideas about the development of self-regulation are often seen as particularly associated with Vygotsky's model of the move from 'other-regulation' to self-regulation, as discussed in Chapter 2. Aspects of young children's social and emotional self-regulation are discussed in more detail in Chapter 3. While all of them are, of necessity, interrelated in young children's development the focus here is particularly on aspects of cognitive self-regulation.

Bronson defines cognitive self-regulation as 'the ability to control attention, to direct and monitor thinking and problem solving, and to engage in independent learning activities' (2000a:3). What seems important here is that such abilities are both conscious and voluntary, that is, that we can choose whether or not to engage in self-regulating behaviour. She emphasizes the interrelationship of motivation and self-regulation, believing that they are inseparable in most situations, particularly for young children. The development of metacognition, an important aspect of such self-regulation, is considered later in this chapter and in Chapter 10 some of the practical implications of the development of self-regulating behaviour are looked at in relation to young children's problem-solving.

Theoretical perspectives on the development of cognitive self-regulation

Theories to account for the development of cognitive self-regulation in young children feature in all of the models of cognitive development outlined in Chapter 2, as well as in a number of other perspectives, such as psychoanalytic and social learning theory perspectives (Bronson 2000a). They provide useful starting points for thinking about what might develop in relation to cognitive processing and it is useful to have them in mind when reading here. The characteristics associated with some of these models are set out here:

Behaviourism: While early behaviourists focused on observable behaviour, more emphasis is now being given to the non-observable behaviour of thinking, with the view that classical and operant conditioning principles of reward and punishment can be used to shape both. Awareness and conscious control of thinking is mediated through language, and children can be taught to regulate their thinking with verbal strategies, self-prompts and rules.

Piagetian: Awareness and control of thinking come about as a result of cognitive development, with the innate self-regulatory processes of equilibration allowing incorporation of new information into existing structures. This ability to control thinking is universal, and linked to a child's age and stage of development. Neo-Piagetian perspectives hold that this process is domain-specific, and that there are domain-specific strategies for thinking and problem-solving.

Information processing: 'Awareness and control are mediated by executive processes...which support control of attention and memory, decision making, goal setting, planning, using strategies, monitoring performance, and metacognitive functions' (Bronson 2000a:129). Children learn to think by developing these functions, in ways that are not always conscious.

Vygotskian: The pre-eminent tool for gaining mastery over behaviour and cognition is language, serving as the primary vehicle for both cultural transmission, and thought and self-regulation. Cognitive self-regulation is an active process, co-constructed by the child with the assistance of others. Sociocultural theorists such as Cole *et al.* (1971) and Rogoff (2003) suggest that 'people of different cultures may think and solve problems in different ways' (Bronson 2000a:22).

(Adapted from Bronson 2000a:113–29)

Whitebread *et al.* (2005) also point to the increased interest in the part played by the development of the brain in the processes of self-regulation, and you may find it useful to refer back to Chapter 4 in this context.

Metacognition

As with self-regulation, there is no universal definition of metacognition. Papaleontiou-Louca defines this 'fuzzy concept' as 'cognition about cognition... thoughts about thoughts, knowledge about knowledge or reflections about actions' (2003:10). Synthesizing the ideas of, particularly, Flavell (1977), seen as the founder of thinking in this area, and Brown (Brown and DeLoache 1983, DeLoache and Brown 1987), a useful working model consists of three closely related elements. These are as follows:

1   metacognitive knowledge (gradually accumulated knowledge about one's own mental processing, tasks and cognitive strategies);
2   metacognitive experience (monitoring one's self-awareness and reflecting upon it);
3   'self-regulation' (control of mental processing, to support appropriate strategy use in a task).

(Whitebread et al. 2005)

Meadows provides a good, if challenging, map of the territory:

> It involves many basic 'on line' metacognitive processes, including: analysing and defining the character of the problem at hand; reflecting upon one's own knowledge (and lack of knowledge) that may be required to solve the problem; devising a plan for attacking the

Box 5.7 Metacognition: Joshua and Jasmeet, aged 4 years

Joshua:
Playing at the sand tray, Joshua is using a bottle top as a scoop to empty the tray.

JOSHUA: This is a good idea. Like this.

Jasmeet:
Having been asked to tidy up, the children begin to throw the dressing up clothes back into the box, but upon trying to close the box discover that they can't. Jasmeet tells the children that they must fold the clothes neatly in order to make them fit. She solves the problem by drawing on existing knowledge.

Observation of Jasmeet reproduced with permission
of Philippa Cooper

Both Joshua and Jasmeet show metacognitive awareness here, analyzing and defining the character of the problem, reflecting upon their own knowledge, and devising a plan for attacking the problem, aspects that Meadows (1993) identifies in her definition of metacognition.

---

problem; checking and monitoring how the plan helps in the problem-solving; revising plan (and perhaps the analysis of the problem) in the light of this monitoring; checking any solution reached; and, generally, orchestrating cognitive processes in relation to the cognitive contents and objectives involved, in the service of whatever is one's goal.

(Meadows 1993:78–9)

As Pramling (1988) suggests, this implies a conscious awareness of one's own learning and thinking, as Joshua and Jasmeet both show, in different ways, in Box 5.7. Look ahead now, too, to Box 7.8 and Abe's comment: 'I don't do thinking, I'm just thinking about my body', and Charlotte in Box 8.2: 'Dad, I've been thinking about it'.

The development of cognitive self-regulation and metacognition

At this point, it is most helpful to look at both of these aspects of knowing about the mind together, as many aspects of young children's development are related to them both. In addition, as I have already suggested, it is difficult to say just where self-regulation ends and metacognition begins.

Bronson (2000b) suggests that the capacity to develop self-regulatory functions of all kinds is affected by both innate factors such as temperament and environmental factors such as interactions with others. Young children's growing physical control gives them opportunities for exploration and experiences that support their cognitive development. Many of the aspects of development outlined throughout this book are important contributors to young children's control of cognitive processing. The early awareness of, and interest in, patterns in their environments, and of cause and effect, noted in the discussion on children's conceptual development in Chapter 8, for example, both reflects and contributes to babies' increasing ability to organize their ideas and thoughts. Early visual scanning comes increasingly under their control, leading to more organized information (Brown and DeLoache 1983). Their growing ability to anticipate and act in accordance with familiar routines contributes to this cognitive organization. There is evidence that, from about six months onwards, babies are capable of making simple plans in order to attain a goal (Karmiloff-Smith 1994). In the following two years young children's memories and abilities at representing past events improve considerably, allowing for a more deliberate approach to selecting goals, and active problem-solving, albeit that they may not yet be very skilled at planning ahead (Bronson 2000a). The explosion of language competence during these years acts as an important support in young children's abilities in organizing and classifying. Even before the age of 2 children will spontaneously correct errors of grammar and pronunciation in their speech (Bruner 1987, Siegler 1998).

This kind of implicit metacognitive knowledge and experience is largely unconscious, and something that we all use without realizing. For example, while you are reading this book, you may be slowing down sometimes, rereading to clarify your thinking, and skim reading at other times. Siegler (1998) comments on its prevalence in young children. Karmiloff-Smith records a mother talking about her son, Kaspar, at 27 months:

Kaspar started to use both English and German names for the same word and seems to know who to use them with: for example he goes to the 'libree' (library) with my friend Deena and he goes to the 'tek' (Bibliotek) with me.

(Karmiloff-Smith 1994:223)

The period from about the age of 3 onwards is marked by more conscious intentionality in young children's behaviour, and thus can be said to be increasingly self-regulated. They are 'learning how to learn and how to solve the problems presented in their environments' (Bronson 2000a:134). Children aged 3 have been shown to be capable of monitoring their problem-solving behaviour, and, at 4, to use strategies and metacognitive processing in puzzle tasks (Sperling et al. 2000). This continues to develop with age. Sperling et al. found that, out of two groups of children (aged 3–4 years and 4–$5\frac{1}{2}$ years), the older group were better able to both predict how well they would be able to perform in a problem-solving task, and, after performance, to evaluate how well they did perform.

Memory

An important element in young children's developing self-regulation and metacognition is their ability to use memory strategies. A general tendency which seems to develop over the period of early childhood is of increasingly conscious control over processes which, while they may emerge initially quite early in life, function better with the more deliberate use of helpful strategies, in recalling both objects and ideas, as discussed in Chapter 1. Children as young as 2-years-old can use rehearsal strategies which help with recall, for example, pointing to or repeatedly glancing at the place of an object that they have been asked to find later (Thornton 2002). Over time children will tend to become better at both doing something deliberate at the time of storage to facilitate later retrieval and in applying more systematic attempts when retrieving (Brown and DeLoache 1983). Three-year-olds may begin to use deliberate strategies such as looking at, and touching, an object, in order to remember it (Brown and DeLoache 1983), thus demonstrating their understanding of the usefulness of doing something to help them remember. However, even at the age of 7 children will tend to overestimate how well they will be able to remember things and underestimate the effort needed for memorization (Thornton 2002).

Knowledge and experience

A number of factors may contribute to young children's less developed skills of self-regulation and metacognition. In Chapter 2 the idea of novicehood was looked at, and young children's relative inexperience may be an important factor here, in not having either sufficient knowledge or strategies for reflecting on their understanding. They may often not know enough about a situation in order to identify its most salient features, an idea looked at in Chapter 8 in relation to young children's conceptual development. They may also not realize that strategies for metacognition and self-regulation are useful in many different situations (Brown and DeLoache 1983), although the extent to which children can usefully transfer strategies across situations is not clearly understood, as we shall see both later in this chapter and in Chapter 10.

Contexts for developing cognitive self-regulation and metacognition

Why is this type of thinking important? Fisher (1990:121) cites research into medical practice which suggests that it is not doctors with the most knowledge of medicine that make the best practitioners but those who know how and when to apply their knowledge. This looks somewhat like Claxton's definition of intelligence, outlined in Chapter 1, as 'knowing what to do when you don't know what to do' (1999a:4). What these doctors may have understood is that, faced with a problem, some basic characteristics of thinking can be applied in most situations, to good effect. Brown and DeLoache (1983) suggest these are:

- *predicting* the consequences of an action or event;
- *checking* the results of one's own actions (did it work?);
- *monitoring* one's ongoing activity (how am I doing?);
- *reality testing* (does this make sense?);
- *coordinating* and *controlling* deliberate attempts to learn and solve problems.

(Brown and DeLoache1983:282, italics in original)

Like Brown and DeLoache, Papaleontiou-Louca proposes a range of strategies that can be applied in a wide range of contexts, suggesting that use of these by young children and those working with them will support 'one of the perennial problems of instruction – that of transfer or generalization of what has been learned' (2003:27–8). Her extensive list includes such strategies as identifying what you know, and what you don't know, generating questions, goal setting, evaluating ways of thinking and acting, role-play, keeping thinking journals, inviting 'thinking aloud' and adult modelling.

In her focus on the importance of promoting consciousness about thinking and introspection in young children she has much in common with Pramling (1988). However, for Pramling, these may not be best achieved through the teaching of potentially transferable metacognitive strategies. Like Bronson, she believes that metacognitive understanding is content and context dependent and best supported by a focus on the relationship of the child to their world. For Pramling, this necessitates the metacognitive teaching of content, rather than strategies:

> We first focus on *what* the child is thinking about (a content). At the second step we focus on *how* the child is thinking about that content. Finally, at the third, we focus on the child's thinking about his own thinking about the content, which is the metacognitive level.

(Pramling 1988:266–7)

Pramling outlines a project with three groups of children aged between 5 and 7 years, working with teachers following the same 'content', but handled in very different ways. Teacher A carried out 'metacognitive dialogues' (1988:270) with the children, focusing the children's attention on different ways of thinking about their learning in their activities. She asked questions such as 'Did you find out anything that you didn't know before?' and 'How would you go about teaching other people all you have learned?' (1988:271). Teacher B's approach was more 'traditionally' didactic, and Teacher C provided materials for play and encouraged modelling work with clay, paper and other materials. When asked to think about their learning six months later, 11 of the 16 children in group A said that they had learned by personal experience, and the remainder went further believing that they had learned by reflection. All of the children in groups B and C either said that that they did not know what they had learned (30 out of 33) or that it was the result of external influence, not themselves. Pramling suggests that part of the reason for this marked difference lay in the continuous focus on the children's ideas of learning by Teacher A. Swan and White (1994) suggest that this can also be done through the use of 'thinking books' in which children are encouraged to write about and reflect upon what they have learnt (rather than, as is so often the case, what they have done). Swan records her purpose in introducing thinking books with the 8-year-old children she was teaching: 'I had introduced the thinking books to encourage children to see purpose in their learning, so that they would have more control over it and would gain a better understanding of what they learned' (Swan and White 1994:25). A number of the practitioners in our research also emphasized ideas of thinking and reflection in their interactions with the children, often asking them metacognitive prompts such as 'What did you think might happen?', 'How do you feel about that?' and 'I wonder why that's there?' (Robson and Hargreaves 2005). In Chapter 7 this modelling of speculative talk is looked at in relation to the work of Paley.

Wood and Attfield (2005) draw on a Vygotskian model to emphasize the value of appropriate, sensitive and responsive adult intervention, whether in adult- or child-initiated activities in which adults create both the conditions and time for reflection. Children, they suggest, should not be left just to find out for themselves but supported in developing greater awareness of their own learning. Joint problem-solving which supports the move from other-regulation to self-regulation may be an important aspect of the adult's role (Bronson 2000a). Whitebread et al. (2005) emphasize how the children themselves can also act in this way and suggests that children learn a great deal about becoming self-regulating learners by watching one another and through peer tutoring. Meadows (1993) also considers the role of peers and suggests the value of conflict and disagreement for metacognitive development.

The roles of adults, and differing perspectives on transferability, are looked at in more detail in Chapter 10, which focuses on approaches to developing young children's thinking through aspects such as problem-solving.

Some implications for practice: a summary

- The importance of all talk, and particularly talk about emotional states, for supporting theory of mind development (Astington and Baird 2004, Bartsch and Wellman 1995).
- The value of narrative contexts, both personal (Bruner 1987) and in children's literature (Szarkowicz 2000), for the development of theory of mind.
- The value of shared pretence for supporting role taking, symbolic transformations and talk about mental states (Dunn 2004a, Vygotsky 1978).
- The most effective self-regulated learning may be promoted by offering choice to the children, opportunities for them to control the level of challenge in tasks and opportunities for them to evaluate both their own work and that of others (Perry et al. cited in Whitebread et al. 2005).
- The value of adult use and modelling of metacognitive strategies, including identifying what you don't know, generating questions and thinking aloud (Papaleontiou-Louca 2003).
- The importance of developing 'metacognitive dialogues' with young children, both oral (Pramling 1988) and written (Swan and White 1994).
- The value of adult–child joint problem-solving for supporting metacognition (Bronson 2000a).
- When adults get involved children may sometimes be more likely to say that they cannot do something. When working with other children, they may be less likely to

question their ability and often gain confidence through mimicking another child (Whitebread *et al*. 2005).

• The most effective response from an adult to a child asking for help may be to direct them to another child who has competence or expertise in the area. Often just watching another child supports metacognitive development (Whitebread *et al*. 2005).

Further reflection

1   Szarkowicz (2000) has used narrative, in the form of story, as a way of exploring false belief. An author such as John Burningham has made extensive use of parallel narratives which embody false belief in his books. Try to find a children's storybook which could be used in this way, and read it with a child(ren). Discuss the story with them, using questions that focus on an understanding of theory of mind.

2   Sunil, aged 3 years 11 months, in the block area:

Sunil sets himself the task of building a tower taller than the teacher.
He begins by using large bricks and places four on top of each other, in a pattern, one horizontally, one vertically.

SUNIL: It makes it tall quicker.

He negotiates with Gurpreet to obtain two smaller bricks, but is beginning to get upset. The teacher suggests they operate a swap shop – Gurpreet agrees and Sunil's building continues. He calls the teacher over to stand next to his tower:

SUNIL: No, it's not tall enough yet, but I can't reach.

The teacher gets a stepladder. On her return he has placed small bricks on top of each other, balancing them. He asks her to stand next to the tower again. She does, and it has not got much taller.

SUNIL: Oh, I need bigger ones again.

Looking at this episode, how, for you, does it show Sunil's awareness of his own knowledge and expertise? Is there evidence of self-regulation and metacognition? What part is being played by the adult?

Further reading

Theory of mind

Astington, J. W. (1994)
Bailey, R. (2002)
Bartsch, K. and Wellman, H.M. (1995)
Cohen, D. (2002) chapter 5
Cutting, A.L. and Dunn, J. (1999)
Dockett, S. (1998)

Dunn, J. (2004a)
Karmiloff-Smith, A. (1994) pp. 222–6
Siegler, R. *et al.* (2003) pp. 260–5
Smith, P. *et al.* (2003) chapter 14
Szarkowicz, D. (2000)
Thornton, S. (2002) pp. 38–40, 63–70
Wellman, H.M. *et al.* (2001)

Self-regulation and metacognition

Bronson, M. (2000a)
Brown, A. and DeLoache, J.S. (1983)
Meadows, S. (1993) pp. 78–81
Papaleontiou-Louca, E. (2003)
Pramling, I. (1988)
Sperling, R.A. *et al.* (2000)
Thornton, S. (2002) pp. 81–2, 216–17
Wood, D. (1998) chapter 4
Wood, E. and Attfield, J. (2005) pp. 69–76

Chapter 6

Observing, describing and documenting children's thinking and understanding

This chapter looks at some of the ways in which close observations of children can be interpreted, drawing particularly on the work of Susan Isaacs and Chris Athey, and on ways of describing children's attitudes or dispositions to thinking and learning, particularly concepts such as involvement, flow and mastery. Developing on from these, it is useful to consider the relationship between the documenting of observations and children's thinking, and the parts played by the children themselves in informing adults' understanding and actions. In recent years, there has been a valuable, and increasing, emphasis on the importance of the children's own 'voices', and the gathering of their own perspectives on their lives (Alderson 2005, Clark and Moss 2001, Morrow 1999, Pramling Samuelson 2004). The chapter concludes with a brief consideration of a particular approach to the description and assessment of thinking, the idea of 'intelligence' and 'intelligence testing'.

Experimental approaches

On first glance, the title of this chapter may appear paradoxical. How can we possibly observe children's thinking and understanding, processes which are essentially occurring inside a person's head? As we saw in Chapter 4, developments in medical techniques allow us the possibility of 'seeing' the brain itself in action, but this, of itself, does not give us a view of young children's thinking and understanding. In addition, these medical and experimental techniques are, of course, not available to practitioners in their daily work with young children nor would it be appropriate for them to be so.

Habituation studies

A common experimental approach in attempting to observe the ideas and thinking of young children, particularly babies, is the use of habituation studies. Habituation is one of the simplest and most fundamental forms of human learning (Siegler *et al.* 2003) and involves the way in which we all show a decline of interest in, or response to, repeated or continued experience. For example, a baby may continue to turn his head and look at a rattle being shaken for some time. Over time, however, he will tend to stop turning his head, show signs of boredom and a new stimulus may be required to restart the head turning. Such behaviour is taken to imply evidence of learning and memory. The decreased response to a stimulus can be taken to suggest that a child has a memory of what it is: 'oh, I know what that is, I've seen/heard/touched/tasted it before, so I don't need to look at it/listen to it/touch it/taste it now'. Presented with an unfamiliar experience, dishabituation occurs: 'I don't think I know what that is' etc. Experimental studies based on this premise can be used to ask a wide range of questions: can babies discriminate between shapes, faces, quantities, for example, and how early in life can they do so? Such studies rely on measurement of observable signals relating to change in a child's behaviour, for example, length of looking at a particular object or display, varying amplitude of sucking on a dummy or pacifier attached to measuring apparatus or changes in heart rate. It is interesting to note that Siegler *et al.* (2003) suggest that speed of habituation is related to general cognitive ability later in life.

The results of such experimental studies may inform practice, but other ways are needed for use in day-to-day work with children. In seeking to observe something which is, in many ways, unobservable, early childhood professionals, psychologists and epistemologists have developed approaches which rely on applying models of thinking, and the use of outward, observable signals which may indicate thinking and understanding, including what children themselves say about their thoughts and actions, as ways of attempting to document thinking and understanding.

Susan Isaacs

Susan Isaacs' influence on the field of early childhood has perhaps been most strongly felt in her emphasis on the value of observation-led records for understanding young children. Her book *Intellectual Growth in Young Children* (1930) provides detailed accounts of episodes at the Malting House School, Cambridge, from 1924 to 1927. The school was initially a small day nursery, for boys aged between 2 and 5, and developed finally into a day- and residential-school for 20 boys and girls, aged up to $8\frac{1}{2}$-years-old. Isaacs was particularly interested in children's interest in the physical and human world around them, and what she saw as their enthusiastic curiosity about everyday life, from drains to traffic direction, to the life cycles of plants, animals and human beings. She believed it was important to provide a counterbalance to what she saw as a greater preoccupation at the time with what she describes as 'self-expression' and 'make-believe' in schools for young children. In her view, it is vital to support both children's imaginations and interest in fantasy and their interest in finding out about the world around them. The two should go hand in hand.

The records of observations in Isaacs' work give an insight into her approach to working with the children and the importance she placed upon children's active exploration, observation and discovery in support of their developing thinking and understanding. She emphasized: 'It is the child's understanding that matters, not our pleasure in explaining' (Isaacs 1930:41). This is well exemplified in the episode described in Box 6.1.

In analysing the observations of children's activities, Isaacs concludes that their efforts at discovery, reasoning and thinking can be categorised under four groups:

1   Applications of knowledge – in particular, the application of knowledge already possessed to new situations or problems, including formal or theoretical applications, imaginative and hypothetical application, make-believe and dramatized knowledge, and comparisons and analogies. The application of knowledge is also evident in the children's practical insights and resourcefulness.

2   Increase of knowledge – gained through experimentation, observation and discovery by the children.

3   Social interchange of knowledge – characterized by children's use of 'why' and other logical questions, and reasoning, and by discussion.

4   Miscellaneous – diverse episodes not easily classified.

(Adapted from Isaacs 1930:49–52)

Box 6.1 The approach of Susan Isaacs

> A rabbit has died during the night at the School.
> One child offers his view that: 'My daddy says that if we put it into water, it will get alive again.'
>
> ISAACS: Shall we do so and see?
>
> The children put the dead rabbit in a bath of water, and hypothesise about it, suggesting that movement means it is alive, and and discussing floating and sinking as indicative of life and death: 'If it floats, it's dead, and if it sinks, it's alive'. They then all help to bury the rabbit.
> The following day two children talk of digging the rabbit up, and suggest it might not be there because it will have 'gone up to the sky'.
>
> ISAACS: Shall we see if it's there?
>
> She says, in conclusion:
> 'They found the rabbit, and the children were very interested to see it still there.'
>
> (Adapted from Isaacs 1930:41)

She emphasizes, however, that no categories are watertight, and that there is considerable overlap, both between the categories themselves and within any one episode involving a child or children.

Initially influenced by psychoanalysts Anna Freud and Melanie Klein, Susan Isaacs nevertheless was clear in her objectives for teachers at the Malting House School that they should not try to act as analysts for the children. The ideal, she says, is that:

> *no* interpretations should appear in the records (of observations)...Only full verbatim records of what was said, and full objective records of what was done should be given.
>
> (Isaacs 1930:1, emphasis in original)

In her view, in any observational situation, adults will always have some impact on the children's behaviour, however involuntary that may be. In addition, any adult selections of observations of children, and their interpretations of children's activities, will always be influenced by their own histories and experiences. France (1986) points to different adult interpretations of similar behaviours in boys and girls, for example.

Isaacs does acknowledge the practical difficulties of taking such full, verbatim, objective records in the course of working with children, and says that, of necessity, the 'on the spot' records of practitioners working with young children may be more summary and fragmentary. As we saw earlier, she disagreed with Piaget's emphasis on stage theory. She concurs with Piaget that use of such developmental scales may be valuable but stresses that 'it can never be allowed to take the place of a direct examination of the full concrete behaviour of the child' (Isaacs 1930:6–7).

Schemas

The work of Chris Athey, in particular her 1990 book *Extending Thought in Young Children*, has been very influential in its contribution to views on the development of young children's thinking and understanding. Athey's work is underpinned by Piaget's notion of cognitive structures (schemas) and his model of conceptual growth. However, whereas Piaget focuses on the limitations of very young children's preoperational thought, Athey focuses more positively on what children can do and on identifying universal patterns or structures of thought. She argues that repeating patterns and actions (schemas) of children's activity represent forms of thought, which can be nourished by appropriate content, in order to support the co-ordination of cognitive structures. These patterns of thinking and learning can be accessed through observations of children's representations, language, mark-making and play, all of which provide evidence of the children's persistent interests. In her view:

> The most easily understood meaning of 'schema' is as follows: 'schemas of action (are) co-ordinated systems of movements and perceptions, which constitute any elementary behaviour capable of being repeated and applied to new situations, e.g. grasping, moving, shaking an object' (Piaget 1962, p. 274). Schemas are patterns of repeatable actions that lead to early categories and then to logical classifications ... A schema, therefore, is a pattern of repeatable behaviour into which experiences are assimilated and that are gradually co-ordinated. Co-ordination leads to higher-level and more powerful schemas.
>
> (Athey 1990:36–7)

Such patterns of repeatable behaviour are evident from very early babyhood onwards and are constantly developing and changing with increasingly complex combinations of schemas as children grow. The co-ordination of schemas, in particular, is related to the development of concepts (see Chapter 8) and is important because 'as schemas are co-ordinated into more and more complex amalgamations, the environment is comprehended at higher levels by the child' (Athey 1990:37).

Building on Athey's work, Arnold cites her own research which suggests that some schemas may be more frequently observed than others in young children. In particular, they include:

- Envelopment – wrapping, covering and enclosing objects, space or oneself.
- Trajectory – moving in, or representing, straight lines and arcs, for example, kicking, punching and graphic representations of straight lines.
- Enclosure – making boundaries around spaces, objects, graphic representations and oneself, for example, painting an enclosing line around a picture.
- Transporting – moving an object or objects from one place to another, or an interest in being moved oneself.
- Connection – joining objects together or joining oneself to things, for example, tying objects together with string.
- Rotation – spinning and turning oneself around, spinning objects, or an interest in things which turn, for example, taps and wheels.
- Going through a boundary – going through a boundary oneself or making an object go through and come out the other side.
- Oblique trajectory – as with trajectory but with a focus on the use of oblique lines.
- Containment – putting an object, objects or oneself inside something which can contain them.

- Transformation – showing an interest in things which change state, for example, water and ice or chocolate.

> (Adapted from Arnold 1999:22. See Bartholomew and Bruce 1993, Meade and Cubey 1995 and Nutbrown 1999 for fuller descriptions of these, and other schemas)

In the example in Box 6.2, Michael displays a combination of both a trajectory and a dynamic vertical schema. As Sam, the observer, notes, he shows this both in what he does (motor level), and in how he talks about his actions (symbolic representation). If we had observational evidence of Michael, at a later stage, talking about his experience in the absence of the bricks themselves, we would also have evidence of 'thought', the third level of functioning Athey describes, alongside motor level and symbolic representation level functioning. *supports this idea but*

Athey and those who have further developed her ideas, such as Nutbrown (1999), place much greater emphasis on the role of other people, particularly adults, in supporting the development of children's schemas than did Piaget. The support of adults in both identifying and nourishing children's schemas, through interaction, and the provision of a supportive environment, is crucial. Athey concludes 'Experience is what "feeds" schemas and extends them' (1990:58). In essence, the role of the adult is to be both proactive with

---

Box 6.2 Michael, aged 3 years 2 months, at nursery school

Michael is sitting at a table with an old set of wooden bricks of various shapes, sizes and colours – cubes, triangular prisms, and rectangular blocks.

1 Michael builds a tower using the bricks
'I'm building a tower'
'I put that on three' – placing a brick on top of another one.
'Then I do this' – he knocks the tower over with a sweep of his hand.
5 His facial expression depicts laughter and smiles, whilst looking at the bricks.
He builds the tower immediately afterwards. This tower falls over by itself.
Again Michael laughs and smiles at the pile of bricks.
He builds the tower again and again. If it does not fall down he pushes it over
10 as before. Each time he laughs and smiles.
He bangs two bricks together: 'I like this'.
He builds another tower. 'You build it very high and go like this; – pushing it over with a sweep of his hand.

In lines 1, 6, 9 and 12 Michael is displaying a trajectory schema. He is accompanying his speech in line 3 with the action of 'on-top-of' schema (Athey, 1990, p.143). He is displaying this on a motor and symbolic level when he has named the stack a 'tower' (line 2), and using vertical trajectory symbolism when describing the tower in line 12.

> Reproduced with permission of Sam Segar

Box 6.3 Joshua, aged 4, at nursery school

Joshua comes into the classroom and goes straight to the woodwork bench. He bangs a couple of nails into a piece of wood. He then comes to the paint table and selects a piece of paper. He takes a brush and makes marks by stabbing the brush down. He then moves the brush in a push pull motion. He moves away from the paint and goes towards the construction area. He picks up two wooden cars and throws them into the home corner. He then gets a pram and takes it outside into the garden where he pushes it around.

Athey talks of 'fitting not flitting' and this applies to Joshua if one looks closely. He is displaying a trajectory schema and is moving from area to area experiencing this. This continued and so did his delight in throwing objects! His interest was discussed and planned for so that he could be supported and extended in his learning. We provided balls hanging from elastic that could be hit with a bat, and targets he could throw balls at. While using these outside he became interested in the guttering and, with support, set this up so he could roll balls down the pipes. Joshua had not been particularly interested in painting before, except for the occasional fleeting visit. He was offered the chance to paint and shown how he could flick the paint so he could splatter it over the table, he was happy spending time doing this.

What would have happened if we had handled Joshua's learning differently? I confess we were sometimes frustrated by his love of throwing things! But we were able to reflect and plan for him drawing upon our knowledge and understanding, what I would consider to be our sound pedagogical nations. Instead of being labelled as a 'naughty' child who would not concentrate, he was viewed as 'strong and capable' and his interest or schema that was at the core of what he was doing was supported.

Reproduced with permission of Lucy Parker

and responsive to the children. Clearly, as with any consideration of the role of the adult, the question of the extent to which adults may themselves 'lead' children's interests is worth putting. In addition, identifying and supporting a child's schemas may require insight and skill on the part of the adult. The example in Box 6.3 highlights the parts played by adults in observing one child's schema and supporting and extending it.

Dispositions

The concept of disposition derives from developmental psychology. Learning dispositions have been described as a combination of motivation and 'situated learning strategies' (Carr 2001:9). Carr suggests that 'situated learning strategies' are knowledge and skills that are being used with a particular purpose in mind, linked to social partners and practices, and tools. She looks at the idea of disposition in the following way:

In everyday speech we often use it like 'temperament': we comment that someone has a 'cheerful disposition'. It is seen as a quality of an individual, something he or she was born with, or an outcome of facilitating circumstances. When motivation is situated, however, as

David Hickey points out, 'context has a fundamental, rather than merely a facilitative role' (1997, p. 177). Lilian Katz made this point when she commented that: 'Dispositions are a very different type of learning from skills and knowledge. They can be thought of as habits of mind, tendencies to respond to situations in certain ways' (1988, p. 30).

(Carr 2001:21)

It follows from this, of course, that not all dispositions are necessarily positive: the dispositions to give up, or to be cruel, are as real as dispositions to persist, or to be kind. A useful way of thinking about the idea of disposition is that it is about children being 'ready, willing and able...a combination of inclination, sensitivity to occasion, and the relevant skill and knowledge' (Carr 2001:21). To learn successfully, one will need to make use of all three of these aspects. For example, in learning to read, the relevant skill and knowledge about the process of reading will, by themselves, ensure that a child learns to read, in a functional sense. However, the inclination to read, and a willingness to do so, will be needed if a child is to really become 'a reader'. Citing Resnick (1987 in Carr 2001:9), Carr suggests that much of learning to be a 'good thinker' is dependent upon being ready or willing to identify opportunities to apply one's capabilities. Perkins and Tishman, in their Project Zero research project Patterns of Thinking, draw out three similar aspects, describing them as the three components of thinking dispositions: inclination, sensitivity and ability. They suggest that 'it is sensitivity, rather than inclination, that appears to be the chief bottleneck in effective intellectual performance' (http://pzweb.harvard.edu/Research/PatThk.htm). Such sensitivity may be related to the kinds of qualities Dweck (2000) describes in her discussion of mastery-orientations (see later in the chapter).

Carr situates learning dispositions centrally within the approach to observation and assessment developed in New Zealand called *Learning Stories* (see Carr 1998 and 2001 for detailed description) and identifies five domains of learning disposition, which themselves are derived from the New Zealand early childhood curriculum *Te Whariki* (Ministry of Education New Zealand 1996). The relationship is shown in Box 6.4.

It may be important, though, to think about such learning dispositions not as end states in themselves but rather as 'dynamic' (Claxton and Carr 2004). Thus, the disposition to persist will not be a once and for all acquisition but a process that displays itself in different ways at different times and along three dimensions: robustness or a tendency to keep responding in a positive way, even under less supportive conditions; breadth or the ability to apply habits of learning across different domains and in different contexts; and richness,

Box 6.4 Five domains of learning disposition and *Te Whariki*

The strands of the New Zealand Curriculum Te Whariki		*The domains of learning disposition* ('*The behaviour we look for*')
Belonging	>	Taking an interest
Well-being	>	Being involved
Exploration	>	Persisting with difficulty, challenge and uncertainty
Communication	>	Expressing a point of view or feeling, communicating with others
Contribution	>	Taking responsibility

marking increased flexibility and complexity and the use of a widening repertoire of strategies (Claxton and Carr 2004).

Carr describes the *Learning Stories* approach as similar to the gathering of narrative-style observations, but 'much more structured' (Carr 2001:96). The five strands and domains set out in Box 6.4 provide a framework for recording and analysing observations of children. In settings using this approach, it is evident that many of the learning stories begin with a primary focus on one area of learning disposition, for example, taking an interest. Carr describes how two processes integrate all 5 areas: *overlapping* and *sequencing*. Overlapping is the process by which different areas often work together, for example, 'Children who have the motivation to tackle and persist with difficulty often express their ideas or feelings in the process' (Carr 2001:97). Sequencing is the way in which one area may follow on from another, as, for example, in the case of a child whose persistence with challenge followed on from his interest and involvement. A practitioner working in an English multi-professional centre which has adopted a *Learning Stories* approach outlines a number of positive impacts on the centre's work. These include practitioners noticing children's interests and schemas more easily, and a shift in practice in the setting to more child-focused planning (Lisa Frank, personal communication). Both of these aspects are important supports for children's thinking and understanding.

Involvement and flow

'Being involved' is identified as one of the five domains of learning disposition described by Margaret Carr (2001). The idea of involvement as an indicator of children's understanding and 'intense mental activity' (Laevers 1999) has been developed by Ferre Laevers in Belgium, and also used by Chris Pascal and Tony Bertram in the United Kingdom, as part of the *Effective Early Learning* (EEL) Project (see Pascal and Bertram 1997). Laevers links involvement with the idea of flow (Csiksentmihalyi 1979) and suggests:

> Involvement goes along with strong motivation, fascination and total implication; there is no distance between person and activity, no calculation of possible benefits... The crucial point is that the satisfaction that goes along with involvement stems from one source, the exploratory drive, the need to get a better grip on reality, the intrinsic interest in how things and people are, the urge to experience and figure out. Finally, involvement only occurs in the small area in which the activity matches the capabilities of the person, that is in the 'zone of proximal development'. One couldn't imagine any condition more favourable to real development. If we want deep level learning we cannot do without involvement.
>
> (Laevers 2000:24–5)

Laevers suggests, then, that involvement is a precondition for 'real development', and also links it with Vygotsky's (1978) idea of the ZPD. He identifies a number of observable 'involvement signals' from which the extent of children's involvement may be deduced. These include concentration, energy, creativity, facial expression and posture, persistence, precision, reaction time, language and satisfaction (Laevers 2000).

In seeking to measure children's involvement, Laevers has developed a five-point rating scale, called the *Leuven Involvement Scale* (LIS):

LEVEL 1:   No activity, or purely stereotypic repetition of very elementary movements.

LEVEL 2:   Frequently interrupted activity (including staring into space, fiddling, dreaming, for approximately half of the time of the observation).

LEVEL 3:   More or less continuous activity, but children appear indifferent to the activity, and do not put in much effort. Action ceases whenever an interesting stimulus appears.

LEVEL 4:   Activity with intense moments. The activity is of real consequence to the child, and involvement is expressed in the signals for as much as half the observation time.

LEVEL 5:   Sustained intense activity. Child's eyes are more or less uninterruptedly focused on the actions and on the material. Surrounding stimuli barely reach the child, and actions are readily performed and require mental effort.

(Adapted from Laevers 1994)

Laevers believes that a key factor of support for the higher levels of involvement is the opportunities children have for choice: 'the more children can choose their own activities, the higher will be their level of involvement' (Laevers 2000:26). His view is supported by Segar (2004), who found consistently higher levels of involvement when children were able to initiate their own activities rather than when directed by an adult. In Chapter 10 the relationship of choice to children's thinking is considered, including differing perspectives on the balance of adult-led and child-initiated activity in early childhood settings. The area of choice and self-directed activity is of some significance in any discussion of children's thinking and understanding.

Involvement is one of two dimensions on which Laevers focuses in assessing the quality of children's experiences. The second dimension is the idea of emotional well-being, looked at in more detail in Chapter 3. In his view, this conceptual framework of well-being and involvement 'challenges the assumption that narrowly defined tests of academic achievement are the only means of measuring educational outcomes' (Laevers 2000:20) a view which can be seen to have elements in common with the ideas of Gardner, in Chapter 2, and later in the chapter.

Csikszentmihalyi, in describing his work with adults, uses the term 'flow' to describe a similar quality of deep involvement, referring particularly to enjoyment, and a desire to repeat an enjoyable experience (sometimes, for example in the case of rock climbers, even when it is dangerous). In his research, adults often described their experiences of 'flow', that is, times when thing were going well, with activities enjoyed for their own sakes, in very similar ways. It is useful to look at his list of subjective dimensions, as commonly cited by the respondents in his research. It is worth reflecting on the extent to which children may exhibit similar characteristics when in a state of flow, and whether these can be seen as indicators of children's thinking:

- concentrated involvement in an activity;
- clear goals;
- immediate feedback related to the goals of the activity;
- little sense of time;
- feeling of control;
- loss of ego and self-consciousness;
- no fear of failure;
- merging of action and awareness;
- a balance between challenges and skills, which can vary over time;
- an activity enjoyed for its own sake.

(Adapted from Csikszentmihalyi 1979:260–2)

A number of these dimensions are often cited as characteristics of 'play'. Csikszentmihalyi draws a distinction between flow and play, suggesting that a state of flow may occur in a wide range of activities, some of which might be seen as 'play' and others, for example, a surgeon performing an operation, which would generally be described as 'work'. For Csikszentmihalyi, play is a structured form for experiencing flow.

Mastery

Mastery is looked at in more detail in Chapter 3, but it is useful to look here at this aspect in relation to observation and description. Dweck describes children as having either a 'helpless' or 'mastery-oriented' reaction, particularly when they experience difficulty or failure (Dweck 2000). As a tool for the observation and description of children's thinking, the focus is on children's approaches to, and motivation for, tackling an activity, and the kinds of problem-solving strategies they use.

Dweck's ideas are useful in helping to look at how children see themselves and whether they appear to be engaged in an activity because they are motivated by improving their own competence or understanding or because they want to gain approbation or avoid negative judgements of their competence. She summarizes these as having a 'learning goal' on the one hand, and a 'performance goal' on the other. She stresses that both goals are normal and universal, and that there is nothing wrong with either of them. The danger, she believes, arises when performance goals are overemphasized, either by the child, or by the adult. Jo Short, an early childhood practitioner, observes how one boy in her nursery seemed to be oriented towards performance goals. In observing him play with construction apparatus, she records him making comments such as 'Do you like this best of all, this thing that I've made?', 'Is it cool now?' (referring to his model). She also notes that he does not give his construction a name, and speculates 'By failing to give his construction a name, is he protecting himself from criticism? He cannot be judged on the end product if it has no specific identity' (Jo Short, personal communication).

As with involvement, Carr (2001) relates this idea of mastery to one of the 5 domains of learning disposition (see earlier): that of persisting with difficulty or uncertainty. However, as Dweck points out, dogged persistence may not always be the best strategy. She suggests that a mastery-oriented response includes 'knowing when to opt out of a task – say, when it is truly beyond someone's current capabilities or when the cost of persisting is too great' (Dweck 2000:13).

The observation in Box 6.5 includes examples of involvement, flow and mastery.

Documentation and thinking

The recording of adults' observations of young children has long been a cornerstone of early childhood practice. Many useful books set out a range of approaches to this kind of documentation (Bartholomew and Bruce 1993, Harding and Meldon-Smith 2000, Sharman et al. 2004), and the ways in which it can support planning and provision. In recent years, however, there has been increasing emphasis on the parts played by the acts of observing and documenting children's activities in supporting children's thinking and understanding (Carr 2001, Edwards et al. 1998). This approach has come to be closely associated with Reggio Emilia, in Northern Italy, in particular.

For practitioners in Reggio Emilia, children's thinking is made visible through a process of documentation using a range of media, and gathered in a variety of ways, including the

Box 6.5 Mark, aged 3 years 2 months, at nursery school

Mark looks at the equipment in the water tray and selects a scoop and a small plastic bottle. He plunges the bottle deep into the water and pours the water onto the scoop. He watches the water spill over the scoop and repeats this sequence five times. A peer initiates verbal interaction with Mark. He gives no response, visually or verbally. Mark puts the bottle back into the water tray. Still holding the scoop, he walks over to the water play storage containers. He looks in each box before selecting a water wheel. He carries it back and places it in the middle of the water tray. He plunges his scoop deep into the water and pours the water into the hole at the top of the wheel. He watches the wheel spin and repeats this three times. He returns to the storage containers and selects a funnel. He returns to the water tray. Still holding the scoop, he places the funnel in the hole at the top of the water wheel. Using the scoop he pours water into the funnel and lowers his body to watch the wheel spin. Mark then kneels on the floor, placing his face closer to the wheel. He pours more water into the funnel, and winces as water splashes his face. He places the scoop back into the tray and stands up. He walks back to the storage containers and selects a cylinder, takes it back to the tray and kneels down again. He plunges the cylinder into the water, then lifts it high to pour the water into the funnel. Mark closes his eyes as the wheel splashes water in all directions.

MARK TO PEER: 'It feels like rain'.

Mark stands up and walks over to the sink, dries his face with a paper towel, and walks over to the block area.

Mark's approach can be described in relation to the dispositions of interest, persistence and responsibility for his own actions (Carr 2001). His 'involvement' is what Csiksentmihalyi (1979) describes as the state of flow. Laevers (2000:24–5) states that 'involvement goes along with strong motivation, fascination and total implication, there is no distance between person and activity'. Mark would score a level 5 on the Leuven Involvement Scale. This is reflected when he does not respond to a peer (however we cannot rule out the question of whether this was a conscious decision, as Mark may not have heard him). He also demonstrated a number of 'involvement signals'. Mark appeared totally absorbed by his work.

Mark demonstrated a sense of mastery through his self-competence and self-efficacy, Dweck suggests that this 'mastery orientation' is the result of Mark's engagement in this activity because he is motivated to improve his own competence and understanding.

Reproduced with permission of Angela Streek

children's own representations and the observations made by adults. This systematically collected documentation of the children's developing ideas, theories and understandings actively shapes thought as children struggle to represent and reflect upon their ideas. Young children's thinking is seen as a collective process and, through discussion and 'provocation', their existing theories and ideas can be reflected on, challenged and modified. It is this intersection of documentation and learning, both group and individual, which supports metacognitive activity and reflection on learning. In collaboration with Howard Gardner and the *Project Zero* team at Harvard University, they suggest that:

> A broad range of documentation (videos, tape recordings, written notes and so on) produced and used *in process* (that is, during the experience) offers the following advantages:
>
> - It makes visible... the nature of the learning processes and strategies used by each child...
> - It enables reading, revisiting and assessment in time and in space, and these actions become an integral part of the knowledge-building process...
> - It seems to be essential for metacognitive processes and for the understanding of children and adults.
>
> (Project Zero and Reggio Children 2001:84,
> emphasis in original)

Assessment, as 'a precious human measuring tool' (Project Zero and Reggio Children 2001:202) is viewed as a central part of this process, which, in itself, opens up new possibilities. Children come together, in the groups in which they have been working, to both assess themselves and each other, by revisiting what they have done, and reflecting on this. Documentation relating to their activity is carefully displayed, reflecting the value placed both upon the activity itself, and the records made of it (Edwards *et al.* 1998). The intention is to both develop attitudes of self-reflection and to deepen children's understanding. They suggest that this process helps children to become more aware of the ways in which their thinking has developed, and view it as analogous to Vygotsky's ZPD. The role of the adult at this point is to highlight to the children the nature of the development in their thinking and understanding.

   While they say they are wary of reducing this process to a prescription, they suggest that there may, nevertheless, be some useful indicators that the learning groups are both supporting and demonstrating understanding, and it is useful to look at these:

a   Children and adults feel they are contributing to a larger, more meaningful whole.
b   The discoveries of individual children become part of the thinking of the learning group.
c   Children express a feeling of continuous growth and awareness that their theories are provisional, and they take pleasure in seeing them modified, developed and advanced.
d   Over time the members of the learning group, alone or as a group, verify, consolidate and apply concepts and competencies acquired in one context to other contexts and domains of knowledge.
e   Children and adults use a language of thinking and emotion.
f   The objective that the group sets for itself is reached by keeping together the procedural and content requirements of the work.
g   Assessment and self-assessment have a strong presence inside the learning group and serve to guide and orient the learning process.
h   Collaboration strategies are an integral part of the group learning process and can determine the quality of learning.

(Project Zero and Reggio Children 2001:247)

Documentation, then, may have a number of potential benefits if the intention is to support and develop children's thinking and understanding, including deepening children's interest, curiosity and understanding, supporting metacognition, enabling children to revisit and reflect upon their own thinking and learning, and aiding memory and recall.

Children's perspectives

In recent years there has been considerable growth of interest in approaches to observing children which seek to gain the perspectives of the children themselves. Such approaches reflect a growing concern to ensure that children are seen as active, willing participants in the process, one which arises partly from greater concern for children's rights (Alderson 2005) and ethical considerations, but also from a growing awareness of the important part played by the children's own views and ideas, both in shaping practice and in supporting adults' and children's understanding.

In the United Kingdom, Alison Clark and Peter Moss have developed an approach to observing and documenting young children's experiences which acknowledges the value of multiple perspectives, including those of the children themselves. Their *Mosaic Approach* uses traditional narrative observations, documentation of parents' views and child conferences, alongside other, more novel techniques such as giving children cameras to photograph places of importance to them, involving children in taking adults on walking tours of their environment, and developing children's maps of their experiences. Initially, Clark and Moss focus on the value this 'framework for listening' (Clark and Moss 2001) has for gaining a complete picture of a child, their interests and their priorities. As their work has developed, it is increasingly clear that such an approach can act as an important tool for children's thinking and reflection. Clark (2005) describes the ways in which the taking of photographs of their 'most important' places by children in an English pre-school setting involved considerable discussion and reflection, the exercise of choice and judgement and the exploration of shared and personal meanings by the children. She suggests that approaches such as *Mosaic* position children as active explorers and meaning-makers rather than as receivers.

Common to both *Mosaic* and practice in Reggio Emilia is an emphasis on hearing the children's voices in a wide range of ways. The product, as expressed in words, pictures, song, dance and any of the other 'hundred languages' of children (Edwards *et al.* 1998) acts both as evidence of, and a tool for, children's thinking and understanding. In so doing, the use of both still and video cameras is invaluable, for 'bring(ing) into their consciousness the children's own high-level thinking in ordinary moments' (Forman 1999:3). Broadhead (2004) describes the ways in which replaying video sequences of the children's play to themselves not only supported this kind of metacognitive activity, but also, through the children's observations and reflections upon what they saw in the video, revealed aspects of their learning which had remained opaque to the adults watching. Forman (1999) speculates that it may be that the video in effect provides children with a space for the physical memory, allowing them more operating memory with which to think about the activity. A practitioner in our research reflects: 'When I've tried to talk to the children about their own learning...I've found they would go off the subject really easily, that they actually find it really hard to know what you're getting at...but a video or photograph can inspire it more (Robson and Hargreaves 2005:90).'

This may be particularly pertinent in relation to younger children. However, as Pramling Samuelson points out, 'toddlers express themselves and communicate with their whole body, and their actions are as trustworthy as spoken language' (2004:5). A similar view was expressed by one of the teachers in our research. Commenting on Nathan (age 4 years 3 months) she suggests that his verbal skills were not yet well enough developed for him to put his thinking into words, instead: 'he was actually just going and doing things, and trying things out by moving bricks, or planks, using different tools. He was actually showing what he was thinking, he was acting out his thought processes' (Robson and Hargreaves 2005: 89). Such statements reaffirm the importance of close observation, and careful listening and watching by adults, if they are to really access children's own perspectives.

Assessing thinking and understanding: measuring intelligence

So far this chapter has looked at ways of observing and describing children's thinking and understanding, which make use of indicators that allow a detailed picture of a child to be built up, with the assessments which are made as a result reflecting the complexity of each child's understanding. These indicators look at children's development across a range of aspects, which include affective as well as cognitive qualities. However, one concept in particular has long been used as a measure of individual difference in cognitive development and that is the notion of intelligence.

As Pollard (1997) suggests, the idea of measuring intelligence is rendered particularly problematic because no one is precisely sure what it even is. As noted in Chapter 1, definitions vary considerably.

Intelligence testing

The idea of measuring intelligence goes back to the nineteenth century and Francis Galton. In the 1880s he had an 'anthropometric' laboratory in the Natural History Museum where, for a small fee, he offered to measure people on a variety of psychophysical tests (Sternberg 1986) including describing their intelligence in relation to the size of their heads (Cohen 2002). It was not until over 20 years later, however, that the first 'intelligence test' was published, by Alfred Binet, in Paris. Binet had been approached by the Paris authorities to develop a way of identifying those children who might not be capable of succeeding in the normal school system, in order that they could be more effectively catered for. First published in 1905, the Binet-Simon (after his colleague, Theophile Simon) intelligence tests were initially used for this purpose but soon gained a much wider following in mainstream education and training. The tests were based on the idea of norms of performance for a given age, from which a child's 'mental age' could be derived. This approach was to prove highly influential in a number of ways, not least of which is that it focuses on individual difference within a given age group, rather than on age-related change, the focus of many theories of cognitive development. Test items in Binet's work were chosen to identify the typical performance of children at different ages, which could then be used to determine a total score for each child. This score was relative to the norm for that age group. Thus, measurement of an individual child's intelligence varied along a continuous scale.

In the century since Binet's work was first developed, ideas of intelligence testing have spread across the world, and form the basis for the use of psychometric testing today. Extensive use of intelligence tests on American soldiers in the First World War set the scene for the proliferation of their use throughout the twentieth century. Psychologists like Burt and Eysenck suggested that it was possible to measure general intelligence or 'g' (a term coined by Charles Spearman, cited in Siegler et al. 2003), as a factor which was independent of experience, knowledge or education. As a consequence, it would then be possible to describe people as either 'intelligent' or not. Siegler *et al.* (2003) describe this as a view of intelligence as a single trait, which influences all aspects of cognitive functioning and is common to all intellectual tasks. Underpinning this general measure is a model of intelligence as 'quickness of mind' (Cohen 2002:131) or the ability to process information quickly. Thus, in measuring intelligence, tests may look at a subject's reaction time (RT) or inspection time (IT) in response to stimuli (Meadows 1993).

Most familiar is the idea of giving an individual's intelligence a numerical value, the 'intelligence quotient' or 'IQ', developed by the German psychologist William Stern in 1912. This is derived in the following way:

$$IQ = \frac{\text{mental age}}{\text{chronological age}} \times 100$$

Thus, an IQ can be established for any individual at any age, which is relative to the rest of that age cohort. The average IQ is set as 100.

Perhaps the most important questions for practitioners working with young children are: what is the content of the measures being used to establish this 'mental age' and how are they being framed to young children? Donaldson (1978) clearly establishes the centrality of context in supporting young children's understanding. In many instances, intelligence tests comprise disembedded items, which may not allow young children to display the true depth of their thinking and understanding. In addition, the content of the tests may focus on a narrow range of areas and prioritize convergent thinking and the 'knowing' of facts rather than aspects such as creativity. This factual knowledge of the world has been called 'crystallized intelligence' (Cattell 1971, Sternberg 1985) or the 'accumulation of schooling, acculturation and other learning experiences' (Meadows 1993:161). In acknowledging the drawbacks of such a narrow focus, developers of other intelligence tests have attempted to draw on other aspects of intelligence, such as 'fluid intelligence' (Cattell 1971, Sternberg 1985), or the ability to draw inferences, to think on the spot, to solve problems and to employ inductive reasoning. Examples of this are the Wechsler Intelligence Test for Children (WISC), and the Wechsler Pre-school and Primary Test of Intelligence (WPPSI), for use with children under 5.

Intelligence testing has proved seductive because it was (and still is, in some quarters) seen as a valid, reliable way of comparing cognitive function. As such, it had widespread use in the United Kingdom in the mid-twentieth century in order to select children for secondary education. However, a range of studies have demonstrated that such tests are not objective, or context-free, and are likely to disadvantage children who receive less coaching in the ways of intelligence tests or who are from cultural backgrounds different from those on whom the tests have been standardized (Pollard 1997). The heavy verbal and linguistic bias of some tests may disadvantage children who are speakers of English as an additional language (where the test is being taken in English!). In addition, those most favoured by such tests seem to be children whose memory and analytical qualities are strongest, at the expense of those with creative and practical qualities. As Claxton says, 'IQ begins to look more like a rather arcane ability, at which only rather peculiar people would (and would wish to) excel, than a crucial quality for living' (1999b:32).

There have been attempts to develop culture- and language-free tests of intelligence, such as the *Raven Progressive Matrices*, which require individuals to complete the missing piece of a pattern, by choosing from a set of six alternatives. However, as Thornton points out, even a test like this assumes that the person taking it has some knowledge of the conventions of testing and is aware of the need to balance speed against accuracy (Thornton 2002). Children from particular cultural backgrounds may be more familiar with such conventions and even the idea of being tested. In addition, children from cultures with no tradition of writing or mark-making may have problems in interpreting such two-dimensional images. The dangers of making cross-cultural comparisons of children based on the same test, or even of using the same test on all children in an average class in much of Europe, North America or Australia, are clear.

Critics of 'IQ' testing

One of the most influential critics of conventional intelligence testing, suggesting that it rests upon a very narrow view of what it is to be intelligent, is Howard Gardner, whose ideas were looked at in Chapter 2. Essentially, Gardner argues that rather than one brain we have a series of semi-autonomous modules, which may sometimes work together, but which may also compete, and which demonstrate a whole range of different intelligences. If we are to truly measure a person's intelligence, Gardner argues, we must find ways that relate to all of these intelligences, not just the narrowly focused verbal, mathematical and spatial aspects which predominate in conventional intelligence testing. For Gardner, there is no reason why a person should score highly on some forms of intelligence and low on others. Pascal and Bertram make a similar point in their discussion of assessment and testing in the early years. They argue for forms of assessment similar to those discussed earlier, which look at a wide range of indicators, 'not simply focusing on those things that are easily measured' (Pascal and Bertram 1999:95). In this they are critical of what they see as a narrow focus on literacy and numeracy in current testing regimes. Such a focus may disadvantage some groups of children, particularly those for whom English is an additional language, and boys. In addition, it does not take account of many children's knowledge, skills, understandings and attitudes in very significant areas of their activity.

Sternberg, similarly, suggests that traditional approaches to testing intelligence have severe limitations. In his view, intelligence is a 'mental activity directed towards purposive adaptation to, and selection and shaping of, real-world environments relevant to one's life' (Sternberg 1985:45). It follows from this that intelligence is situated within sociocultural contexts, and may differ from one culture to another, dependent upon experience, and upon what is valued. His triarchic theory of intelligence comprises three subtheories. The first or 'experiential' subtheory, concerns the task itself and is concerned with how effectively a person learns a new skill. The second, 'contextual' subtheory, looks at the ways in which people adapt to, select and shape their environments. Sternberg suggests that this may be best measured via tasks which look at social and practical skills. The third subtheory is called the componential subtheory and considers information processing aspects of tasks and focuses on the different strategies people might use in solving a task. This third subtheory, which focuses more on metacognitive skills, may be relatively independent of context, but Sternberg concludes that the other two subtheories in his definition of intelligence are, in the case of the 'experiential', more culturally relative, and in the case of the 'contextual', context dependent. Consequently, Sternberg argues that behaviour is not intelligent in the abstract, but in context. The person who jumps into a river to save the life of someone he sees drowning is, we would tend to think, behaving more intelligently than the person who stands on the riverbank calculating the specific density of the drowning man as he sinks below the water, however well he is able to perform the calculation.

To return to the idea of intelligence as 'innate, general cognitive ability' (Burt in White 2002:78), the inevitable consequence of such a viewpoint is that intelligence owes much to our genetic inheritance, that it is a product of our nature, more than it is a result of our experiences. Siegler *et al.* (2003) suggest that no issue in psychology has been responsible for more acrimonious debate than the relationship of heredity and environment to intelligence. In Thornton's (2002) view, the relative importance of nature and nurture will vary according to situation. The area as a whole is probably best summed up by Meadows:

> The only sensible position to take, it seems to me, is that intelligence is affected by one's genes both directly as they work to produce a more or less adequately functioning brain and indirectly through one's kin's behaviour and the environment one seeks out and elicits oneself; but that it is also malleable, affected by the environments to which one becomes adapted.
>
> (1993:184)

To summarize here, the idea that there are many forms of intelligent behaviour, all of which are influenced by the social and cultural contexts in which they occur, suggests that 'intelligence' as a narrowly understood concept of general ability may not be especially useful in the assessment of young children's thinking and understanding. In addition, the idea that 'individual human minds can be characterized as having a given level of general intelligence' (Thornton 2002:179) is a theory, and not a fact. Furthermore, knowing a child's score on an IQ test may be of little value in informing practitioners about how they should proceed in order to support that child's further development.

Some implications for practice

The practical implications of observing, describing and documenting young children's thinking and understanding are implicit throughout the discussion in this chapter. Observation is, of itself, a practical support in informing adults working with young children about all aspects of their behaviour, including their persistent concerns (Athey 1990) and their dispositions for learning (Carr 2001), such as involvement (Laevers 1999) and mastery (Dweck 2000). It plays a valuable part in making children's thinking 'visible' (Project Zero and Reggio Children 2001) in which children's own involvement in the process is critical (Clark and Moss 2001).

Further reflection

With their permission, make a narrative observation of a child or a group of children, or find a recorded example in the references for this chapter. Look at it in the light of the range of approaches discussed in this section, for example using Laevers' involvement signals, or Carr's domains of learning disposition.

1 Does each approach add to your understanding in different ways?
2 Are the approaches complimentary to one another, or do they conflict?
3 Would different approaches be more or less useful in different contexts?

Further reading

Schema

Athey, C. (1990)
Meade, A. and Cubey, P. (1995) pp. 2–4 and 16–45
Nutbrown, C. (1999) chapters 2 and 4

Dispositions

Carr, M. (1998, 2001)
Claxton, G. and Carr, M. (2004)

Involvement, flow and mastery

Carr, M. (2001)
Csikszentmihalyi, M. (1979)
Dweck, C. S. (2000)
Laevers, F. (1999, 2000)
Pascal, C. and Bertram, T. (1997)

Documentation and children's perspectives

Carr, M. (2001)
Clark, A. and Moss, P. (2001)
Edwards, C. *et al*. (1998)
Project Zero and Reggio Children (2001)

Intelligence

Cohen, D. (2002) chapter 7
Gardner, H. (1983, 1991)
Meadows, S. (1993) chapter 3
Siegler, R. *et al*. (2003) chapters 3 and 8
Thornton, S. (2002)

Language, communication and thought

In this chapter the focus is on the role of language, particularly spoken language, and communication, in young children's thinking and understanding. We look at the curious, inquiring minds of young children, and at their efforts to make sense of their world, through talking, questioning, playing and interacting with others, in the contexts of home and early childhood settings. Thornton suggests that the development of language is 'the most striking achievement of infancy' (2002:42). How this happens and how children acquire language remains a contested area, and theories to account for the acquisition of language are briefly considered later in the chapter. The main interest here, though, is in the relationship of language to children's thinking, and on the role of language as a tool for thinking (Vygotsky 1978, 1986), which can be used 'to organise, sequence and clarify thinking, ideas, feelings and events' (DfEE 2000:58).

To what purposes do we put language?

The ability to use language to communicate, and to make sense of experience, is a uniquely human attribute. This highly flexible and constantly evolving symbolic system provides a means for humans to represent and communicate their thoughts and ideas. Halliday argues that language enables human beings 'to build a mental picture of reality, to make sense of their experience, of what goes on around them and inside them' (1985:101). While, as we shall see, some of this may be a solitary process, the uniqueness of language is in the ways in which it facilitates communication and the sharing of this sense-making process. As Astington (1994) points out, our thoughts are shared with others in language. Mercer suggests that this is what makes language qualitatively different from other communication systems, in that it 'provides us with a means for thinking together, for jointly creating knowledge and understanding' (2000:15) and for making better sense of the world together. We use language to convey our beliefs and desires to others, to make things happen (Astington 1994), to differentiate between ourselves and others, to take advantage of the things that people before us have discovered about the world (Gopnik *et al.* 1999) and, as Wells (1987:53) says, 'just to remain in contact'. Claxton suggests:

> The ability to talk to ourselves supports the development of physical skills. Listening to and telling stories helps people to make sense of challenging and puzzling situations. And language also enables us to develop our powers of memory.
>
> (Claxton1999b:133)

So while language could be said to be a single system used for two purposes, namely representation and communication (Astington and Baird 2004), these two purposes interact with one another, with acts of communication serving to support representation and vice versa. How does this happen? What is the relationship between language and thought?

The relationship between language and thought

In order to explore this relationship, it is worth looking very briefly at the main theories of how children come to learn to speak in the first place. Flavell's assertion that 'Draconian measures would be needed to *prevent* most children from learning to talk' (Flavell in Thornton 2002:44, emphasis in original) reflects Trevarthen's (1995) views considered in Chapters 2 and 3. Theoretical perspectives about how this drive to communicate is built upon fall into approaches which place varying emphases on the role of innate properties and environmental experience. Behaviourist approaches in the 1950s suggested that language was acquired as a result of conditioning with children imitating the speech they heard around them. If that were the case, however, we should not expect to see children generating their own grammars and the kinds of expressions with which we are all familiar. Children's comments such as 'my stick breaked', or 'the bath's unfilling' demonstrate the application of grammatical rules which are, in many instances, correct, but which, as here, cause problems in the face of irregular forms, common in English. Partly in response to the behaviourists' ideas, a variety of theorists, of whom Noam Chomsky is best known, suggested that language is too complex to learn from experience alone, so there must be some innate, pre-existing structure that enables young children to acquire it. Chomsky calls this the Language Acquisition Device or 'LAD', and it relates to the modular ideas of cognition referred to in Chapter 2 as well as to some of the current thinking about brain development looked at in Chapter 4. This perspective, known as a nativist approach, proposes that there is a universal grammar (UG) or set of unconscious rules common to all languages, that humans are pre-programmed with this and that they are innately predisposed to learn language (Chomsky 1957).

Chomsky's theories have undergone considerable development and reformation since they first appeared (Trott *et al.* 2004) and have been taken forward, most notably by Pinker, in his claim that we all have a 'language instinct' (1994). Thornton, however, refers to a range of studies which may suggest that, while predisposed to be social and to interact with others, babies may not be born with an innate predisposition to learn grammar, and that overgeneralizations like 'breaked' are not evidence of a specific focus on grammar rules but part of 'the very much more general cognitive tendency to extract generalizations from a collection of concrete examples' (Thornton 2002:58).

A more general criticism of the nativist viewpoint is that it does not take sufficient account of the part played by pre-verbal communication, of the communicative aspect of language and of the parts played by babies' relationships with the important people around them. This more interactionist viewpoint has much in common with sociocultural perspectives on children's cognition and positions language learning more within general ideas of cognition.

Siegler (1998:169) outlines three possible relationships between language and thought:

1   language shapes thought;
2   thought shapes language;
3   language and thought influence each other.

Language shapes thought

The first of these positions, the so-called Sapir-Whorf hypothesis, represents an approach known as linguistic determinism. It is based on the idea that language moulds thought so profoundly that 'the "real world" is to a large extent unconsciously built up by the language habits of the group' (Sapir, cited in Siegler 1998:169). For young children, then, the language they learn will determine the thoughts that they have, and initiation into the language uses of their community will be an initiation into the ways of thinking and living in that community (Whitehead 2004). A 'weaker' version of the hypothesis suggests that language 'influences' rather than 'determines' thought (Lee and Das Gupta 1995). Evidence for the linguistic determinist view derives largely from studies of language acquisition across different language communities. Sapir, for example, noted that Native North American Wintu speakers must pay attention to whether the knowledge they are talking about comes from hearsay or direct observation in deciding whether to put a suffix onto verbs. In English such a decision is based upon tense and time of occurrence (Pinker 1994). Motluk (2002) discusses a range of other studies.

The linguistic determinist view has been strongly challenged by psychologists such as Pinker (1994) on several grounds. Methodologically, Pinker suggests that Whorf and Sapir provide circular arguments to make their claim: 'Apaches speak differently, so they must think differently. How do we know they think differently? Just listen to the way they speak!' (Pinker 1994:61). He also argues that the linguistic practices they set out may not be accurate reflections of the cultures they claim to represent, and cites critical studies conducted since formation of the Sapir-Whorf hypothesis. In his view, and that of the majority of psychologists and linguists today (Motluk 2002), the idea that language determines thought has little to recommend it. Pinker points out that people think in images as well as words and in abstract logical propositions. He suggests that people are well able to distinguish in their thinking between different meanings for the same word (spring, hop, key . . .), or even for different strings of words, and, that being so, 'if there can be two thoughts corresponding to one word, thoughts can't be words' (Pinker 1994:79). In his view, people do not think in English or any other language, but in a language of thought which he calls mentalese, richer in some ways than any spoken language, and simpler in others. Donaldson seems to be suggesting something similar:

> Thinking is an activity in which we engage. We need our representational resources to make the activity effective, but the resources are varied, and they are not the same as the thought they sustain.
>
> (Donaldson 1992:104)

The children in Box 7.1 would appear to demonstrate this idea, as they struggle to put their thoughts into words. One possible practical implication here must be that, in any sphere of learning, if thought does proceed without language, rote verbal approaches to teaching and learning will not be sufficient to develop understanding.

Thought shapes language

What, then, of the two other propositions, that thought shapes language, or that language and thought influence each other? These two represent the most fundamental disagreement between Piaget and Vygotsky, who devotes a considerable part of *Thought and Language*

Box 7.1 Rachel, aged $4\frac{1}{2}$ years, and Rabi, aged 4 years 3 months in the nursery

Rachel:

Sian, Rachel and John (the teacher) were having a discussion about a picnic.

JOHN: If it's nice we're going to have it outside but if it rains we're going to have it on the carpet.

SIAN: Yeah if it rains we don't want to have soggy sandwiches.

JOHN: Or soggy crisps!

SIAN: Or soggy drink!

RACHEL: Drinks won't get soggy, they'll...they're...just, they'll more drink.

Rabi, at fruit time in a small group:

RABI: John, John, the apple...can I have two pieces? (Rabi takes a piece of apple and also a piece of orange. He lingers over eating the orange, sees John looking and grins.)

RABI: I like orange, it's got (pause), it's got, taste!

Pinker (1994) maintains that higher order thought processes are independent of language, He says they are conducted by a different process which he calls mentalese. These two observation would seem to support that. Rachel knows that the quality of sogginess doesn't change with the addition of more liquid but, as the hesitation shows, she can't find the right words to explain dilution. In the end she does very well. Rabi is also a victim of the same problem – he knows that oranges have flavour, but can't find that word to describe it.

Reproduced with permission of John Griffiths

(Vygotsky 1986) to arguing against Piaget's position. For Piaget, language is a system for representing thought (see Chapter 2) with the processes of thought having been derived from action. He argues that language is a medium, or way of representing, which 'exerts no formative effects on the structure of thinking' (Wood 1998:28). As a result, children's language will always be unable to convey what is not already established as a thought. Thus, for Piaget, thought shapes, or leads, children's language. He also argues that early language is egocentric, and only becomes socialised with the advent of concrete operations, that is, at the age of about 7 years. The early conversations of children, he says, are more like monologues than dialogues, and when a child uses egocentric talk 'he does not bother to know to whom he is speaking nor whether he is being listened to' (Piaget 1959:9). As with Piaget's general view of development, this is 'chiefly because he (the child) does not attempt to place himself at the point of view of his hearer' (Piaget 1959:9). Only with the development of concrete operations does speech take on a genuinely communicative function, and egocentric speech then dies away, to be replaced by socialized speech.

Language and thought influence each other

Vygotsky asserts that his own 'theoretical position (is) in exactly an opposite direction' to Piaget (Vygotsky 1986:11). For Vygotsky, 'the true direction of the development of thinking is not from the individual to the social, but from the social to the individual' (Vygotsky

Box 7.2 Anna, aged 1 year 8 months in the nursery

Anna is standing at a sand tray with three other children and a nursery nurse. She tries out different play items before settling on two spades. She quietly transfers sand from the spade in one hand to the spade in the other by pouring, repeating this action over and over again. Every few minutes she spontaneously speaks out loud, seemingly to herself, repeating the words:

Pour, pour, pour
Catch it, catch it
Careful.

Anna's verbalizations during the task can be defined as egocentric speech. She appears to be ensuring her success by giving herself reminders about how to conduct the activity. Furrow (1984) defines this as 'self-regulatory' utterance.

Reproduced with permission of Rachel Spencer

1986:36). Childhood speech, in Vygotsky's model, is not a personal, egocentric matter but social and communicative from the outset. He argues that children's speech is *intended* to communicate, even if they are not always successful in this aim. A baby's gestures and speech help him to control his world, through the agency of other people. In addition, Vygotsky believes that what Piaget saw as children's egocentric speech is an instrument of thought: 'it serves mental orientation, conscious understanding; it helps in overcoming difficulties' (Vygotsky 1986:228). He points to evidence from his work which shows that egocentric speech is most prolific when children are struggling with symbolic representation. For Vygotsky this speech does not disappear, but becomes internalized, to form inner speech, or verbal thought, and may also resurface in spoken form when older children and adults are thinking through problems. Thus, egocentric speech is a tool for representing the world and a means of self-regulation or metacognition. In this way, speech comes to form what Vygotsky terms the higher mental processes. Box 7.2 shows a small, but typical, snippet of egocentric speech. It is worth taking the time to reflect on whether you see it as a display of thought, entirely for the self, as Piaget suggests, or whether you see it as having a role in helping to shape Anna's thinking, and communicative in intent.

For Vygotsky, then, in 'an inspired compromise between the views of Whorf and Piaget' (Whitehead 2004:74), language and thought influence each other. Vygotsky outlines what he sees as the developmental path here:

We consider that the total development runs as follows: The primary function of speech, in both children and adults, is communication, social contact. The earliest speech of the child is therefore essentially social. At first it is global and multifunctional; later its functions become differentiated. At a certain age the social speech of the child is quite sharply divided into egocentric speech and communicative speech ... Egocentric speech emerges when the child transfers social, collaborative forms of behaviour to the sphere of inner-personal psychic functions ... Egocentric speech as a separate linguistic form is the highly important genetic link in the transition from vocal to inner speech.

(Vygotsky 1986:34–5)

It is this interactionist perspective which has assumed the most influence in recent years, and the view that the role played by language in children's thinking is both communicative (cultural tool) and sense-making (psychological tool) is reflected in the work of, among others, Jerome Bruner (see Chapter 2), Tizard and Hughes (2002) and Wells (1987). Wells suggests that children are active seekers of meaning:

> In learning through talk – as in learning to talk – children are active constructors of their own knowledge. What they need is evidence, guidance and support. Parents who treat their children as equal partners in conversation, following their lead and negotiating meanings and purposes, are not only helping their children to talk, they are also enabling them to discover how to learn *through* talk.
>
> (Wells 1987:65, emphasis in original)

Wells takes Vygotsky's ideas further, suggesting that language is more than just a cultural and psychological tool. Rather, we should conceptualize it as a whole tool-kit, because of the great range of functional varieties it serves in order to meet our cultural needs (Wells in Mercer 2000).

Thinking about language: the path to metalinguistic awareness

At the same time as children are, in Wells' (1987) words, learning *through* talk and learning *to* talk, they are also thinking and learning *about* talk. Children's attempts to make sense of spoken language, of its structure, content and functions, reveal much about their thinking. The ability to reflect and talk deliberately, and knowingly, about language, is called metalinguistic awareness. Conclusions about when this occurs in young children vary. Barratt-Pugh and Rohl suggest that many researchers 'agree on somewhere between the ages of three and seven' (2000:67), while Thornton (2002) suggests it occurs at about age 6. She cites evidence of studies from Karmiloff-Smith which suggest that, before this age, children have difficulty in reflecting either upon language as a thing in its own right or on the structural properties of language.

While this explicit reflection on language may not be available to very young children, there are, though, many ways in which they are both developing and displaying their understanding of language from the very beginnings of life, in ways which show clear evidence of their thinking. Bilingual children may have a particular advantage here. Their experiences of code 'switching' and 'mixing' ('Maman, I've trouved the book', as my bilingual nephew said to his mother), and of manipulating language as a formal system, are just the kinds of characteristics associated with metalinguistic awareness (Romaine 2004, Whitehead 2002, 2004).

Grammar

The way in which young children develop an understanding of grammar provides a good demonstration of their implicit thinking about language. I pointed earlier to the very familiar ways in which children seem to overgeneralize their understanding, making errors such as 'my stick breaked', which uses a regular past tense ending for an irregular verb, or creating a plural form such as 'childs'. Clearly, in most instances, a child has not heard an adult using these word forms, so it cannot be just imitation. Similarly, children may create one part of speech from another, in this case, a verb from an adverb: 'Shall I off the lights?' as one 3-year-old said to me. Children are, in so doing, revealing their understanding of aspects of language, such as the rules for creating past tenses and plurals. Wood cites Karmiloff-Smith's view that such over generalizations serve an important diagnostic role in that they are important indicators of conceptual change and reorganization (Wood 1998). It is not, as Chukovsky (1963) says, the children's fault that language does not adhere to strict rules of logic. This may have very important practical implications in that it suggests that children's receptive ability (to listen and understand) may often be in advance of their productive ability (to speak) (Wood 1998). If this is so, then evaluation of a child's understanding and competence based solely on the ways in which they can talk about something may not be entirely reliable.

Language play

A key way in which young children may be displaying their understanding of language is in the ways in which they play with it. Crystal (1998) suggests that language play begins very early in life, and is at the core of babies' interactions with their carers, in the form of motherese (see later in the chapter), songs and rhymes, all of which are accompanied by non-verbal ways of communicating, including eye contact, and physical interactions such as tickling and cuddling. As he says, the message given to babies is that these sorts of interactions, and the verbal exchanges that go along with them, are fun. It is not long before babies are spontaneously engaging with this play with language on their own, at first as a kind of 'vocal play' with noises which may serve a symbolic function (car and telephone sounds, for example), and then, at around the age of 2, more explicit manipulation of language (Crystal 1998). These monologues, of which those recorded by Ruth Weir (in Garvey 1977) are the most famous, reveal children taking language apart and reorganizing it in ways which demonstrate their awareness of language as a system.

In the same way, children then engage in verbal play with others. This social language play necessitates that each player is able to interpret the meaning of the other(s). Telling

Box 7.3 Ella and Emily, both aged 2 years 8 months at the playdough table

ELLA: My mummy says that I am her little princess
EMILY: My gran says that I'm her carrot top
ELLA: You can't wear a carrot, you have a stripey top on
EMILY: No, she calls me carrot top because my hair is red
ELLA: But your hair isn't red, it's not carrot either
EMILY: What colour is my hair then?
ELLA: I know, it's like a penny, isn't it
EMILY: No, it's like a carrot
ELLA: Ok, penny carrot
EMILY: Ok, Ella bella wella
ELLA: Ok, penny carrot silly billy
EMILY: Ella bella wella annabella
ELLA: Penny carrot silly billy Emily
EMILY: Ella bella wella silly billy princess annabella

your friend a joke, at whatever age, is an indication of your awareness of the other person's mental state (Lee and Das Gupta 1995), which is an important aspect of the development of theory of mind, discussed in Chapter 5. Garvey categorizes children's social play with language in three ways: 'spontaneous rhyming and word play; play with fantasy and nonsense; and play with speech acts and discourse conventions' (Garvey 1977:69). The first and third of these, rhyming and word play and play with speech acts and discourse conventions, are illustrated in that of the two girls in Box 7.3. This type of word play is almost inevitably spontaneous and reveals much about children's understanding of language.

The second of Garvey's categories, play with fantasy and nonsense, requires children to have sophisticated understandings, both of language and of the world. As Whitehead points out, 'jokes and nonsense depend on knowing the right way to do things' (Whitehead 2002:38–9). Without such an understanding, the humour of the joke is often lost. Gifford gives a lovely example of a 'number joke', which not only illustrates the ways in which nonsense play is apparent in all areas of a child's experience, but also the close links it can have with positive emotion. She records Jermain, a boy in the nursery: 'Jermain pointed to number four on the hundred square carpet, shouted "91!" at me and ran off laughing' (2004a:88). The best-known examples of children's nonsense language play, and their 'topsy turvies', or inversion of reality, are in Chukovsky, who asserts that such topsy turvies 'strengthen (not weaken) the child's awareness of reality' (Chukovsky 1963:104). The example in Box 7.4 illustrates one kind of topsy turvy, in Jack's play on words and ideas.

Children's misconceptions about grammar, their curiosity about language, and their play with it, reveal both the beginnings of metalinguistic awareness, and their thinking more

Box 7.4 Jack, aged $3\frac{1}{2}$, early one morning, at home with his mother

Jack goes into his mother's room. It is still dark outside so she asks him to go back to bed. He says he doesn't want to, and that he wants to play. His mother says that he should go back to bed and daydream. When she later goes to his bedroom door she hears him 'reading' quietly to himself, muttering the lines of the book *Night monkey, day monkey*, by Julia Donaldson, that he has learnt off by heart, under his breath. When she walks in he says:

JACK: Mummy, I'm daydreaming . . . and nightdreaming.

They both laugh, and Jack gets out of bed.

Dunn (1988) maintains that children are building on their knowledge of the world when they play with language. This concurs with the views of Chukovsky (1963) who suggests that humour is a developmental process: 'the more aware the child is of the correct relationship of things . . . the more comical does this violation appear to him. He has become so sure of truths that he can even play with them (1963:99). When Jack talks of 'nightdreaming' he knows it is funny, as he laughed after he said it. Chukovsky refers to these word games as 'topsy turvies'. According to him they are not just a diversion, but are a serious mental effort that helps confirm reality.

I often propose that the children 'daydream' when they ask what they can do: it may be that Jack was making a joke to check his theory that there is such a thing as 'nightdreaming'.

Reproduced with permission of Kathryn Torres

generally. This kind of play may be very particular to early childhood, helping children to achieve mastery of spoken language, the major need for which will tend to have passed by the age of 8 (Chukovsky 1963). As such, it may be a particularly significant aspect of the relationship between young children's language and thought. For the remainder of this chapter we shall look at some of the contexts in which children's language efforts occur.

'Motherese' or infant-directed speech

For the great majority of children, communication and language begin in the home, with other family members. The ways in which those family members attune their own language to the child, providing child-contingent language, is well documented. Characteristics include use of a higher pitch than normal, exaggerated changes of pitch, frequent use of a child's name, restriction of semantic and syntactic content, running commentary on a child's actions, repetition, questions, expansion of the child's utterances, and gestures such as lip smacking, although perhaps not all at the same time! Much research has focused, in particular, on the ways in which primary carers, especially mothers, seem to unconsciously do this, using 'motherese' or 'caregiver speech' with their children. More recent research has looked at the ways in which a baby's siblings, and other young children outside the family, act in the same way. This has led to the phenomenon now often being termed 'infant-directed speech'. The example in Box 7.5 shows one such episode. What is particularly noteworthy here is the young age of the two boys using this type of speech to comfort their sister. Bruner (1988) suggests that 4-year-olds will use motherese with younger children. In the example here, Sean is not yet 3. As Rebecca, the crèche worker involved, points out, Sean, in particular,

Box 7.5 Ciara, aged 1 year 4 months, Sean, aged 2 years 11 months and Mark, aged 4 years 2 months (siblings) at the crèche

Ciara, Sean and Mark have been at the crèche for an hour. Ciara is beginning to be distressed, is close to tears, and has a worried expression. Soon Sean and Mark, who have been playing elsewhere in the room, come over to comfort her.

SEAN: Ok, Ciara, is ok (tickles her tummy quite roughly) Tickle tickle.
CRECHE WORKER: Sean, gently with Ciara, don't hurt her.
SEAN: My not hurt her, is ok, Ciara like it (reaches to her again) Tickle tickle.
MARK: It's okay, Ciara does like it, we always play with Ciara.

Ciara is still sniffling, but seems calmer.

MARK: Hey, Ciara Ciara, it's okay, Sean and Marky here, mummy coming, back soon.
SEAN: Yes, Ciara, mummy *and* daddy come soon.

Ciara has stopped crying. Mark returns to his activity, Sean sits beside Ciara.

SEAN: Hey Ciri Ciri, tickle tickle, you like that don't you, yes you do, Ciara. Sean tickle tickle you. All better now, Ciara is all better, you laughing now, tickle tickle make you laugh, my make you laugh, happy Ciara, Ciara happy now, yes you are.

Reproduced with permission of Rebecca Shuttleworth

seems to have unconsciously picked up this way of comforting babies from the behaviour of others, for example his parents and staff at the crèche. His speech to Ciara is different to the ways in which he talks to both the adult involved and to his brother. What Wells (1987) also shows is that infant-directed speech is evoked by the child as well as by the carer or older sibling, suggesting that very young children are able to think about and control such exchanges.

Babies themselves show a preference for infant-directed speech (Siegler *et al.* 2002). In addition, the use of repetition and clear enunciation of speech sounds may support children's acquisition of language (Gopnik *et al.* 1999). Thornton (2002) links infant-directed speech with ideas of scaffolding, suggesting that adults' use of it can help children to make connections between events in the world and word meanings. It is important to bear in mind, however, that this form of interaction is not universal. Meadows (1993:310) suggests that infant-directed speech is a cultural phenomenon, most often used in Western middle-class households. Heath (1983) describes the ways in which the black, working-class children in her study grew up among adults who used narrative prompts and questions such as 'Did you see Maggie's dog yesterday?', as ways of initiating conversation, and did not engage in motherese at all. In some cultures, children may be ignored conversationally until they are older, or only addressed using correct syntax (Siegler *et al.* 2003). The fact that most children, given normal developmental factors, rapidly become confident language users, suggests that infant-directed speech is not a prerequisite for language development, and does not affect the eventual levels of mastery of language that children achieve (Siegler *et al.* 2003).

Conversation and questions, questions, questions...

Communication begins, as we have seen, in the earliest moments of a child's life. Children's early protoconversations (Trevarthen 1995) with their carers lay the foundations of later verbal communication. The intersubjective exchange of gestures, eye contact and sounds is the beginning of turn taking, shared meaning making and inferring what is in your conversational partner's mind. Box 7.6 shows Josh, a boy of 8 months, initiating and sustaining an interaction of which he is very clearly in control, while he explores the boundaries of what he is doing. Throughout the interaction, not a word is spoken, but Josh has clearly communicated his interest and involvement in the game. By about 2–3 months of age, babies begin to make their first language-like sounds (Karmiloff-Smith 1994), and the world of spoken language and conversation unfolds.

Conversation

Wells (1987) suggests that young children's conversation is generally purposeful and goal-directed. That is, in talking to those around them, children are interested in achieving other ends – getting what they want, keeping in contact with others, sharing things of

Box 7.6 Josh, aged 8 months 3 weeks

Josh is on the train with his mother. He pulls off his hat and drops it on the floor. A woman sitting opposite picks it up and gives it to him. He looks at her and drops it again, she picks it up again and passes it to him. This routine is repeated continuously over the three minute train ride.

Box 7.7 Boy, aged 2, out with his mother

BOY: (looking up at a plane flying overhead) that noise?
MOTHER: That's a plane.
BOY: Nanny plane.
MOTHER: Yes, nanny went on a plane.

interest – aims that they share with their conversational partners at home. They also share experiences. So, for much of a child's early life, children's conversations in their homes and communities are highly context-bound and characterized by 'the desire to understand and to be understood' (Vygotsky 1986:56). They draw upon the shared knowledge and understanding of all participants, and thus are often elliptical and fragmentary. The brief conversation between a mother and her son in Box 7.7 illustrates this shared knowledge and experience between family members.

The success of such a conversation, as an exchange of language and thinking, is dependent upon the shared knowledge and understanding of the participants. However, just as important is the way in which the mother assumes that her son has something important to say, and that he is intent on conveying meaning. She takes what her son says, expands it using the shared knowledge they have and together they jointly construct a meaning which satisfies them both. Wells believes that, in so doing, children gradually come to reflect on action as they speak, and that, eventually, as in Vygotsky's model of language and thought, this dialogue begins to be carried on internally instead. In addition, participation in conversations like these may contribute to an understanding of perspective and an awareness of mental states so central to the development of theory of mind (Astington and Baird 2004). They suggest that, while the relationship between language and theory of mind is complex and interdependent, there are nevertheless ways in which language plays a role in the development of perspective taking that is independent of social communication *per se*. Cutting and Dunn (1999) speculate on the part played by gender here, suggesting that narrative ability may play a more pivotal role for girls than boys in the development of false-belief understanding (see Chapter 5 for fuller discussion of these features of theory of mind).

Wells (1987) and Tizard and Hughes (2002) found that the features of conversation noted earlier were particularly characteristic of conversation at home. The sheer quantity of shared experience gave children and adults much to talk about, and the fact that much of the conversation took place in situations of 1 adult to 1, or 2, children, gave the children many more opportunities to initiate and sustain conversation, and to do so in spontaneous and unplanned ways. Opportunities for conversations between an individual adult and child in early childhood settings will be less plentiful than in the home and there will be far fewer shared contexts. Katz and Chard (2000) suggest that project work characteristic of the kind found in settings in Reggio Emilia (see Chapter 10) can provide rich contexts for conversations between adults and children and between the children themselves, and shared experiences of events which can be thought about and discussed. Paley (1986, 2004) reaches similar conclusions about the importance of creating a shared culture in the nursery.

Wells also stresses that the seeming disparity between home and school should not be taken necessarily to be disadvantageous. He suggests that settings need to focus on ways in which they can broaden the range of children's experiences, and 'help them (the children) develop the sustained and deliberate attention to a topic or activity that makes systematic learning possible' (Wells 1987:67). Above all, he suggests, nurseries and schools can help children to become more reflectively aware of what they already know and still need to know, in ways that enable them to take increasing responsibility for their own learning.

Questions and the search for understanding

One very characteristic form of young children's interactions is questioning. Ask the parents of young children about the questions they ask and many of them will give you a rueful look which suggests that perhaps there can be such a thing as too many. For the young child, however, there can never be too many questions. Tizard and Hughes (2002) record the 3- and 4-year-olds in their research asking an average of 26 questions an hour at home. The mother in Box 7.8 records her son asking 17 questions in less than 15 minutes. In Chapter 1 the question of whether children's thinking is qualitatively different from adult thinking was discussed. Challenging Piagetian notions of children's questions as indicators of their intellectual limitations, Tizard and Hughes suggest that it is children's limited conceptual framework and comparative ignorance and inexperience that is the issue, not a fault in their ability to apply logic (Tizard and Hughes 2002). One of the ways in which children seek to close the gaps in their experiences is through asking questions. Children's questions reveal a lot about what they do and do not understand, their misconceptions and their interests. Their questions may not, however, all require an answer. What children may often be doing is using their own questions to help them to shape and clarify their thinking by thinking aloud in the way that Vygotsky describes.

Children demonstrate considerable persistence in their desires to clarify their thinking. Interestingly, Tizard and Hughes (2002) record that those children who asked the most searching questions were often most likely to have parents who answered them most fully, and, of course, that the parents who were most likely to answer their children's questions were the ones with children most likely to ask. A characteristic form of question for 3-year-olds is repeated use of 'why' questions (Isaacs 1930). Tizard and Hughes record that about a quarter of all of the questions posed by girls in their study were 'why' questions (their study did not include boys). However, they also point out that it is not just the use of 'why' which is important, rather it is the intention behind the question which matters. Children's intentions in asking questions, they suggest, revolve around seeking new information or explanations, puzzling over something they do not understand or trying to make sense of apparent anomalies in their limited knowledge of the world. They describe this process in children as engagement in 'passages of intellectual search' (2002). They recount incidences of the 4-year-old children in their research repeatedly returning to a topic, and persistently, and logically, questioning their mothers, often when the conversation has apparently moved on, in their drive to make sense. Paley makes a similar point about the children in her kindergarten:

> confusion – mine or theirs – is as natural a condition as clarity. The natural response to confusion is to keep trying to connect what you already know to what you don't know.
> (Paley 1986:131)

Characteristic of these passages of intellectual search were children's awareness of, and interest in, other people's viewpoints, including the use of inference, and the application of 'rigorous logic' (Tizard and Hughes 2002:103). They suggest that such behaviour may be particularly characteristic of children in the age range of 3–5 years. By the age of 4, they argue, dialogue, and exploration with words, is as important as physical exploration may be for the younger child:

> The children in this study seemed in some sense aware that their conceptual framework was not yet substantial enough to cope with their experiences, and engaged themselves actively in the process of improving their intellectual scaffolding. The passages of intellectual search seemed particularly useful in this process, and indicated that the children were at some level aware that protracted dialogue with adults was a useful way of developing their conceptual knowledge.
>
> (Tizard and Hughes 2002:105–6)

Box 7.8 shows this persistent questioning in a 5 year-old boy.

Box 7.8 Abe, aged 5, at home with his mother

Abe is looking through a 'body' book with his mother. He repeatedly asks questions relating to the pictures in the book. For reasons of space many of her responses to him have not been included. He poses a new question as soon as he gets an answer.

ABE: Is your bones the same shape as your face?
       What happens when you spike yourself? (looking at picture of hedgehog).
       How do you talk?
MUM: From a thing called your voice box.
ABE: Are there lots of voices?
       How do your nose wiggle? (Wiggling his nose.)
       How does your teeth make a noise?
       Does bones melt inside your tongue, by water going on it?
       What's in your blood?

Mum shows him a picture of a blood vessel and the cells inside it.

ABE: But this is a picture, what does it really look like?
       What happens if you eat the same time and you have a ride the same time?
          (on a fairground ride).
       What about if you eat sweets all day?
       What gives you energy?
       How do you know your arms are going to move? (Looking at a picture of the
          brain and muscles.)
MUM: Your brain sends a message to your arm muscles.
ABE: How does he stop?
MUM: How does who stop?
ABE: The brain.
MUM: Are you thinking?
ABE: I don't do thinking, I'm just thinking about my body.
       What does your heart look like? Do ladies have their heart in their boobies?
MUM: No, under their boobies.
ABE: Will their heart get squashed by their boobies?

Reproduced with permission of Sam Segar

Several possible implications for practice arise from Tizard and Hughes' work:

- They found that most of the 'intellectually challenging' conversations at home took place at times of relative leisure, such as mother and daughter sharing a meal, or during a one-to-one story session. The activity orientation of life in early childhood settings may offer fewer opportunities for such times.
- They recommend greater emphasis on feeding children with 'a great deal more general knowledge', which may include 'going beyond the school walls more' (2002:220), much as Athey (1990) suggests (see Chapter 6).
- They suggest that professionals have much to learn from studying parents and children at home.
- They counsel strongly against underestimating children's abilities and interests.

Research by Siraj-Blatchford *et al.* (2002) looked at the development of thinking skills in a range of settings with 3–5-year-olds in England. They emphasize the importance of what they term 'sustained shared thinking' in developing children's thinking skills. They found such episodes of sustained shared thinking happened most often in talk between a child and an adult, or between an adult and a child pair. The larger the group, they conclude, the less likely were such episodes, and the more likely it was that interactions would be monitorial, or involve direct teaching in which children might have fewer opportunities for extending their thinking. Practitioners in our research said similar things, believing that size of group played an important part in supporting children's thinking. One practitioner said that they had focused particularly on pair discussion, because the children worked well together in pairs, and did not feel threatened by each other (Robson and Hargreaves 2005). The National Oracy Project in England (1990) advocates pair discussion, particularly where younger or quieter children are concerned. Another practitioner in our research suggested that groups of about four children were supportive of children's thinking because 'more ideas may be coming through from children in a small group'. Bennett and Dunne, in their study of co-operative grouping, come to a similar conclusion, suggesting that groups of 3 or 4 allow for 'lines of communication' (1992:115) that are not too complex to be manageable.

Young children's use of narrative

To take up Wells' (1987) point that children are active meaning-makers, there is much evidence to suggest that narrative, in the form of children's own storying ('the act of creating narratives', Whitehead 2004:111), plays an important role in this process, allowing children to represent their experiences and deepen their understanding, thereby creating 'brain fictions' (Gregory 1977:394) that support hypotheses about the ways in which the world works. Wells suggests that 'Storying is the most fundamental way of grappling with new experience' (1987:206), and 'the way in which the mind itself works' (1987:197). In this, Whitehead (2002) stresses the link between narrative and the organization and function of memory. Narrative is not, however, just an individual act, but intimately bound up with our cultural and communal histories, providing children with 'ways into the shared beliefs and meaning making strategies' (Whitehead 2002:34) of their culture. As such, the practice of using narrative to make sense of experience begins very early in life. As Wells suggests, 'Even before they can talk, infants begin to construct a mental model of their world' (1987:196), in the form of mental stories about perceptual information and the events of their lives. Children's earliest spoken narratives arise directly out of conversation, as children relate incidents, and hear them related by others: 'My stick breaked', the example used earlier, is a story in miniature. Bruner (1987) describes how children learn to make sense of the world as they develop the ability to tell stories about it. Later on, these stories reflect children's developing understanding of the language of literature. Wally, at 5 years old, is clearly experienced in the language of books, and in thinking about how literary, rather than oral, form sounds:

> Once there was a boy hunter. His little sister didn't like him so he ran away. So he found a baby girl lion.
>
> ('Wally', in Paley 1981:29)

It is in the work of Paley that some of the richest examples can be found. The contexts for the children's narratives often revolve around real and imagined events in their lives: birthdays, going to stay with a friend, shooting the bad guys. Underpinning many of these contexts, in both their narratives and in pretend play (see later in the text) are the three themes of friendship, fairness and fantasy (1986:124). These, Paley believes, are the things that really matter to the children, and she recounts how, in the kindergarten when they were up for discussion as part of the children's narratives, 'participation zoomed upwards' (1986:124). In paying close attention to the children's narratives, Paley suggests that the connections they make about their knowledge and understanding, their facility with structuring, reinventing and explaining the world, are made more apparent to those listening. Astington (1994) also suggests that one of the things that Paley is doing which is important to the development of children's thinking is her own use of words and expressions *about* thinking, as she comments on the children's narratives: 'oh, I think I know what reminded you of that' or 'are you wondering', for example. She says:

> In Paley's classroom the talk is not just about things in the world, it is also about the children's thoughts about things in the world.
>
> (Astington 1994:185)

In so doing, Astington suggests, the children's understanding of how they think and learn, a central part of metacognition, is made more consciously explicit to them. Pramling (1988) expresses a similar view, in her suggestion that a focus on the relationship of the child to the world promotes the development of metacognition. In Chapter 5 the part played by narrative in the development and study of children's theory of mind is also emphasized.

Young children's talk in pretend play

The role of play, particularly pretend play, is considered throughout this book. In the context of language and communication, the role of sociodramatic play, which involves interaction and verbal communication between two or more players, may be highly significant for the development of young children's thinking. Bergen suggests: 'Pretend play requires the ability to transform objects and actions symbolically, it is furthered by interactive social dialogue and negotiation, and it involves role taking, script knowledge, and improvisation' (Bergen 2002:2).

As she points out, what is not clear is the extent to which language, pretence and cognition develop as 'parts of an integrated, reciprocally developing system' (2002:2) or whether it is the experience of pretend play which has a positive impact on children's language and cognition. In her synthesis of recent research, she concludes that engagement in 'high-quality' (2002:6) pretence may assist children's linguistic development. As Kenner *et al.* (1996) demonstrate, it may also provide contexts in which children can most confidently display their linguistic competence. Dockett (1998) also points to evidence suggesting that children's involvement in shared pretence, of which communication is an essential part, has a positive impact on cognitive development, particularly theory of mind. This is looked at in more detail in Chapter 5 but children's language use in this context is worth considering. Underpinning such language use is the act of symbolic transformation, which requires the players to define those transformations verbally to each other in order to establish a shared frame of meaning.

Pretend communication and metacommunication

Dockett (1998:113) draws a distinction between two types of language use in sociodramatic pretend play. The first is pretend communication, which describes children's talk when in role. When they do this, children take on another person's ways of speaking, tone of voice, even particular vocabulary. In so doing, what they are demonstrating is their ability to take on another's perspective, and to think about how that person might act, and what they might say.

The second way in which children use language in their play is in order to talk about the play. This is referred to as metacommunication, or 'verbal statements or actions that explain how messages about pretend play should be interpreted' (Farver, cited in Dockett 1998:113), and, importantly, convey the message 'this is play', signalling that the behaviour it encompasses is symbolic (Giffin 1984). Dockett expands on this idea, and suggests that metacommunications serve several important functions:

> On one level, they serve to separate, in an explicit manner, real from pretend. More importantly, metacommunications are understood by the players on these two different levels. Even when players step outside the play frame, or outside their adopted role, to issue a direction or rebuke, neither they nor the other players seem to experience confusion about the reality or the pretense [*sic*]. On another level, metacommunications frame the play by setting the context and offering guidance and direction as to the ongoing nature of the play. When children add to, or respond to, their partner's ideas and actions in the play, they extend the shared meanings already established.
>
> (Dockett 1998:113)

Giffin suggests that children's metacommunications will range along a continuum from ones which are very much within-frame ('Mommy, I did something nice for you. I made you a wedding ring cake', Giffin 1984:81) to out-of frame proposals such as 'let's pretend that'. In so doing, children are making implicit choices about the extent to which pretence is maintained, and are demonstrating 'evolved skills in human communication' (Giffin 1984:96).

Metaplay

Children's metacommunications occur as part of metaplay, a more general term for the act of stepping outside of the play in order to think or communicate about it. Trawick-Smith's typology of metaplay behaviours reveals how complex and varied this act is for young children. He identifies three distinct categories of metaplay behaviour, each of which is further categorized:

1   Metaplay Initiations: 'behaviors [*sic*] in which children halted role-playing-in progress to: 1.) initiate a new play activity, or 2.) engage peers in conversations or physical interactions related to play themes' (Trawick-Smith 1998:436):

    i   announcing symbolic transformations;
    ii   announcing/narrating make-believe actions;
    iii   requests for clarification about make believe;
    iv   announcing characters' internal mental states;
    v   persuading peers;
    vi   initiatives concerning object ownership.

2   Metaplay Responses: physical or verbal responses to the play-related behaviours and comments of peers:

    i   disagreeing/not complying;
    ii   agreeing/complying;
    iii   answering/providing clarification;
    iv   protecting objects/maintaining ownership.

3   Metaplay Constructions: physical actions, sometimes accompanied by verbalizations, involving constructing a play setting:

    i   nonverbal constructions;
    ii   constructions with verbalizations.

(Adapted from Trawick-Smith 1998)

What is clear from this typology is the pivotal role played by language in children's metaplay. Only a small number of Trawick-Smith's categorizations have a non-verbal element, and most depend on talk. As with many other aspects of development, children's metaplay seems to increase markedly over time, possibly as a function of children's increased social and cognitive competence. Trawick-Smith records a 20-fold increase between the ages of 2 and 5 years, for example. Metaplay initiations accounted for over half of all interactions, in all three of the age groups Trawick-Smith studied (2-year-olds, 3–4-year-olds and 5-year-olds). Interestingly, it was the youngest children who showed the most incidences of interactions involving persuading peers. Even at the age of 2, children seem to understand that other children have separate minds that need persuading around to their point of view. Box 7.9 illustrates many of the aspects discussed earlier. Here, Jake and Sam negotiate characters and roles, engage in a range of metaplay interactions and use pretend communication to sustain their play.

What are the practical implications here? In order to support this form of language use, it may be important for adults to model such usage in play themselves, and to support the creation of shared meanings through play. Trawick-Smith (1998:450) also speculates that non-realistic objects such as blocks and cardboard boxes may be particularly useful aspects

Box 7.9 Jake, aged 4 years 10 months and Sam, aged 4 years 9 months at Nursery School

---

Jake and Sam are playing outdoors. There are wheeled toys, a changeable traffic light, and a wooden shop with empty crates. They have been playing with the traffic light, when Jake says:

JAKE: Hey, Sam, let's do grown-up things. Let's play going to the shops. (They walk over to the shop.) Do you want to be the daddy or the lady?
SAM: I want to be the man in the shop.
JAKE: You can't. You have to be the lady coz there's a lady in my shop and she gives me sweets.
SAM: I want to be the daddy then.
JAKE: OK. (He walks round and positins himself behing the counter, and speaks in a slightly higher voice) Good morning, how may I help you?
SAM: I'd like to buy some carrots please.
JAKE: No, no, you want to buy sweets for your little boy.
SAM: OK, I want to buy some carrots and some sweets please.

Jake makes a grabbing action into the baskets and holds out a fist to Sam.

JAKE: Here we are, lots of carrots. What sweets do you want?
SAM: Nice ones, I don't like the hard ones. Granny has hard sweets, they're not nice.
JAKE: Here we are, these ones are soft. Are they for your boy?
SAM: Yes, he likes soft chewy ones.
JAKE: I bet he's getting very big just like his dad.

Reproduced with permission of Angela Streek

---

of provision, because their non-representational nature supports speculative talk and discussion about what they might become in the play episode, with the possibilities this has for developing both metacognition and theory of mind. Umek and Musek (2001) suggest that a certain level of skill at representing ideas in play may be a crucial factor here, and demonstrate in their research that younger children (aged 3–4 years) might need more structured, representational, play materials such as dolls, pots and pans, and cutlery. By contrast, Broadhead, in her research on social and co-operative skill development in children aged 4–5 years, found that themed role play areas which were resourced with structured play materials (home corners, shops, cafes) tended to produce 'social' play (some, but limited, reciprocal language and action), but not 'highly social' (increased reciprocity) or co-operative play. She and her co-researchers speculate that this could be because, while the themed role-play areas related to the children's experiences, they might be more closed in their potential for stimulating play themes and the social interactions required in negotiating roles, talking about the play and announcing symbolic transformations. As a result, they set up areas resourced, as Trawick-Smith (1998) suggests, with items such as pieces of fabric, empty boxes and clothes horses. One child dubbed this area 'the whatever you want it to be place' (Broadhead 2004:73). What they found when they observed and documented the resultant play was an increase of highly social and co-operative activity, part of which was enhanced language use. Hall and Robinson (2003) also point to the part played by this kind of role-play in the development of children's understanding and use of the symbolic language of literacy.

Baron-Cohen (2004) suggests that boys may get involved in more solitary pretence, for example, superhero play, with girls engaging in group play more frequently. Holland (2003) also points out that gun and weapon play, the very type of pretend play which many boys often prefer, is routinely banned in many settings, thus preventing access to a site for meaning-making, and consequent language and communication activity, which is most valued, and enjoyed, by them.

The role of adults in supporting young children's thinking through talk

The important role played by adults in supporting the development of children's thinking through talk has been stressed at various points in this chapter. In relation to those adults working with young children in settings, Coles provides a useful summary, in his suggestions that adults working with young children need to have:

- sensitivity to the child's current state and an understanding of the child's level of ability and immediate interests;
- sensitivity to the meanings he or she is trying to communicate and a desire to help and encourage interaction where both participants have equal space and discourse status;
- the ability to be a sympathetic listener rather than a propensity to dominate the situation and make it adult led (being 'genuinely curious', Paley 1986);
- skill in responding to the meaning intended – just as a good conversationalist would with people of any age – and to have genuine concern to achieve a mutual understanding (analogous to Mercer's idea of an 'intermental development zone', or IDZ, Mercer 2000:141).

(Coles 1996:10)

Coles' points raise a series of issues central to any consideration of professional practice in working with young children. Educators in Reggio Emilia (Project Zero and Reggio Children 2001) suggest that young children's thinking is a collective process, dependent upon discussion and 'provocation' to challenge existing theories and ideas, with adults playing a vital, but equal, part in this discursive process alongside the children. The extent to which such equality occurs in practice may be different, and adult domination of conversation in schools and nurseries is well documented, alongside the possible reasons for it (Hughes and Westgate 1988, Tizard and Hughes 2002, Wells 1987). Wood (1998) comments on the prevalence of adults' questions, in particular 'closed' questions used to elicit and check children's knowledge, where the questioner clearly already knows the answer. Such questions may provoke little more than one-word responses, and not serve as the starting points for rich conversational experiences. Siraj-Blatchford *et al.* emphasize the importance of more open-ended questions for supporting children's thinking, and suggest that adult interventions in the most effective settings in their study 'were most often in the form of questions that provoke speculation and extend the imagination' (2002:47). Medcalf-Davenport (2003) reports more elaborated talk by both girls and boys when they were given greater opportunities for discussion, rather than responding to closed questions. Just allowing children more 'thinking time' before they are expected to respond can result in dramatic improvements in the quality of their responses (Wood 1998).

Adult emphasis on the use of questions as a way of eliciting knowledge may result in children viewing all questions used by them as a form of assessment (Kenner *et al.* 1996). Wood (1998) asks whether questions are even the best way to find out about a child's thinking. Instead, he suggests that adult speculation and hypothesizing, and closer adult listening, may be more productive. In so doing, adults may be creating more 'space' for the children's own ideas to come out. Hughes and Westgate (1988) noted the greater input of the children, and their use of talk for a wider range of purposes, in classroom contexts where adults, and teachers in particular, were able to create this space, either by being physically absent, and encouraging child-child talk, or 'pedagogically' absent (i.e. by not taking an instructive role). In this, they differ from the conclusions of Siraj-Blatchford *et al.* that 'when adults manage to find time to talk to children individually or in child pairs, then these interactions are likely to be the most "stretching" interactions' (2002:59). In our research, practitioners emphasized the value (and difficulty!) of finding time to let children's talk develop (Robson and Hargreaves 2005).

Some implications for practice: a summary

Along with the discussion of the adult's role mentioned earlier, a wide range of practical implications have been discussed throughout this chapter, and it is useful to briefly summarize some of them here:

- The value of 'evidence, guidance and support' (Wells 1987:65) from adults in talking with children, and an attitude of equal partnership in conversation, for supporting children's thinking and understanding *through* talk (Wells 1987).
- The value of project work characteristic of the kind developed in Reggio Emilia for providing contexts for conversation and shared experiences (Katz and Chard 2000).
- The importance of creating a shared culture in the nursery (Paley 1986, 2004).
- Settings could focus on ways in which they can broaden the range of children's experiences (Wells 1987:67). This may include feeding children with 'a great deal more general knowledge', and 'going beyond the school walls more' (Tizard and Hughes 2002:220).
- Nurseries and schools can help children to become more reflectively aware of what they already know and still need to know, in ways that enable them to take increasing responsibility for their own learning (Wells 1987). Explicit talk about thinking with young children may help to make them more consciously aware of their thinking (Astington 1994, Pramling 1988).
- The importance of supporting children's questions and 'passages of intellectual search' (Tizard and Hughes 2002).
- The importance of times of relative leisure for intellectually challenging conversations (Tizard and Hughes 2002). Attention to how professionals can find such opportunities in settings may be important.
- Size of group may be important for 'sustained shared thinking' (Siraj-Blatchford *et al.* 2002).
- Children's narratives may be particularly important starting points for supporting and developing their thinking (Paley 1986, Wells 1987).
- Pretend play, particularly sociodramatic play, may be valuable in the ways in which it provides opportunities for children to best display their linguistic competence (Kenner *et al.* 1996), and in how it supports both pretend communication and

metacommunication (Dockett 1998). Adult modelling and involvement, and non-representational resources, may be important supports in pretend play (Broadhead 2004, Trawick-Smith 1998).

Further reflection

1   Write your response to the following query, which appeared in *New Scientist* (6 July 2002):

I think in English, but my Swedish friend thinks in Swedish. How do deaf people, who have never heard words in any language, think?
    When I think, I think using words and sentences. Although I can't remember for certain, I don't think I knew any form of language as a baby, so how do babies think?

2   The following observation comes from Athey (1990:140):

Gary (4:2:16) asked the teacher if he could 'read' to her. After they settled he said, 'Look!' and swivelled a pencil. The teacher expressed interest and said, 'You made that turn round, didn't you? You made it *'rotate'*. Much later Gary showed the teacher a picture of a cement mixer in a book. The teacher said, 'That's interesting, you have found something else that goes round, that rotates. Can you think of anything else that *rotates*?' After a pause Gary replied, 'Yes, a candy-floss maker'.

Do you think that the teacher here is supporting the development of Gary's thinking? If so, in what ways? What could she have said or done next?

Further reading

The relationship between language and thought

Donaldson, M. (1992) chapter 7
Mercer, N. (2000)
Piaget, J. (1959)
Pinker, S. (1994)
Thornton, S. (2002) chapter 3
Vygotsky, L. (1986)
Wood, D. (1998) pp. 27–31

Metalinguistic awareness

Chukovsky, K. (1963)
Crystal, D. (1998)
Garvey, C. (1977)

Whitehead, M. (2002, 2004)
Wood, D. (1998) chapter 5

Language at home and in early childhood settings

Bergen, D. (2002)
Dockett, S. (1998)
Gopnik, A. *et al*. (1999) chapter 4
Heath, S.B. (1983)
Karmiloff-Smith, A. (1994) chapter 4
Meadows, S. (1993) pp. 309–33
Mercer, N. (2000)
Paley, V.G. (1981, 1986)
Tizard, B. and Hughes, M. (2002)
Trawick-Smith, J. (1998)
Wells, G. (1987)

Chapter 8

Knowing about the world
The development of children's concepts

This chapter looks at the ways in which young children develop their understandings of the world around them. We shall look first at what might be meant by 'conceptual development' and at perspectives on how this occurs in young children, and then consider specific aspects of young children's scientific, mathematical, geographical and historical thinking. As Lee and Das Gupta point out, however, this is an area of research 'in which there is little certainty and much theorizing' (1995:117), arising from both psychological and philosophical standpoints.

What are concepts?

Concepts are the ideas and understandings we each have which enable us to group together objects, events and abstractions and, in particular, relationships. Some of these concepts may be considered universal, while others are clearly culturally specific and involve different ways of categorizing things according to social practice (Rogoff 2003, Siegler 1998). White supports Wittgenstein's claim that concepts are 'public phenomena', and that a key role of adults is to induct children into this 'public heritage' (White 2002:53). The number of possible concepts is infinite, and they are just as likely to be about the mundane and everyday (pencils, socks and teacups) as they are to be about more abstract ideas such as truth, beauty and speed. In our daily lives we constantly define new concepts in response to situations. Until we go to visit Granny we have no real need to construct a concept of 'things we must take on our visit to Granny' (Meadows 1993:105). Concepts, then, are mental models we construct to explain the world around us, which help us to deal with things and events more efficiently. As Siegler suggests: 'Concepts allow us to organize our experience into coherent patterns and to draw inferences in situations in which we lack direct experience...Concepts also save us mental effort by allowing us to apply previous knowledge to new situations' (Siegler 1998:213).

Clearly, such a process is extremely useful. It can help us to cope with new and unfamiliar situations, to employ what knowledge and experience we already have and to use our understanding most effectively. It can tell us how to react emotionally to experiences, as, for example, when we react cautiously to all unfamiliar dogs after having been bitten by one (Siegler *et al.* 2003). The alternative, as Meadows suggests, is chaos: 'Without concepts we could not predict, could not remember, could not communicate at all exactly, could not act appropriately with other people. The world which flows by us has to be organised if we are to survive' (Meadows 1993:101).

Children's conceptual development is part of their general cognitive development, and throughout this chapter you may find it useful to think back to many of the ideas looked at in Chapters 2 and 3. Piaget's idea of schema, looked at both in Chapter 2, and in Chapter 6 in discussion of Chris Athey's work, for example, is particularly relevant to any discussion of conceptual development. It is also impossible to look at concept development independent of language. In Chapter 7 different perspectives on the relationship of language to thought were discussed, and many of the perspectives outlined there, for example, Vygotsky's views about the interdependence of language and thought, are relevant in this context, too. Concepts, as 'public phenomena' (White 2002:53) are expressed in language, and some aspects of language, such as naming, may contribute to the development of concepts by supporting the process of categorization (Lee and Das Gupta 1995:130). However, as Pinker suggests: 'If you learned that *wapiti* was another name for an elk, you could take all the facts connected to the word *elk* and instantly transfer them to the *wapiti*' (1997:86), suggesting that we have a level of representation which is specific to the concepts behind the words themselves.

How do children's concepts develop?

Both Vygotsky and Piaget would suggest that young children are not skilled at forming and using concepts, in particular that they cannot form representations based on defining features (Siegler 1998). Piaget found that, at the preoperational stage, children could not categorize objects according to taxonomic principles, for example grouping all of the 'red' things together, or making a set of 'vehicles'. Instead, he found that children grouped things according to thematic principles, such as a cake and a table, because you put a cake on a table. Piaget suggests that children's conceptual development follows a path similar to their general cognitive development and is largely a move from the concrete to the abstract. For Piaget, children's thinking is qualitatively different to that of adults, and their knowledge structures are different at each stage of development. Cognitive conflict, which arises as children try to resolve anomalies in their understanding as a result of their experiences, results in wholesale, global restructuring of knowledge and stage change.

Vygotsky hypothesizes that children pass through three stages of conceptual development. In the first stage they form thematic concepts, as described earlier, then chain concepts, in which the basis for classification seems to change during the process of sorting. So, for example, a young child might group a few red things together, then a few circles of red and blue, then a few blue things and so on. The third stage, where children form true concepts based on stable, salient criteria, is, for Vygotsky 'quite a late achievement' (Meadows 1993:107). Thus, for both Vygotsky and Piaget, young children's conceptual understanding is fundamentally different to that of older children and adults.

The past 30 years have seen these ideas come under increasing scrutiny, and current thinking suggests that the idea that children structure knowledge differently at different stages may be an oversimplification (Meadows 1993). Siegler, for example, points to research which suggests that children as young as 1 year old can form taxonomic concepts, an ability Piaget and Vygotsky suggest is not present in 4- and 5-year-olds (1998). He concludes that the reasons that they did not seem to do so in Piaget and Vygotsky's experimental situations were that, first, children might find the thematic relationships more interesting than the taxonomic one: 'Young children might put dogs and frisbees together, rather than dogs and bears, because they find the relationship between dogs and frisbees more interesting' (Siegler 1998:217). Second, he suggests, Piaget and Vygotsky both underestimate the role of specific content knowledge in conceptual understanding. Quite simply, young children may not always have the necessary knowledge and experience to know what the defining features are that enable categories to be formed. This latter reason seems to be at the heart of any difference between young children's conceptual understanding and that of older children and adults. Developmental changes seem to be more about differentiation and elaboration rather than fundamental changes in the whole basis of conceptualization. What is central to this process is children's knowledge, for example, their event knowledge and experience. A good example of this is Arnold's (1999) description of the scientific concepts that Georgia is most concerned with from the ages of 2–5 years. The three listed are food allergy, childbirth and changes of state. Of these, two have particular significance in Georgia's life: she experiences the impact of childbirth when her brother, Harry, is born when she is 2, and he has potentially life-threatening food allergies.

Knowledge and experience, then, and the information gained from them, play a central part in shaping how we reason and form concepts (Thornton 2002). Siegler *et al.* (2003) suggest that this is the main reason why a characteristic form of young children's thinking touched on in Chapter 1, magical thinking, dies away with age, as young children increase their knowledge about the world, and as they have experiences that challenge their beliefs, for example, about the existence of the tooth fairy.

Categorization

The tendency to form concepts seems to be a basic part of what it is to be human, a kind of 'explanatory drive' (Gopnik *et al.* 1999:85). Babies form them from their earliest days. Karmiloff-Smith (1994:42) suggests that babies have a 'very simple template' of the human face from birth, which quickly develops into a general concept of a face, before recognition of individual faces. She also suggests that babies know a lot about concepts such as size, space and depth from the very beginning. After about five days, she recounts, babies will only reach for things like mobiles that are within their grasp.

It is primarily through the use of their senses that babies first begin to explore, and develop concepts about, the world around them. Gopnik *et al.* suggest that humans have 'a special kind of knowledge that enables us to translate the information at our senses into representations of objects' (1999:62). The brain 'systematically transforms' (1999:62) the wealth of sensory information it receives, and, in so doing, organises that information into a complex, but coherent network. Catherwood (1999) suggests that babies can see categorical similarities at the age of about 3–4 months, notably of what are generally referred to as 'basic' categories, for example, 'car', and possibly even at a higher level, for example, 'vehicles'. These perceptual categorizations arise from the 'heuristic inferences' (Thornton 2002:108) babies and young children make as a result of their experience of the world. Meadows suggests that what may be central to this process is children's representation of meaningful events in their lives or 'General Event Representation' (GER) (Meadows 1993:111). Many of the 'events' of children's lives are highly routinized: getting up, going to the shops, having a drink, playing 'Peekaboo' games, for example. Children's representations of these routines, she argues, help them to attach meaning to them, and also support comparisons with other routines. She cites Nelson, in her suggestion that GERs could be the 'basic building blocks' (Meadows 1993:112) of cognitive development, and particularly of aspects such as categorization, patterning, making inferences and cause – effect relations, so important in conceptual development.

GERs may play an important part in the development of children's ability to categorize, in particular, in moving from basic categories to the development of hierarchies of category.

As they develop beyond babyhood, children show an increased understanding of both category hierarchies and causal connections (Siegler *et al.* 2003). Looking at category hierarchies, Rosch (cited in Lee and Das Gupta 1995) suggests that such categorization comprises three levels. Young children generally learn these three levels of categorization in a similar order. First, children form 'basic' level categories, as in 'car', earlier, then 'superordinate' level categories, as in 'vehicle', the class to which all cars belong. The third level of category formation is known as 'subordinate' and deals with finer discrimination of the basic level, for example, type of car. Another example of the relationship between the three levels would be animal (superordinate), cat (basic) and Siamese (subordinate). Children generally tend to form basic level categories first because these usually have a number of consistent characteristics. In cats, for example, these include fur, whiskers, size and 'meow'. The characteristics of the superordinate level, animal, are less consistent. Subordinate category characteristics are consistent, as in the basic level, but require children to make finer discriminations: differences in fur length and colour in cats, for example.

Sorting objects in terms of their categories tends to improve with age. Three-year-olds are generally able to sort by basic level categorization, but only half as likely to be able to sort by superordinate level as 4-year-olds (Lee and Das Gupta 1995). The role of adults in supporting the development of children's superordinate and subordinate categorization formation may be important here, with parents and carers often using basic-level examples to illustrate these: 'animals are creatures like cats', or 'a daffodil is a kind of flower, it's yellow, it's not very tall, and it comes up in the spring'.

Causal relationships and categorization

This approach to categorization focuses strongly on the perceptual, that is, grouping on the basis of observable physical characteristics. It is very useful in everyday contexts (Thornton 2002) but cannot account for all of the 'events' of children's lives. What is needed, and what tends to develop later in infancy, is children's conceptual understanding of causal relationships, although Gopnik *et al.* (1999) suggest that there is evidence of babies making causal connections from as early as 3 months of age. Thornton (2002) suggests that Carey's (1985) study of the concept of animacy, that is, whether things are alive or dead, is an example of how children's reasoning changes from perceptual to conceptual or 'principled' inference, based upon being able to make causal category definitions. For Thornton, this development represents a radical change, which 'provides the child with a new and more powerful basis for reasoning, better suited to formal, analytical thinking' (2002:117). In addition, she suggests that it illustrates the difference between Piaget's perspective that new knowledge arises out of a change in the 'mental tools' available to children and the more current view that increased knowledge supports the development of new ways of thinking. Put simply, 'what you know determines how you reason' (Thornton 2002:118).

As Thornton points out, this may explain why children's reasoning can be so different from one context to another. Elsewhere here we have looked at the idea of novicehood and noted that children are initially novices at everything but develop expertise in particular areas or domains as a result of their experiences, which will, of course, differ from child to child. This domain-specific knowledge may be particularly important in the development of key aspects of conceptual understanding such as inferential and analogical reasoning and the identification and use of problem-solving strategies (Thornton 2002). The accumulation of knowledge and expertise means that the expert can recognize a problem as familiar, and is also able to call upon previous experience in solving that problem more quickly and effectively. What the expert does not have to do is to run through the whole of a procedure in order to arrive at the best solution; she already knows that a particular approach will 'work'. Children's early knowledge tends to be heavily procedural (knowing how to do things). Over time, children generally get better at accessing their knowledge without having to use this procedural knowledge, and come to rely more on 'declarative' (knowing that) knowledge (Meadows 1993).

Thus, it seems likely that young children's approaches to forming and using concepts may not be qualitatively different to those of older children and adults, rather that they differ in their ability to use 'the intellectual system' (Lee and Das Gupta 1995:128). We have seen that young children are capable, for example, of categorizing objects on taxonomic grounds, contrary to Piaget's and Vygotsky's beliefs. In addition, there is evidence to suggest that use of thematic grouping does not die with age, and that adults, too, use such grouping (Meadows 1993). Knowledge seems to be key to the development of young children's concepts, and 'where children are knowledgeable and encouraged to discuss their knowledge they seem to have concepts very like those of adults' (Meadows 1993:115).

Some implications for practice in supporting the development of children's concepts – part 1: experience and adult roles

All of this suggests that the provision of rich experiences which support the acquisition of knowledge and understanding will be key to children's conceptual development, from their earliest days. Goldschmied and Jackson (2004) believe that the provision of 'treasure baskets' and heuristic play provides babies and toddlers with opportunities to make connections in their knowledge and understanding. In playing with a treasure basket, babies are able to explore objects through all of their senses: touching, smelling, mouthing, looking at and listening to a broad variety of natural materials. The role of experience is also borne out in Hatano and Inagaki's (1992) studies of young children's care for goldfish. They concluded that those children who had experience of caring for goldfish tended to be able to make use of this knowledge and experience in analogous situations, such as in thinking about the characteristics of frogs, for example. In this, they were able to make conceptual inferences more advanced than those of their classmates who had no direct experience but who had merely observed their teachers caring for animals in the kindergarten. That is, they had developed conceptual knowledge which they were able to transfer to a new situation. This supports Watson's view that children should be given opportunities 'to develop expertise (domain-specific knowledge) in areas that interest them' (1997:15). A key context for supporting the development of such interconnections is children's play (Claxton 1999b).

One final element of Vygotsky's ideas may be important to consider here. Vygotsky suggests that there are two types of conceptual development, the 'formal' or 'scientific' ones learned as part of the process of schooling, and the 'everyday' ones, acquired in context (1986:194). In his view, both types interact in children's development, and complement one another, with home concepts being built on by scientific ones, and those, in turn, modifying the home concepts. The implication here may be that 'educational practices have to build on the child's everyday concepts but also to reach into the future where experiences can be created in school and combined with other subject matter concepts (scientific concepts)' (Hedegaard 2005:14).

The role of the adult, White (2002) suggests, is to explain, give examples and monitor children's understanding, because, in his view, children will not just pick concepts up. The implication of Navarra's (1955) observations of his son is that careful, sensitive observation is important if adults are to notice, and support, conceptual change. Such observation may reveal children showing their understanding of concepts in many ways, through action as much as through language (MacNaughton and Williams 2004).

Willig (1990:13) suggests that five strategies, in particular, are important in extending children's conceptual development, all of which can be seen to have a relationship to the models of cognitive development outlined in Chapter 2.

- matching teaching material to the ability of the learner;
- disturbing the learner's existing ideas;
- teaching by telling;
- learning from observing;
- learning by thinking about thinking.

Willig's suggestion that 'teaching by telling' (1990:18) is an important strategy in extending children's conceptual development emphasizes 'meaningful reception learning' (1990:18) rather than any kind of rote learning. Nevertheless, it seems somewhat at odds with Duckworth's assertion that 'Simply telling children the truth about something could not make them understand it' (1987:32). Box 1.1, in Chapter 1, illustrates this dilemma and suggests that repeated opportunities which explore and challenge children's thinking will be necessary in order to support the development of concepts, and, even then, when faced with the novel, children will often revert back to earlier intuitions (Driver 1983). Paley describes a similar episode, in which the children, faced with a very large, heavy bag of sand in the middle of the kindergarten, 'invent' pulleys and levers in order to move the bag. She later tells them a story in which a man needs to move a heavy rock in front of the entrance to his cave, and asks the children what advice they could have given him. Their responses include no reference to the kinds of strategies they devised when faced with a similar predicament. As she reflects: 'The adult should not underestimate the young child's tendency to revert to earlier thinking; new concepts have not been "learned" but are only in temporary custody. They are glimpsed and tried out but are not permanent possessions' (Paley 1981:101).

Further general implications for practice in supporting young children's conceptual development are set out at the end of this chapter. The remainder of the chapter focuses on some specific areas of conceptual development, in particular at ones such as number, space and time, that are 'so important, so pervasive, that they merit special attention' (Siegler 1998:226), using examples here to draw general implications. Although these are considered in 'subject' areas, there is, of course, considerable overlap between these domains, and emphasis is on the holistic way in which children themselves think about things. Looking at children's concepts of 'time', for example, reveals aspects of their mathematical, historical and scientific thinking, at the very least. In addition, there is no suggestion that these are the only aspects of young children's conceptual development of value to consider, merely that there is not sufficient space here to look at everything.

Young children's scientific thinking

A good example of young children's holistic thinking is their understanding of 'living' and 'non-living' things. There are many accounts of children's concepts in this area (see, in particular, Carey 1985), and the ways in which they attempt to resolve conflicts in their understanding of life and death: if you bury a dead rabbit it will grow again (see Box 6.1), trees are not alive because they do not move and so on. Babies distinguish early on between animate creatures and inanimate objects, on the basis of movement (Thornton 2002). However, this understanding, and the ability to categorize things and creatures as animate or inanimate develops over a long period of time, and it is not until around the age of 10 that children will have the 'received model' (Selley 1999) of the concept of 'living' and 'non-living' (Carey 1985). Willig (1993) cites research showing confusion in young children's minds about whether dolls are inanimate objects, at least until the age of 6 years (for example, 46 per cent of 3-year-olds made errors about this). Willig's data also shows children's considerable uncertainty about the status of other groups, such as fish, insects and dead animals. As Thornton (2002) suggests, in the early years children will tend to make their inferences about concepts, in this case about animacy, on perceptual grounds: the more a thing 'looks' like the prototypical animate creature, the more likely it is to be assessed as alive. On this basis, dolls look like a better proposition than, say, trees, for a young child. In addition, children's experiences of stories, television programmes and films, where dolls can be just as animate and 'alive' as humans, may have an impact on their thinking.

Children's confusion about death and its permanency is reflected in questions such as 'Is Mrs Z still dead?' (Navarra 1955:96) and in their play where people often die and come alive again. Lofdahl relates a 'funeral' play episode between two girls, aged $3\frac{1}{2}$ and 4 years, who play out scattering flowers over a body in a grave in order to make it come alive again. The comment of Maja, one of the girls, also illustrates how children form concepts as a result of the language they hear around them and try out this language in order to negotiate understanding. Her comment: 'You can just wake up when you feel the flowers on your body' (Lofdahl 2005:13) may come from hearing people talk about dead people 'going to sleep', alongside a propensity in young children for 'magical thinking' (Paley 1981, Siegler *et al.* 2003) noted earlier. What children lack, Carey (1985) suggests, is sufficient biological knowledge which would enable them to create unified categories of 'living' and 'non-living' things.

'Knowing' and ways of thinking

The accumulation of such knowledge will take time. In addition, it will not, by itself, be enough. Nunes suggests that scientific knowledge is about particular 'ways of thinking' (1995:194) and is much more than the accumulation of 'facts'. She uses the example that children can 'know' that the world is a sphere, but their thinking about the world may be governed more by a view of it as flat, with the sky above and the earth below. Similarly, the two girls in Lofdahl's (2005) study might, in some sense, 'know' that one does not come alive again, but still think that one does. For Nunes, the facts are meaningless unless the concepts to which they relate become part of our thinking. In describing the development of one boy's ('L.B.') scientific concepts over a period of two years, Navarra similarly concludes that development was not just a matter of 'knowing' more:

> Individual experiences and items of information that grew out of L.B.'s activity were continually related and integrated into ever larger, interlocking conceptual patterns. L.B.'s conceptual growth was not merely an additive process in which new information was accumulated. It was, rather, an evaluative process in which the integration of new information could bring about a basic reconstruction in the conceptual framework.
>
> (Navarra 1955:121)

Arnold concurs, in her observations on Georgia, and the process by which many different elements of a particular concept come together over time, and are reflected in the schemas Georgia explores in her play (Arnold 1999). In so doing, Georgia can be seen asking questions of herself and others, hypothesizing about ideas and then testing these out. Navarra's work is set within the dominant perspective of its time, that of Piaget, with his emphasis on new knowledge arising out of a change in the 'mental tools' available to children. However, it is also possible to read Navarra's observations as a demonstration of the more current view that increased knowledge supports the development of new ways of thinking. A good example of this process is the development of L.B.'s increasingly differentiated concepts of smoke and steam. A very brief selection is shown in Box 8.1, and illustrates L.B.'s active search for meaning and his increasing use of stable characteristics to denote a concept.

Alternative frameworks

What is clear from the examples we have looked at is that young children's experiences can result in them developing concepts which may look different to those of older children and

Box 8.1 L.B., aged between 3 years 2 months and 4 years 8 months

August 1951	(Watching his aunt dusting a rosebush with a spraygun) Is that smoke?
August 1951	(Looking at haze and fog on the sea) Where's the smoke coming from?
October 1951	(Watching his mother iron clothes) What's that – smoke? Where is that coming from? Is there something that makes it smoke?
October 1951	(Watching a car being steam cleaned) What's he doing to the car? Is the car burning on fire? (His father replies: No, he's using steam to clean the car).
February 1952	(Watching boiling water being poured) Hey! Look at all that steam! Are you going to drink that? Where is all that smoke going to?
April 1952	(In a steam-filled bathroom) Look at all the smoke.
April 1952	(In a steam-filled bathroom) Hey, mommy, where does all this steam come from – from the water?... This *is* steamy. (Mother says: What do you mean – steamy?) L.B.: It's all wet.
August 1952	(Smoke is coming out of the chimney of the house next door) Where's that coming from? Is that happening because they want to take a bath? How come no smoke isn't coming out of ours? Isn't our heat on?
February 1953	(L.B. has a hot cup of bouillon for his lunch. His mother tells him to 'wait until it cools off'. He eats the rest of his lunch first) Is it cool now? (Mother says: I don't know) L.B.: Yes, it's cool now' cause there's no steam. (Mother: Does that mean it's cool?) L.B.: Yes. (Mother: Doesn't steam come from cool things?) L.B.: No, only when it's hot.
	(Adapted from Navarra 1951:39–44)

Box 8.2 Charlotte, aged 5 years 9 months, in conversation at home with her father

CHARLOTTE: Dad, I've been thinking about it and I think there must be two suns. One goes round the world and makes days and nights. The other always stays in front of Africa, because it's always hot in Africa.

Charlotte lives in England, but her uncle lives in Africa, and he has told her that it is hot there all the time. Her father is also a physicist, and has shown her books about astronomy, and they have talked about the earth moving around the sun, so on one level she 'knows' that there is only one sun. How, then, can she make sense of this when she knows that the sun gives heat, and her uncle has told her it is hot all the time in Africa? Charlotte attempts to resolve this cognitive conflict by inventing a second sun, an alternative framework which provides, for her, a consistent model for explaining the situation. What is also interesting here is that the remark was generated spontaneously by Charlotte herself, and her metacognitive opening statement 'I've been thinking about it' suggests her understanding about what it means to think.

adults (although adults, too, may have concepts which do not match the received models). As we have noted, this is more the result of lack of experience than of qualitatively different ways of thinking. In Box 7.8 we saw Abe's hypothesis that 'ladies have their hearts in their boobies'. This is a reasonable conclusion for Abe to draw on the basis of his knowledge that our hearts are in our chests and women's breasts are on their chests; so he invents a reality where hearts are inside them. Such ideas have often been referred to as 'misconceptions' in young children's scientific thinking. However, a more useful way of considering them is as 'alternative frameworks' (Driver 1983), which are perfectly logical conclusions on the basis of individual children's understanding and experience. Arguably, this is often what 'real' scientists do, when they invent *ad hoc* hypotheses to make sense of the world. Box 8.2 illustrates one such alternative framework. Much more discussion and experience may be needed to move Charlotte's current concept closer to that conventionally held.

Supporting the development of young children's scientific concepts

In seeking to support the development of young children's scientific concepts, as with other areas of conceptual development, attention to both process and content will be important. Careful observation and exploration of children's current understanding (Valanides *et al.* 2000), and sensitive intervention by those working with young children will be the most worthwhile starting points. Wadsworth suggests that awareness of the different kinds of ideas children hold will be important for adults in supporting the development of young children's scientific understanding:

- anthropomorphic views: 'don't cry, little worm';
- egocentric views: 'we've got to go to bed, we can't sleep when it is light';
- ideas based on colloquial use of language: Maja's understanding of 'waking' from the dead (p. 135);

- ideas based on limited experience and observations: as with Abe in Box 7.8;
- stylized representations: children often draw the sun with lines radiating out, but this does not mean that they understand light travels in straight lines.

(Adapted from Wadsworth 1997)

Gura (1992) also remarks on the positive impact on children's thinking as a result of watching other children engaged in similar activities, for example blockplay, and on the ways in which adults can help to structure children's enquiry and exploration.

Finally, it is worth returning here to Vygotsky's (1986) idea of 'everyday' and 'scientific' or 'formal' concepts. He suggests that young children's concepts arise out of their everyday experiences, and, as a result of particular experiences, children generalize to wider concepts. He sees the learning of scientific, or formal, concepts proceeding in the other direction, from the general to the particular. This may be useful in looking at some potential difficulties that children may experience in developing concepts in the area of science itself. Nunes (1995) suggests that they fall into four categories. First, scientific concepts involve us in making distinctions we might not ordinarily make in life, for example between temperature and heat. Second, many scientific concepts represent intensive rather than extensive quantities. Extensive quantities are derived from units of measurement, for example, the centimetre. Intensive measurements involve ratios, for example density is measured as a ratio of mass to volume. Third, scientific concepts often require reasoning about non-perceptible aspects of the physical world, for example, molecules and atoms. Finally, children have already developed some knowledge about the physical world which differs from the established scientific concept, and may have alternative frameworks, as outlined earlier. While elements of these difficulties assume their greatest relevance in relation to older children, it is nevertheless worth noting them here.

Children thinking mathematically

Young children's conceptual understanding in mathematics is an area of some controversy, centred upon the question of whether or not they 'have genuine mathematical experiences' (Bryant 1997:53). In looking at children's mathematical thinking, the chief focus here is on number, for two reasons: first, because number underpins all other aspects of mathematics, including shape, space and measurement, and second, because it is in this area that some of the questions about young children's mathematical understanding are best, and most easily, explored. The following section, on young children's geographical thinking, looks at spatial cognition, which is also highly relevant here.

Understanding number

In order to look at what develops, it is useful to begin by clarifying the two basic types of number knowledge, as these will be referred to here. The first is cardinality, or the absolute numerical size of any set or group. Thus, the last number reached when counting stands for the total number of things counted. The second is ordinality, which refers to the relational properties of numbers. Numbers are always said in the same order, and always stand in the same relationship to one another in the sense of being greater or less. You are reading the eighth chapter of this book, perhaps drinking a second cup of coffee, and the number 5 will always be bigger than the number 3.

Given Piaget's interest in the development of children's logical thinking, it should come as no surprise that he devoted considerable time and effort to exploring children's understanding of number, although much of it looks in more detail at older children. This is because, for Piaget, young children, while they might be able to use number words and sequences, and even to apply these to objects and actions, do so without real understanding (Bryant 1997). Piaget suggests that children need to have an understanding of both the cardinal and ordinal properties of numbers, and the key operations of classification (putting a set of things together) and seriation (putting the set in order) that accompany them (Piaget 1952). Research since Piaget, particularly that involving naturalistic observation, suggests much earlier competence (Donaldson 1978, Gelman and Gallistel 1978, Hughes 1986). This leads Blakemore and Frith to conclude that Piaget was 'simply wrong' (2005:50) in his views about young children's number concepts.

What develops?

From the very earliest days, babies demonstrate an interest in pattern ('a key element in mathematical thinking', Fisher 1990:207), developing an early ability to distinguish between the faces they see around them. Research evidence suggests that babies of only a few months (Karmiloff-Smith 1994, Siegler 1998), or even neonates (Pound 2004), have some sense of cardinality, and can discriminate 1 object from 2, and 2 from 3. They also seem to have some understanding of adding and subtracting such small numbers (Pinker 1997, Siegler 1998). In so doing, they seem to be making use of a perceptual process called subitizing, in which we recognize the quantity of a set of objects, and apply a number to it without actually counting them. By the age of 2, children make frequent reference to number words, although this is often idiosyncratic, and may show little reference to the corresponding objects (Meadows 1993). Up to this point, then, children may not be counting, in the sense of accurately assigning a number to a set of objects too big to be subitized, by tagging each object with a number. Maclellan (1997) suggests that this is a skill which underpins an understanding of number, and it may not be eident until around the age of 4 (Siegler 1998).

Fuson (cited in Munn 1997) outlines a developmental sequence for counting, suggesting that children initially imitate a string of words when saying a number word sequence, alongside some understanding of appropriate contexts for counting. This is followed by a stage where children begin to count things as an activity in itself, coordinating pointing, naming and object. The third stage is where children integrate counting and cardinality, including considering 'how many?' type questions. This highlights an important point, that number concepts are acquired as part of a process of cultural transmission. Young children both hear and see adults and older children around them using numbers, and are very often inducted into naming and counting by them. Munn sees this sequence of development as essentially Vygotskian:

> First, counting appears on the social plane, between people, with children's activity supported by language and goals. After considerable experience of this joint action, children internalize the cultural practice of counting. It then appears on the psychological plane, at which point children are able to direct their counting according to adult principles.
>
> (Munn 1997:18)

Gelman and Gallistel suggest that the development of counting marks understanding of a number of counting principles, which will, in general, be evident by the age of 5 years, but in some children by as young as 3 (1978). The first three of these principles are 'how to count' ones: the one-to-one principle (you can assign one and only one number word to each object), the stable order principle (numbers are always assigned in the same order) and the cardinal principle (the last number counted represents the value of the set). The fourth principle is the order irrelevance principle, requiring an understanding that the order in which things are counted is irrelevant. The fifth principle, the abstraction principle, means that any set of objects can be counted (Gelman and Gallistel 1978). Their conclusion that young children understand these principles, and therefore know what it means to count, is very different from that of Piaget. Other research has challenged Gelman and Gallistel's proposition that children understand and use these principles in order to learn to count, suggesting that the process works in the opposite direction, and that children can use counting skilfully before understanding underlying principles (Siegler *et al*. 2003). Munn (1997) suggests that this has important implications for practice. Here, it is important to note that these differences of view exist but are not yet conclusively resolved.

The second type of number knowledge children will need is ordinal knowledge, concerning the relative values or positions of numbers. This knowledge, of which the most basic concepts are 'more' and 'less', develops a little later than cardinality, but is still apparent by the age of about 18 months. Again, as with cardinality, evidence of development seems to be displayed partly as skill in handling larger numbers, and in being able to make sense of questions such as 'Which is more? Four apples or six?'

Language in mathematics

The relationship of ordinal knowledge to an understanding of ideas such as more and less highlights a wider issue here that is concerned with language in mathematics. Understanding of mathematics is mediated through language, and children's understanding of 'mathematical' problems, both contextual ones such as 'how many forks do I need to put on the table if everyone needs to have one?' and abstract number problems such as 'what is 2 and 1 more?' can only be understood if you know what these words mean, and understand that, in a mathematical context, they have a very precise meaning. Words like 'more' and 'less' are used much more ambiguously in everyday speech – we even have an expression 'more or less' to mean 'approximate' or 'roughly equal'! How is a child to reliably know in which context these words are being used? A practitioner working in a London nursery told the children that, as part of their celebration of Chinese New Year that they would be having 'Chinese take away', at which point one boy burst into tears, saying 'Oh no, I can't do adding yet!' (Esther Whalley, personal communication). Box 8.3 provides a good example of this. Reflecting later, Paley says that, had she put her inquiries in dramatic form, the children would have understood. However, it may also be that the children were unclear of the language she used, and even that, for them, the questions had little point.

Gura (1992) suggests that adults need to support the development of children's mathematical understanding and the language needed to go with it, as a simultaneous process:

> Rather than seeing the development of mathematical ideas as a two-step process, with action and abstraction preceding language, they should be viewed as an integrated process. The adult role then becomes one of helping the child to develop both the understandings and the corresponding language through shared activity.
>
> (Gura 1992:93)

Box 8.3 Vivian Paley at snack time

Of the eight children at my snack table, six ask for peanut butter and jelly on their crackers, one wants plain peanut butter, and one, plain jelly. My question: What did I make more of, peanut butter and jelly or plain peanut butter? The children stare at me blankly and no one answers.

'What I mean is, did more people ask for peanut butter and jelly or did more want plain peanut butter?' Silence. 'I'll count the children who are eating peanut butter and jelly.' I count to six. 'And only Barney has peanut butter.'

Because Barney likes peanut butter,' Mollie explains.

'Yes but did I make more sandwiches that have both peanut butter and jelly?'

'Because we like peanut butter *and* jelly', Frederick responds patiently.

(Paley 1986:131)

'Everyday' and 'formal' mathematics

Thus far, the focus has been largely on children's acquisition of conceptual understanding in mathematics as part of their daily lives, that is, 'everyday' understanding. Rogoff (2003) and Nunes (1995) both illustrate how competent children of all ages can show themselves to be in contexts which are familiar to them, often using informal, mental strategies. Carr (1992) describes a framework of the social purposes for which children use mathematics in their everyday lives:

- to indicate comparative status: 'I'm four, you're big';
- to rehearse a culturally significant sequence: in songs, games etc;
- to recognize culturally significant symbols: in the home, indicating measures (e.g. on heaters), indicating 'how many';
- to solve interesting problems: making and fixing things, checking and timing.

(adapted from Carr 1992:4–5)

What is not altogether clear is how this everyday expertise translates to the more formal (Vygotsky's 'scientific' understanding) conceptual understanding which is increasingly emphasized as children get older. Both Rogoff (2003) and Nunes (2005), in fact, show how the competence children show in their everyday mathematics can often evaporate in school contexts, where different ways of thinking and different procedures are emphasized. This, in keeping with the general conclusions drawn by, among others, Donaldson (1978), has led to a belief in the importance of setting children's mathematical learning in embedded contexts which have meaning for them. Hughes (1986) suggests that children show greater competence in number activities embedded in everyday contexts, and where they are able to handle or see the objects, rather than when tasks are set in more abstract, formal codes.

As a result, many early childhood settings emphasize everyday activities, such as cooking, as contexts for mathematical activities. While this may be valuable in many ways, Gifford (2004a) also points out that many distractions, not the least of which will be an interest in eating the food cooked, may militate against developing the mathematical aspects of the activity. In addition, everyday contexts will tend to make use of very different units: one orange at snack time, and 150 g of flour for the cakes (Gifford 2004a). She also cites

Walkerdine's argument that this 'everyday life' is both culturally bound and often gendered (Walkerdine cited in Gifford 2004a). While not arguing against the value of connecting with children's home lives, Gifford makes the important point that this will require practitioners to have some understanding of what the children's individual home lives are actually like and also knowledge of the kinds of number experiences children have had.

The kinds of activities Gifford records the 3- and 4-year-old children in her study engaging in cognitively with numbers were not always set in everyday contexts. The cognitive activities were:

- making connections – pleasure in discovery;
- predicting – *'cognitive thrill'* of risk taking and problem solving;
- rehearsal – satisfaction in achievement;
- representation – creativity and satisfaction;
- spotting mistakes and incongruities – humour in *'number jokes'* and playfulness, both enhancing and protecting self-esteem.

(Gifford 2004a:96, emphasis in original)

They were each often accompanied by clear indications of positive emotions like excitement, leading her to conclude that these cognitive–emotional aspects combined to form 'hooks' (2004a:93), which engaged the children. She suggests a number of key mathematics teaching strategies for the early years, including helping children make connections, challenging misconceptions, providing opportunities for representation and discussion, instructing and demonstrating, thinking aloud, providing immersion and apprenticeship opportunities, sharing and scaffolding problem-solving, and giving feedback (Gifford 2004b:104). This has much in common with Pinker's (1997) view that the passage from 'intuitive' to 'school' mathematics is one which requires attention to, and induction into, specific mathematical concepts.

Children's geographical thinking

Children's geographical thinking is about the way in which they locate themselves, and then others, physically in space, but, just as importantly, it is about their social and cultural location, and their sense of belonging. This will include their view of themselves in relation to others, both their immediate family and community, and the wider world.

Spatial orientation

Knowing the shape of our environment 'represents a domain of early cognitive strength for young children' (Clements 2004:278) and can be seen from early babyhood onwards, although developing spatial orientation competencies is a long process. In attempting to chart this development, Siegler (1998) suggests that we represent spatial location in three ways:

1   egocentric representation: in relation to ourselves, and our own position;
2   landmark representation: by locating significant landmarks in the environment;
3   allocentric representation: by use of an abstract framework of maps, or coordinates.

(Adapted from Siegler 1998:229)

In the earliest stages, babies' understanding of space is 'egocentric', in that it is tied to their own position within it. The ability to move – to shuffle, crawl and eventually walk – marks (literally!) a huge step forward. In moving, babies are able to engage all of their senses, and can take more perceptual notice of their surroundings, and the significant landmarks they encounter. The active process of cognitive mapping, that is, the mental maps of the spatial environment we all carry around with us, gathers pace. Karmiloff-Smith quotes an example from a parent's diary, describing her 14-month-old daughter:

> She's become a real explorer. Took her the other day to my friend's house and though she'd never been there before, she went all over the place, opening cupboards – really nosey – and going in and out of different rooms. She'd occasionally pop her head around the door, though, to see if we were still there, and then off she'd go again. Once she got her fingers caught, so then she bawled. Otherwise she seemed really happy.
>
> (Karmiloff-Smith 1994:79)

Exploration, Karmiloff-Smith says, fuels the desire for more exploration. At first, children's mental maps are fragmented, and not linked together, but gradually they connect, to form a much bigger picture, in which landmarks are highlighted, and which give each child a growing sense of their place in the world. This process highlights the importance of experience and, in particular, experience as part of a culture. Learning about place is intimately bound up with one's own place in the physical, cultural and social spaces we inhabit. Kearins (cited in Siegler 1998) points to the need for highly developed spatial thinking in Australian aboriginal children as an example. Knowing the location of widely spaced wells and creeks may be the difference between life and death for aboriginals who spend much of their time on the move, in desert areas. Comparing the performance of Australian aboriginal children with white Australian children raised in the city, Kearins found that, not only did the aboriginal children show superior memory for spatial location, they also used different strategies from the urban children for remembering. The aboriginal children tended to be silent and concentrated on the look of things, while urban children rehearsed the names of the objects. Siegler (1998) suggests that both types of strategy fit the children's predominant needs: the one for verbal efficacy, the other for surviving in the bush.

What of the third of Siegler's three categories of representation, the allocentric? This requires more complex orchestration of spatial information, from multiple perspectives. Siegler (1998) suggests that children who are 1 year old can be shown to have a basic allocentric sense, and are able to make use of information in situations where they have no specific landmarks available to help them. By the age of 4 children are able to negotiate their way around a simple maze using a map (Willig 1990), can interpret a range of symbols, such as those for roads, rivers and parks, on a map, and have begun to be able to use co-ordinates, for example on a simple grid (Palmer 1994). A number of factors may be important in the development of this environmental cognition. These include experience (Palmer, 1994, for example, cites research pointing to enhanced route learning in children who had the opportunity to walk the route rather than just look at a slide presentation or video), greater familiarity with a wider range of environments, and exposure to the particular ideas and social conventions of mapmaking and map-reading (Clements 2004, Haste 1987, Heal and Cook 1998).

Box 8.4 Sarah, aged 3 years 11 months, at nursery, sitting with two friends at the graphics table

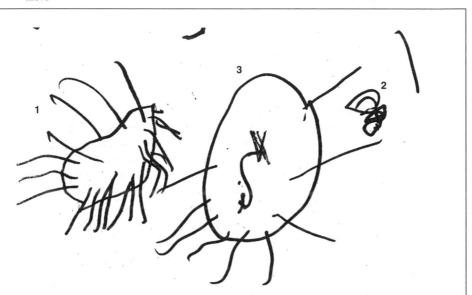

SARAH: I'm going to make a treasure map (reaches for a sheet of paper and draws a circle – see 1 on drawing). This is the way to Sunderland (starts pulling lines from the edge of the circle out, and continues until lines are radiating out all way round the circle). This is my treasure map too; it's my treasure map and my Sunderland map! These are the traffic lights (adds three circular marks – see 2 on drawing, then another large circle – see 3 on drawing). And then you go over a path to Sunderland, and then you go over another path, then you go over another path, then you go over another path, then another path, then another path, then another path, then another path, then another path (each time she says this she adds another line radiating out from the second circle). And that's the way to Sunderland! (Smiles and pats paper).

In her mark making Sarah shows a core and radial schema as she represents her understanding not only of maps but also the movement she associates with going to Sunderland. Each radial line added to figure 3 is directly accompanied by her vocalization that 'you go over another path', an example of what Matthews (2004) sees as the child's interest in representing not only figures but movement too. His observations support Athey's research, which found children verbalizing about both objects and action when involved in graphical representation.

Reproduced with permission of Lisa Guy

Children's personal maps

Children's early personal recorded maps are generated as part of their graphic representations of the world, and often incorporate marks which may stand for a number of ideas and concepts, and which change meaning as they are being made. Box 8.4 illustrates this well, as Sarah's map moves from being a map of the journey to Sunderland, to a treasure map and back again.

The landmarks that children depict will tend to express the personal meanings that these things have for them. In this, they may not differ significantly from adults. Haste (1987) describes research showing adults' representations of their home towns. Like children, they tend to incorporate features that are meaningful for them on a personal level, such as particular buildings and landmarks. Haste (1987) stresses that such representations are not, though, purely idiosyncratic, but serve as shared representations, that the rest of the social group could understand. An account of a project in Reggio Emilia illustrates these ideas well (Piazza and Barozzi 2001). In this project, two groups of 5- and 6-year-olds (a group of 3 girls and a group of 3 boys) develop their own maps of the city. As Piazza and Barozzi note, the end results look very different, although this difference is more in the kinds of ideas represented than in the form each map takes. The girls' map depicts 'a city full of relationships and life' (2001:234), and seems to reflect an interest in the places in which they live, go shopping, play and go to school. The boys' map is 'full of functions and connections' (2001:241), in which topological landmarks like the station, the sewers and the electricity system seem to reflect their interest in an 'urban network'. Piazza and Barozzi also note the different behaviours of the groups in developing their maps. The girls engage in informative and negotiating talk with one another. For the boys, they say, 'dialogue seems to be identified more in the silences, in the shared looks' (2001:244). While it would be invidious to draw conclusions from one episode, a consideration of gender may nevertheless be important here.

Fisher (1990:230) outlines a developmental path in children's mapmaking, from simple schematic drawings, where features are generally represented in elevation, that is, seen from the side rather than from above, through the mixing of both plan and elevation in the same map, and finally to a more complex plan view, which includes abstract representations of objects, and in which the relationship of one place to another is set out clearly. As with map-reading, this kind of mapmaking requires considerable skills of abstraction and symbolization. In this, Rogoff suggests that Western 'schooling seems to foster perceptual skills in analysis of two-dimensional patterns and in the use of graphic conventions to represent depth in two dimensions' (2003:242). As such, this kind of skill may be more valued, and more explicitly developed, in some cultural contexts than others.

Children's understanding of history

Much of the accepted thinking about children's historical concepts, often based upon Piaget's conclusions, has, until relatively recently, tended to focus on children's imperfect understanding of temporal relationships, and difficulties in having a sense of the passage of time. Many of the core concepts of history – order, duration, change, continuity, past and present – are, in many respects, abstract and challenging ideas, full understanding of which may only be achieved in late childhood (Lee and Das Gupta 1995). In addition, an understanding of the 'complex interacting concepts' of speed, space and number, necessary for the measurement of time, emerges slowly (Cooper 2002:9). However, as Hoodless points out, 'a failure to understand the accurate quantification of time is not the same thing as failing to have any concept of time' (1996a:101), and there is much evidence to suggest that even very young children have a sense of the order of events (Hartley 1993, Siegler 1998).

Experiencing and understanding order and sequence

From their earliest days babies are developing a sense of past and present. Their recognition of the familiar face of a carer rests upon their ability to connect the past, via memory (I've seen that face before!), to the present. At about 3 months there is evidence of their ability to detect a repetitive sequence, and by about a year they are able to do this after only one experience of an event, and also to put in sequence a pair of actions that they have seen. By about 20 months, they can reproduce a sequence of three events, indicating that they are able to form a mental representation of first, next, and last (Siegler *et al.* 2003). Over time, they develop the ability to do this with an increasing number of events, although there may be an interesting parallel here with the idea of thematic categorization, discussed earlier. Cooper cites research with 4- and 5-year-old children, in which, asked to sequence photographs of themselves, they chose what were often seen as idiosyncratic criteria rather than temporal ones, for example, the most recent picture next to a baby one (Cooper 2002). Is this perhaps just a more interesting way of looking at the activity than a conventional timeline, in much the same way that Siegler (1998) suggests in his discussion of children's general conceptual development? Fraisse (cited in Hoodless 1996b) seems also to link this with the development of expertise and declarative knowledge, also considered earlier, in his suggestion that, over time, children's increased experience and knowledge facilitates the processing of the perceptual information in front of them.

Up to this point, much of children's understanding of time will be concerned with personal experience. A wider understanding of 'historical' time, and the passage of time, will require some understanding of personal, clock and calendar time (Cooper 2002). This understanding becomes increasingly apparent in children's language, with references to the past, for example, evident in children's talk from about the age of 2 onwards (Lee and Das Gupta 1995). At the age of 2 years 8 months my daughter talked about 'bedtime o'clock', and Hoodless (1996a) records the 3- and 4-year-olds she observed spontaneously referring to clock times, as well as words such as 'morning' and 'daytime'.

Estimating and 'telling' the time

As Siegler *et al.* (2003) point out, estimating the duration of events is harder than remembering the order in which they occur. As a consequence, such capability tends to develop later, although, by the age of 5, if they are given helpful feedback, children can make reasonably accurate estimations of time periods of up to half a minute (Siegler *et al.* 2003). Hoodless records the 7-year-old children in her study speculating and hypothesizing about how long an event took. As she suggests, though, duration can seem to vary considerably, depending upon the type of experience. As one child says 'like in assembly, it feels like a long time' (Hoodless 1996a:105). In Box 8.5, Emma, a much younger child, is clearly grappling with this issue of the variability of perceived time.

Hoodless suggest several strategies which children use in order to support their developing concept of historical time. They carry with them implications for practice. She describes the children using:

- sequencing strategies: evident in narratives as well as on other occasions,
- noticing differences and similarities: involving concepts of classification,
- location and the process of historical inquiry: an awareness of people living in the same place at different times,
- imagining and speculating about the past: through exploring possibilities, and thinking about 'what could have happened'.

(Adapted from Hoodless 1996a:109–15)

Box 8.5 Emma, aged 4 years 1 month, at home with her mother, sitting colouring

EMMA: Mummy, when it's night time how do clocks go faster?

MUM: What do you mean?

EMMA: Well, when it's night time and you go the sleep its 7 o' clock and then you fall asleep and it's morning really quickly.

MUM: Oh, I see. You mean time *seems* to go quicker when you're asleep.

EMMA: Yeah...is there a man inside the clocks pushing the...the handles round quicker when you fall to sleep?

MUM: Do you men the hands on the clock?

EMMA: Yeah the hands. It makes it go faster.

MUM: Well, when you're asleep, the clocks don't really go faster. It just seems to because when you're asleep, you're so busy having dreams that time *feels* like it goes really quickly.

EMMA: So when I'm busy having dreaming the time goes faster?

MUM: Well, it's like when Nanny goes on holiday. You always think that a week is a long time but when you're busy with school and things, time seems to go really fast and she's back before you know it!

EMMA: The clocks don't really go fast then do they? Just at night time when you can't see them. And when Daddy wakes up for work, the clock goes slower because he's stopped dreaming.

MUM: That's an interesting idea Emma.

It seems that Emma thinks that the clock, a representational tool of time, is time itself – it is something you can see – and because time appears to pass more quickly when she is asleep, something must happen to make it go faster. In her final comment Emma appears to have grasped the concept that her mother tries to explain to her, but then she reverts back to the idea that clocks do go faster 'at night time when you can't see them' and links this to dreams as a cause, i.e. when you dream time goes faster, when you stop dreaming time goes back to normal.

Reproduced with permission of Kirsty Mclelland

Some implications for practice in supporting the development of children's concepts – part 2: narrative and play

Narrative, both the children's own narratives and oral and written stories, as well as play, are central to how young children both develop and display their conceptual understanding. The idea that children's own narratives are ways in which they make sense of the world was considered in Chapter 7. These narratives contain many elements of children's conceptual understanding. For example, children's narratives will show their historical and geographical understanding of chronology, sequencing, the use of devices such as the past tense, and of the vocabulary of time and place, including that 'borrowed' from story: 'once upon a time', 'a long time ago', 'far, far away' and so on. They are rooted in a child's social and cultural experiences.

In the same way, published narratives are sequential, embody the idea of the passage of time, and also often explicitly use the language of time, place and mathematics. Consider, for example, the idea of the passage of time in *Once There Were Giants* by Martin Waddell, *Kipper's Birthday* by Mick Inkpen or a traditional tale such as *Sleeping Beauty*. Likewise, stories such as *Titch* by Pat Hutchins, 'provide a venue for reflecting on number in common social purposes' (Carr 1992:9), such as comparing status, an activity which has great personal meaning for young children, as noted earlier. At the same time, while they 'are not "true" in the same way that conceptual understanding purports to be true' (Claxton 1999b:136–7) stories provide opportunities for children to use inferential cues from text and illustration, to hypothesize and to consider alternative pasts, futures, places and identities. Wells suggests that stories provide 'a richer mental model of the world and a vocabulary with which to talk about it' (1987:151–2). For children, this richer mental model can give them opportunities to explore ideas and situations both within and outside their personal experience and help them to make sense of these. Such opportunities have clear links with the development of abstract thinking, and may be used, among other things, to support children's schemas and nourish their thinking (Nutbrown 1999).

The centrality of play, and a playful approach, as a vehicle for developing young children's thinking and understanding is a theme which runs throughout this book. In Chapter 5 it was considered in relation to understanding other minds and in Chapter 7 in the context of language. Here, it may be useful to distinguish between spontaneous pretend play and that which occurs in themed 'role-play' areas. I have already noted the importance of children's spontaneous pretence and of resources which allow children to create 'whatever you want it to be' places (Broadhead 2004:73). At the same time, many early childhood professionals, theorists and researchers suggest the cognitive value of themed areas (Cooper 2004, Hall and Abbott 1991, Hall and Robinson 2003, Wood and Attfield 2005). Cooper (2002) suggests that pretend play of all kinds allows children to explore the boundaries between imagination and reality, important, for example, in history which is concerned with a past reality which no longer exists, and in geography where places may be geographically distant. At the same time, children have opportunities to explore both their own cultural and social identities and those of others. Cooper (2004) looks at how this can be supported both indoors and, importantly, outside too. McCaldon comments on the impact on a group of 4- and 5-year-old children's opportunities to engage in play about 'the past':

> It was in the play situation that they were able to understand historical items, explore their uses, demonstrate their understandings, refine their understandings in the light of other children's knowledge, and generally operate in a way which integrated much of their growing knowledge about the past. It is as if playing made sense of it all.
>
> (McCaldon 1991:69)

Further reflection

Look at the following observation, which brings together many of the ideas and concepts considered in this chapter. How might you describe and explain both Charlie's and Harry's conceptual understanding?

Charlie, 3 years 3 months and Harry, 4½; are in the garden with Charlie's mother.

CHARLIE: (To Harry) Hey, look, the plane! (grabs mum's arm) Look, mum, plane!
MUM: Oh, yes, I wonder what nice places they've been to.
CHARLIE: Been to grandma's!
MUM: Yeah, they might have been to Oz (Australia).
HARRY: I'm going to my grandma's for tea.
CHARLIE: On the plane?
HARRY: No, in the car.
CHARLIE: But you can't go in daddy's car cos it's long and the sea.
MUM: (Laughing) Oh no, Charlie, Harry's grandma doesn't live in Australia.
HARRY: No, she lives near the park.
CHARLIE: Oh.
HARRY: Another one (pointing to another plane). They might be going on holiday.
CHARLIE: Not all to grandma's then?
HARRY: No, maybe to Spain.
CHARLIE: Cos holiday's long?
HARRY: Yeah, too far to drive.

Reproduced with permission of Joanna Johnson

Further reading

Carey, S. (1985)
Cooper, H. (2002)
Gifford, S. (2004a)
Gopnik, A. *et al.* (1999) chapter 3
Hoodless, P. (1996a)
Karmiloff-Smith, A. (1994) chapter 1 in particular, but see throughout
Meadows, S. (1993) pp. 97–156
Munn, P. (1997)
Navarra, J. (1955)
Nutbrown, C. (1999) chapter 7
Palmer, J. (1994)
Siegler, R. (1998) chapter 7
Siegler, R. *et al.* (2003) chapter 7
Thornton, S. (2002) chapter 5
Valanides, N. *et al.* (2000)
White, J. (2002) chapter 2
Willig, J. (1990)

Chapter 9

Young children's visual thinking

This chapter looks at aspects of the relationship between visual representation and thinking. In a number of other parts of this book young children's visual thinking and visual representation have been seen to be an integral, and vital, part of their developing thinking. Bruner's (1966) description of an iconic mode of representation, and Gardner's (1983) category of spatial intelligence, considered in Chapter 2, are underpinning aspects of their theories of cognitive development. For Athey (1990), children's schemas (see Chapter 6) are very often represented in graphic modes. For practitioners in Reggio Emilia, visual representation encompasses some of the 'hundred languages' that children use to represent their experiences and their ideas.

Children's mark-making, drawing, painting and 2- and 3-dimensional representation are sometimes considered as aspects of 'creative development' (DfEE 2000), along with other areas such as movement, dance and music. I am mindful that all of these other areas deserve attention, but feel that this is best done by others with much more expertise than mine (see, for example, Pound 2003, Storr 1993, Trevarthen 2002 for musical thinking). The focus in this chapter is on the ways in which children use visual representation both as a tool for making sense and meaning, and as a way of communicating. Young children's creativity is a very important part of this, but it is also a part of every other aspect of their lives, not confined to particular subjects. The National Advisory Committee on Creative and Cultural Education (NACCCE) define creativity as 'imaginative activity fashioned so as to produce outcomes that are both original and of value' (1999:29). In keeping with this definition, creativity and creative thinking is looked at in more detail in the following chapter and should be read as including all areas of young children's experience.

The relationship of visual representation to young children's thinking

What, then, is the relationship of young children's drawing, and mark-making of all kinds, to their thinking? Arnheim (1969) suggests that all thinking, not just that related to visual experience, is basically perceptual in nature, and that our perceptual response to the world is at the heart of all of our thinking. In visual representation, the perceptual and the conceptual come together, and 'there is no basic difference in this respect between what happens when a person looks at the world directly and when he sits with his eyes closed and "thinks," (Arnheim 1969:13). For Vygotsky (1978), visual thinking is a vital cognitive process, in which visual images, graphic symbols and models are important tools for mediating cognition (Vygotsky 1978). Children's own visual representations support the creation of personal meaning, and are as vital a narrative form as speech and movement for young children (Anning and Ring 2004). They are important aspects of the development of metacognitive thinking and perspective taking (Brooks 2004, Reggio Children 1996). Our perception of shape, an interest evident from the earliest days of life, marks the beginnings of concept formation (Arnheim 1969).

Visual representation acts also as an important means of communication for young children. Through drawing, painting and other 2- and 3-dimensional representations, young children can express their ideas, thoughts and theories visually. These may be for themselves, part of what Vygotsky would regard as thinking aloud, as well as for sharing with others. In so doing, they are developing shared, collaborative meanings and creating a forum for reflection, as the 5- and 6-year-old children quoted below demonstrate. The discussion centres on the children's drawings, which illustrate their personal theories of how a fax gets from their centre in Reggio Emilia, to another in Washington DC:

> ROBERTA: See? In Alioscia's drawing you can see how a fax gets to America. It goes inside a pipe, so it doesn't get lost on the way.
> ALIOSCIA: It's a long pipe that goes around the things that it runs into on the trip.
> MATTEO: But you can't tell where it starts and where it goes to. You can't tell which way it goes.
> ALESSANDRA: You can tell in Roberta's drawing. You can see that the fax goes over the sea. America is on the other side of the world, on the other side of the ocean.
> ROBERTA: In Lucia's drawing you can tell that America is on the other side of the world – it's real far away.
>
> (Project Zero and Reggio Children 2001:224)

As Perkins (1994) suggests, this kind of reflection can also be on 'public' works of art, as well as the children's own representations, and may be especially supportive in the development of some very basic thinking dispositions, including personal engagement and connection making. He suggests that looking at art 'recruits many kinds and styles of cognition – visual processing, analytical thinking, posing questions, testing hypotheses, verbal reasoning and more' (1994:5).

Children's early mark-making is also often seen as an important precursor to later literacy learning (Matthews 2003), although, as Brooks points out, for young children drawing may, at least initially, be a much more powerful tool, in that 'it is immediately holistic and interactive in ways that writing is not' (2004:49). Anning and Ring also emphasize the importance of not positioning drawing as somehow less valuable than writing, and as 'only a "temporary" holding form of symbolic representation leading to mastery of the "higher level" ability to form letters and numbers' (Anning and Ring 2004:118). Notwithstanding the validity of Anning and Ring's (2004) warning, studying young children's efforts in this area can nevertheless be useful for supporting insights into children's understanding of the language sign system. Box 9.1 shows the combination of image and letterforms in the drawing of Charlotte, aged 4 years 7 months It reveals much about this 4-year-old girl's understanding, including directionality, the use of a horizontal axis and space. The repeated use of 'H' and 'P' are her early attempts at writing the word 'happy'.

Views on the development of visual representation

At a physiological level, much is, of course, known about the development of the visual system and visual perception (Pinker 1997, Siegler *et al.* 2003, Smith *et al.* 2003). Pinker

Box 9.1 Charlotte, aged 4 years 7 months, spontaneous mark-making at home

(1997) emphasizes mental imagery as an important aspect of cognition, and others, such as Sylwester (1998), stress the important part played by the arts in general, as well as art in particular, in developing and nourishing the brain.

In developing their thinking and understanding, very young children use movement to explore their world. As we noted earlier, young babies are also interested in shape, form, movement and all types of patterning. Matthews (1994, 2003) suggests that young children develop their mark-making skills, initially using whatever comes to hand, for example, food and drink, as a natural consequence of their physical movement. He identifies three types of movement that are particularly important for all later mark-making, whether it is with porridge or a pencil: vertical arcs (downward swiping), horizontal arcs (wiping or fanning – see Box 9.2), and push–pull (reaching and grasping) movements. These, he suggests, develop early in life, and make their appearance in the order shown here, over a period of about 2-weeks-old to the fourth month (Matthews 2003). What feeds this development is social interaction with others, and this supports babies in developing strategies for exploring and investigating their world. An understanding that these exploratory movements with whatever comes to hand cause a mark to be made is, for Matthews, 'the most basic principle of drawing' (2003:54).

Piaget's model

One particularly influential account of how children's visual representation develops comes from the work of Piaget (1962). He, in turn, drew on the work of Luquet (cited in Matthews 2003). Put briefly, Piaget's model identifies a first, meaningless (for Piaget) scribbling stage.

Box 9.2 Isabella, aged 2 years 7 months, at home

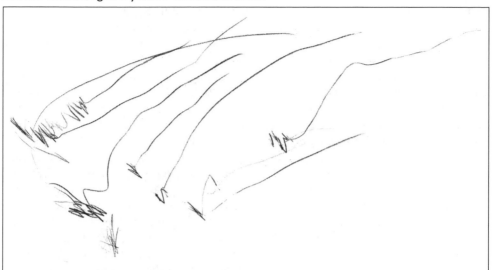

The horizontal arcs Matthews (2003) identifies as an early motor movement are now used to make marks, to which Isabella attributes a meaning of roads, paths and streets.

This is followed by a stage he refers to as fortuitous realism, in which there is no initial intention to represent an object, but children fortuitously see a likeness to something in the marks that they make. Kellogg (1969) concurs with Piaget here, suggesting that such marks are more to do with movement than representation. Piaget's model is completed with two further stages. In the first, 'intellectual realism', children represent what they know, or intellectually understand, about an object or scene, rather than what they actually see in front of them. For example, children know that people have two eyes, and will draw both of these on a figure, even when that figure is being drawn from a side view. The final stage of visual realism reverses this, and children then draw what they see even if it conflicts with what they know.

Researchers since Piaget have further developed the idea of stages in the development of children's visual representation. Lowenfeld and Brittain (1982) outline six stages. Kellogg (1969), using large samples of children's drawings, attempts to describe universal stages of drawing. As Anning and Ring (2004) point out, the focus is on cognition in these approaches, with less emphasis being placed on the relationship of affective, aesthetic and psycho-motor aspects to children's visual thinking.

Chris Athey

The work of Chris Athey (1990), first looked at in Chapter 6, is particularly helpful in describing young children's visual representation. While the overall aims of Athey's work are concerned with exploring and documenting commonalities and continuities in children's spontaneous thought and behaviour, and thus encompass more than visual representation, the evidence from children's mark-making and visual representation is integral to Athey's conclusions. Like Piaget, she outlines a series of developmental sequences of behaviour, from early motor behaviours to thought. She differs from him, however, in her emphasis on what children *can* do, and on how their representations highlight their persistent concerns, rather than seeing them as steps on a path to visual realism. Athey classifies children's activity as a range of schemas (see Chapter 6), which are expressed in four ways: through motor actions; symbolically (graphic representations, action representations and speech representations); functional dependency relationships (children showing understanding of cause and effect) and thought. While all of these coexist, they are each also more closely associated with particular ages. In Athey's research with children aged between 2 and 5 years, motor action schemas were present in largest numbers at age 3 years 1 month, symbolic representations at age 4 years 1 month, and thought representations at 4 years 5 months.

Of all of the graphic representations recorded, Athey distinguishes these into 24 different types of mark, which are then further subdivided into two groups of straight lines and curves. She also subdivides marks into a number of space orders, for example, the proximity between marks, vertical order between figures, or representation of 'in front of' or 'behind'. Athey identifies a developmental sequence in young children's drawings, using these three groups of lines, curves and space orders. She stresses that the ages at which schemas appear cannot be generalized, because experience and context will influence this. In documenting a continuum for the development of lines, Athey suggests:

> Given the opportunity, young children draw *lines*, make *lines* with and objects that can be aligned and run in *linear directions*. They construct *circular enclosures* and run in *circular directions*. They construct and draw *zig-zag configurations* and they run in *zig-zag directions*.
>
> (Athey 1990:90, emphasis in original)

A developmental sequence for curves begins with circular scribble, followed by circular enclosure, or core and radial, ovals, semi-circles (closed and open), helix, spirals, concentric circles and multiple loops (Athey 1990). Box 8.4 in Chapter 8 illustrates one girl's use of a core and radial schema. As Athey's comment (earlier) emphasizes, children's graphic representations are one of the ways in which they represent their interests and persistent concerns, alongside other symbolic representation, motor action and thought. All of them act together to develop young children's schemas, as they make connections and develop concepts.

Revising stage theories

The models of developmental stages in drawing outlined by Piaget (1962) and Lowenfeld and Brittain (1982) proved highly influential, but in recent years, they have been subject to examination and revision. Anning and Ring (2004) point out that they all represent a deficit view of young children's drawing, in their focus on the goal of visual realism (as I emphasized earlier, Athey's model of stages does not imply a deficit view). Duffy (1998) believes that young children's visual representations are much more purposeful, and less a matter of unintentional scribbling, than either Piaget (1962) or Kellogg (1969) would suggest. She cites young children's awareness of composition, shown, for example, in the careful, deliberate ways in which they place new marks with reference to existing ones.

A strong critic of Piaget's model is Matthews, who suggests that the reason that children do not produce visually realistic pictures is not because they cannot do so, but may be more to do with their desire to represent what, for them, is 'the truth about the structure and characteristics of the object' (Matthews 2003:97). He includes examples of young children depicting objects and scenes in visually realistic ways at a much younger age than Piaget's theory would suggest they could, and suggests that children do not pass neatly from one stage to another, but develop along a continuum which draws on information from 'different perceptual channels, including touch and movement and also involving language and concepts' (2003:97). For Arnheim (1969), like Matthews, this perceptual process is a very active one, a matter of thinking and not just seeing. As the artist, Paul Klee, says: 'art does not reproduce what can be seen: it makes things visible' (Marnat 1974), an idea echoed in the collaborative project *Making Learning Visible* (Project Zero and Reggio Children 2001).

As with other aspects of Piagetian theory, criticism of Piaget's model has also focused on the cultural specificity of his ideas about children's visual representation. Butterworth and Harris (1994) show examples of very different, culturally defined, conventions for representing objects. These conventions are learned in cultures, and are not related to intellectual ability. Lee and Das Gupta (1995) look at the different ways in which children across the world depict the human figure. Some aspects show cross-cultural consistency, albeit with local variation: use of either tadpole or stick-like figures, for example. Other conventions may be more local, for example, common depiction of genitalia in African children's drawings, rarely seen in Western children's drawings. While the evidence used here may now be rather dated, and not reflect either the complexity of the world, or the possible impact of globalization on the kinds of images young children see, it does suggest that the use of children's drawings as indicators of their intellectual development may need very careful consideration.

One very common approach in this area has, for many years, been use of the 'draw a person' test, developed by Goodenough and later revised by Harris (Kellogg 1969). In this test, children are asked to draw 'the very best picture that you can' (Fisher 1990:236) of a man or woman. The result is scored, with points earned for inclusion of basic figure elements and features, for example, arms and legs attached to trunk, inclusion of eyebrows and so on. This score is then regarded as indicative of cognitive maturity. Like all so-called intelligence tests (see Chapter 6), the Goodenough test is standardized on a particular population (in this case North American children) and thus inapplicable to all populations indiscriminately. Just as fundamentally, however, both Matthews (2003) and Kellogg (1969) suggest that children do not learn to draw as a result of observation from life, but as a result of their own mark-making efforts, a phenomenon not acknowledged in such a test, which relies on perceptual information being used to support conceptual understanding. What children choose to include in their picture of a man or woman may reflect their interest at that time, rather than a particular level of ability. Box 9.3 shows the response of one girl to the 'draw a person' test at the age of 3 years 7 months. While it would not score very highly on this test, it is, nevertheless, a very sophisticated response, which shows just what Charlotte was noticing about people at that time.

What (and how) do children represent?

The answer to this question is, of course, everything, but, at an individual level, it will be personal to them (Duffy 1998), and reflect what matters to them (Arnheim 1969, Matthews

Box 9.3 Charlotte, aged 3 years 7 months, at home, asked to 'draw a person'

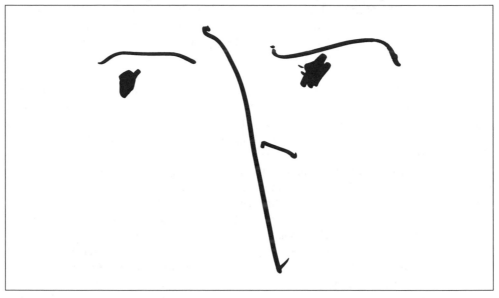

2003). Anning and Ring demonstrate how strongly this is influenced by their experiences, both at home and in early childhood settings. They suggest three particular aspects of this cultural influence:

1   The contrasting expectations of what it meant to be male and female modelled by parents, friends, siblings and extended families within their home communities;
2   the impact of media and commercial interests on their choice of what and how to represent their understandings and feelings;
3   the cultural expectations of what it is to be a friend in pre-school and infant school settings.

(Anning and Ring 2004:103)

Anning and Ring (2004) document how, at home, the drawing (and play) themes of the girls in their study often revolved around domestic doll play, while the boys often engaged in more dynamic themes, involving action, movement and speed. When they then went to nursery and school, the girls often found more continuity, with their depiction of figures in their drawings being encouraged more than the boys' action representations (Anning and Ring 2004). This may have important consequences for boys' thinking and understanding, if the themes which are significant for them are not among those that seem to be validated by the adults around them.

Young children's representations, then, will include objects, people and scenes but also ideas such as movement and action, as Athey (1990) and Anning and Ring (2004) indicate. Duffy identifies four categories, and suggests that children's representations may include

Box 9.4 Nathan, aged $4\frac{1}{2}$ years, in the nursery

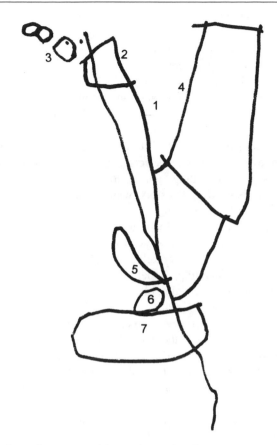

Nathan has just dicated a story to his teacher, when he says:

Now I'm going to write a story. (He starts with the circular shapes at 3.)
Once upon a time and he went down the path a long, long. (At this point he trails the pen down the page at 1.)
Then he crossed the path (drawing the loop at 2).
Then he walked up the steps (holding his pen over 3, then drawing the box shape at 4)
That's him, walking around.
(He draws the smaller enclosures at 5,6 and 7 without commenting, then the sequence of dots at 3) Then he went up the lane. Then he took 2 steps, 4 steps, 6 steps.
Nathan grins hugely, puts his pen down and goes off to play with Ethan.

Nathan is attributing representational meaning to his marks, although they do not yet resemble the meaning he is attributing to them. For Athey (1990), thinking is what happens when considering the changes between two states. In mature thinking, this happens symbolically without the two end states necessarily being available to the thinker, whilst children play out these changes in state by manipulating the concrete objects. Nathan's verbalization of changes in states can be seen as the precursor to symbolic thinking.

Reproduced with permission of John Griffiths

one, or a combination, of them:

1   configurative aspects – to do with space;
2   dynamic aspects – to do with action;
3   specific viewpoints – drawn from a particular view point;
4   object specific – to do with the main features of an object.

(Duffy 1998:60)

Box 8.4, in Chapter 8, and Box 9.4 both illustrate aspects of this combination. Box 9.4 features both configurative and dynamic aspects, and also illustrates young children's integration of different ways of representing their experience, and the importance of a narrative framework. Here, Nathan is drawing his story, while relating it in words. Interestingly, he also refers to his drawing as 'writing' here.

The examples illustrated so far have focused on mark-making and drawing with pens, pencils and crayons, but the many other ways of representing their worlds visually are as important for young children, both by themselves, but also in multi-modal ways, combining found materials with drawing, painting, model making and construction. Anning and Ring (2004) comment on the empowering nature of children's opportunities to be so fluid in their representations.

Children's visual representations in paint support exploration of light and colour, their use of textiles and other materials give them opportunities to explore texture, touch and feel. Increasingly, the value of children using video cameras, still cameras and computers to play with their thoughts (Reggio Children 1996) is recognized: 'the computer produces phenomena that put their systems of perceiving the world, of gathering information and constructing thought and behavior [sic], "off-balance" ' (Reggio Children 1996:102). Box 9.5 shows one boy's use of the interactive whiteboard in his nursery to represent his ideas.

Children's three-dimensional representations in a range of media including modelling with malleable media such as dough and clay; sculpting; and construction with blocks, construction toys and woodwork, give children opportunities to develop representations in ways that are unavailable to them in two dimensions (Duffy 1998). Gura suggests that blockplay, for example, 'can be used to say certain kinds of things more powerfully than words or words alone can say' (1992:27). Models and constructions have insides and outsides, tops, bottoms, sides, fronts and backs. They can often be walked around, looked at from different viewpoints and perhaps entered. They may also more readily lend themselves to collaborative activity. Matthews (2003) stresses the value of supporting children in using materials in their three-dimensional representations in novel, multi-modal ways, which 'transgress' their functional categories. He uses the example of his son who, having looked at a picture in a book of a rocket taking off with flames shooting from its combustion chamber, then builds a three-dimensional representation of the flames out of blocks, laying them on top of the open book. Such a view has much in common with both Trawick-Smith's (1998) emphasis on the use of non-representational materials in the development of metaplay, and Hutt *et al*'s. (1989) views on the cognitive value of supporting children's own associations between materials.

Look back now at the observation recorded in Further reflection point 2 in Chapter 5. This episode of block play features the 'heaping' (Matthews 2003:118) of objects in three-dimensional representation, often the first way in which children classify objects (Athey 1990).

Box 9.5 Arun, in the nursery

Arun rarely uses traditional media to represent. He was keen to access the smartboard and subsequently spent some time depicting his favourite Superhero, Spiderman, during his adventures. The smartboard afforded Arun with an avenue for his drawing that was acceptable to, and valid for, him. Though physical, direct experience with the smartboard, Arun's creativity was supported as his body senses gathered 'evidence' (Prentice 1994:127), and allowed him to express his ideas and make 'powerful intelligent hypotheses' (Mathews 2003:01).

Reproduced with permission of Lynn Bartlett

Some implications for practice in developing children's visual thinking

- The importance of experience – Athey (1990) and Brooks (2004), for example, both emphasize the value of experience gained through visits in feeding young children's thinking, and in providing opportunities for visual representation. Experience is what feeds young children's schemas (Athey 1990).
- Children need time, to interact with materials, with adults, and with each other (Escobedo 1999), in order to develop their visual thinking and representation.
- It may be through their observations of the shapes in their own representations that children start to notice shapes in the environment, not, as is generally thought, the other way around (Matthews 2003).

- Instruction in drawing from observation may not be useful. Matthews suggests that 'premature instruction in drawing from observation damages development' (2003:109), and that 'sometimes, interaction means doing *nothing*' (2003:110, emphasis in original).
- The importance of adult involvement in ways which will 'support and extend children's learning and development by adding the information or skill they need at the point they need it' (Duffy 1998:94–5).
- The value for children of interactions with other drawing 'users', more experienced than themselves, who can comment on the processes children are using, developing the vocabulary of mark-making. Anning and Ring (2004) suggest the value of adults drawing alongside children, Matthews (2003) stresses the need for adults to go beyond the 'very nice' response to a child's drawing, and to comment in ways which not only communicate an interest in what a child has done, but also provide a vocabulary for talking about it.
- The value of supporting the development of children's personal reflections, both on their own representations (Brooks 2004) and on those of others (Nimmo 1998, Project Zero and Reggio Children 2001). Brooks positions this within a Vygotskian framework, suggesting that children's representations operate at both an interpersonal level, where 'drawing is the mediator for an interpersonal dialogic exchange' (Brooks 2004:47) and an intrapersonal level, where drawing can help children integrate new knowledge with previous ideas and experiences, and where discussion focuses on the construction of representation.

Further reflection

1   Do you think that there is a universal sequence in the development of drawing?

2   What part is played by culture in young children's visual thinking?

Further reading

Athey, C. (1990)
Brooks, M. (2004)
Duffy, B. (1998)
Gardner (1983, 1993)
Matthews, J. (2003)
Meadows, S. (1993) pp. 94–101

Chapter 10

Approaches to developing young children's thinking and understanding

In this chapter the focus is on ways in which young children's thinking may be developed and supported. A range of published approaches aimed at developing thinking are considered, including those informed by ideas of philosophy for children. More generally, young children's creative and critical thinking and problem-solving are considered. These terms are often explicitly stated as aims in many programmes, and problem-solving, in particular, is often conflated with thinking skills (Johnson 2001). It is valuable to consider what each might mean and what potential benefits they might have for young children's cognitive development. The starting point here is the possible practical implementation of the ideas, theory and research of the preceding nine chapters.

Developing 'good' thinkers

The rationale for developing young children's thinking is underpinned by ideas arising from the different theories of cognition considered in Chapter 2, alongside other aspects such as metacognitive development and self-regulation in Chapter 5. Mc Guinness (1999), like others, suggests that a focus on the development of 'thinking skills' is valuable because it supports active cognitive processes which make for better learning. A fundamental question, however, is what we might mean by 'better' here, and what 'good' thinking looks like. Fisher suggests that an important role for those supporting young children's thinking is to focus attention on 'knowing how' (procedural knowledge) rather than 'knowing that' (declarative knowledge). He also makes the following point:

> If learning is making sense of experience, and thinking is how we learn, then improving children's thinking will help them make more sense of learning and of life.
>
> (Fisher www.teachingthinking.net/Thinkskills.htm)

Costello (2000) takes this argument further, and suggests that the teaching of thinking skills is an essential element in the avoidance of indoctrination in school.

Initiatives and ideas for supporting young children's thinking are often referred to as 'teaching thinking', 'teaching thinking skills', or even 'teaching children to think', as if, somehow, they were not doing so already. None of these terms seems entirely appropriate as a way of looking at the area. The problem with a term like 'teaching thinking' is that it tends to imply a narrow range of functions for those *doing* the 'teaching', rather than focusing on what it might mean to learn to be a good thinker. The 'catchall phrase' (Lipman 2003:162) of 'thinking skills' is used very broadly, to apply to anything from very specific to very general abilities, and thus can be taken to mean a very wide range of processes and actions. In addition, the word 'skill' suggests that it is a matter, on the learner's part, of applying procedures for thinking, in much the same way that one might have acquired the skill of riding a bike, or using scissors. While it may be possible to suggest that thinking can be characterized as a skill because it can be improved by practice (White 2002), the development of young children's thinking and understanding will be much more than this, and include supporting positive dispositions to use such skills in appropriate situations, and attitudes of 'delight' in so doing (Coles and Robinson 1991a:14). Johnson (2001) points out that, in many aspects of activity, to have mastered a skill is often taken to mean that one can exercise it *without* thinking!

Traditionally, this idea of skill and cognitive ability has been the defining principle of 'good' thinking (Project Zero Patterns of Thinking, http://pzweb.harvard.edu./Research/ PatThk.htm). In recent years, however, greater emphasis has been placed upon a wider view. The Patterns of Thinking project, led by David Perkins and Shari Tishman, reflects a more current view that it is much more than this:

> Certainly, good thinkers have skills. But they also have more. Passions, attitudes, values and habits of mind all play key roles in thinking, and, in large part, it is these elements that determine whether learners use their thinking skills when it counts. In short, good thinkers have the right 'thinking dispositions'.
>
> (Project Zero Patterns of Thinking, http://pzweb.harvard.edu./
> Research/PatThk.htm)

'Good' thinkers may have a repertoire of strategies for thinking, be able to think reflectively about their own thinking, be confident in their attitude to thinking, and willing to take risks in their thinking and learn from mistakes. Meadows suggests that 'In short they will be people who enjoy thinking' (1993:333).

This may seem to be at odds with the premise outlined in the subtitle to Claxton's *Hare Brain Tortoise Mind* (1998): *Why Intelligence Increases When You Think Less*. However, what Claxton is arguing for is less reliance on one particular form of thinking, which he calls 'd-mode' ('deliberate-mode') thinking. This form of thinking is characterized by logic, precision, clarity, generalizations and explicit language. Whereas, of course, this way of thinking is important, Claxton suggests that it should not be the only way of thinking that we develop and value. As described in Chapter 1, he believes that the mind has three 'processing speeds', including one which is more playful and contemplative. He argues that too much emphasis on the 'deliberate' or 'd-mode' of thinking can prevent us from looking at problems and ideas in different ways, and warns:

> If we see d-mode as the only form of intelligence, we must suppose, when it fails, that we are not 'bright' enough, or did not think 'hard' enough, or have not got enough 'data'. The lesson we learn from such failures is that we must develop better models, collect more data, and ponder more carefully. What we do not learn is that we may have been thinking *in the wrong way*.
>
> (Claxton 1998:12, emphasis in original)

He suggests that the slower ways of thinking and knowing are just as important because they make use of sensations, images, feelings and hunches as well as clear, conscious thoughts, which can help us to connect different inputs in new ways, and because confusion and uncertainty (allowed in these slower ways) may precede the development of a good idea. One practitioner in our research emphasized the value of children having the opportunity 'just to "be" really', saying that this required time and space. She suggested that outdoor activity provides a particularly good context here, possibly allowing children more time to stand back, watch, take their time and reflect (Robson and Hargreaves 2005:87).

Models for teaching thinking

In recent years there has been considerable interest in the explicit development of children's thinking. Two recent Department for Education and Skills Research Reports in England, for example, have both had as part of their brief to investigate ways of developing young children's thinking (Moyles *et al.* 2002, Siraj-Blatchford *et al.* 2002). Across the world, a wide range of programmes have been developed, with, McGuinness (1999) suggests, a common aim of developing thinking to a qualitatively higher level. The Thinking Skills Review Group propose as a working definition that such initiatives are:

> Approaches or programmes which identify for learners translatable, mental processes and/or which require learners to plan, describe and evaluate their thinking and learning. These can therefore be characterized as approaches or programmes which:
>
> - require learners to articulate and evaluate specific learning approaches; and/or
> - identify specific cognitive and related affective or conative processes that are amenable to instruction.
>
> (Thinking Skills Review Group 2004:1)

Put more succinctly, these are programmes which specify both what is to be learned and how it is to be taught. While the majority of these have tended to focus on work with older children (and, as a result, tend to refer to teachers rather than other adults working with children), it is worth looking at the findings with regard to some of these, as well as those programmes which have involved younger children. McGuinness categorizes approaches into three 'models for delivering thinking skills' (1999):

1   interventions that can be directed towards enhancing thinking skills through structured programmes which are additional to the normal curriculum: for example Feuerstein's *Instrumental Enrichment* programme (1980) or *The Somerset Thinking Skills Course* (Blagg *et al.* 1988);
2   approaches that target subject-specific learning such as science, mathematics, geography: for example, *Cognitive Acceleration through Science Education (CASE)* (Adey and Shayer 1994);
3   infusion across the curriculum through systematic identification of opportunities within the normal curriculum for thinking skills development: for example, Swartz *et al.* (1998).

(Adapted from McGuinness 1999)

Trickey and Topping (2004) also identify a fourth category, which they call 'Multi-method' programmes. They suggest that approaches such as Dawes *et al.*'s *Thinking Together* approach (2000), and *Philosophy for Children* (Lipman 2003, Lipman *et al.* 1980) can be seen as multi-method programmes, fitting into more than one of McGuinness' three categories.

There are a number of problems associated with evaluating the efficacy of such programmes, including whether any gains are long-term (McGuinness 1999), how soon they are evident (Adey and Shayer 1994) and the possibility of the so-called Hawthorne effect, where separating out the impact of a programme over and above that of any novel, enthusiastically applied intervention may be difficult. Methodologically, the evaluations of some of these programmes have also been criticized (Claxton 1999b). All of these factors lead Trickey and Topping (2004) and Wilson (2000) to urge caution in interpreting the available data.

Are some models more effective than others?

Taking these caveats into account, some general conclusions are becoming evident. Coles and Robinson (1991a) suggest that the main criticism of the first approach in McGuinness' categorization is that this skills approach is reductionist and fragmentary, with limited transfer of skills learnt to new contexts, a view with which Gardner (1993) concurs. This idea of transferability is seen as key – Leat (1999:388) describes it as the 'Holy Grail'. It has proved to be a major challenge, with big claims sometimes being made for particular programmes, not always substantiated by evaluation (Claxton 1999b). McGuinness (1999) suggests that the more successful approaches tend to have strong theoretical underpinnings, well-designed and contextualized materials, explicit pedagogies and good teacher support. In keeping with the accepted views on the value of embedding children's learning in meaningful contexts (Donaldson 1978), the most successful interventions seem to be those which take an embedded approach (Whitebread 2000a). In particular, they are ones directed at 'cognitive apprenticeship', which includes scaffolding techniques and metacognitive and self-regulatory approaches (Thinking Skills Review Group 2004, Whitebread 2000a), similar to those referred to by Swartz (2000) as infusion approaches. Characteristically, these are approaches which emphasize classroom talk and interaction (Thinking Skills Review Group 2004), where adult interventions such as scaffolding, modelling and questioning make their own thinking explicit to the children, and where the children themselves are required to articulate their thinking, and can enjoy 'playing around with ideas' (Whitebread 2000a:155). An example of such an approach, Whitebread suggests, is Lipman's *Philosophy for Children* (see later in the chapter). He also commends ideas such as the *Thinking Books* (Swan and White 1994) referred to in Chapter 5. Coles and Robinson (1991a) and McGuinness (1999) suggest that Lipman's work, and Feuerstein's *Instrumental Enrichment* programme have both been rigorously tested and evaluated and shown to work in a number of settings. Lipman's ideas, in particular, McGuinness (1999) suggests, may have an impact on the quality of discussion, on children's abilities in forming questions, and on their self-esteem.

The Thinking Skills Review Group's Systematic Review (2004) of the area concludes that a majority of the programmes they looked at demonstrate a positive impact as a result of the programme and none show a negative impact. Of these, the most impressive at age 16, in terms of transferability of learning and thinking to new contexts, is CASE (Adey and Shayer 1994). This Piagetian approach has been adapted for younger age groups, with one programme targeted at children aged 5 and 6 years, called *Let's Think!* (Robertson 2004). Robertson suggests that, as a result of the programme, children both developed their thinking ability and learned more effectively across the curriculum. Critical success factors she identifies are that the programme is valued by the school as a whole, that collaborative work is supported and developed by the teachers and that teachers are prepared to respond positively to challenges about any preconceptions they have of children (Robertson 2004).

Swartz, similarly, suggests that his infusion approach supports transferability, and steers a path between the abstraction of the structured approaches extra to the normal curriculum, which he describes as teaching *of* thinking, and methods which, while they promote deep understanding of the curricular content, do not emphasize the processes of thinking, an approach he labels teaching *for* thinking (Swartz *et al*. 1998). In his infusion model children are supported in raising questions and drawing inferences that might be useful in any context, not just the particular one they are engaged in at that moment.

Finally, the Thinking Skills Review Group caution that the impact of thinking skills approaches may not be the same for all children. Their review suggests greater impact on 'low attaining pupils, particularly when using metacognitive strategies' (2000:39). However, they do cite one study which suggests the opposite, finding the greatest impact on higher attaining children. Overall, they suggest that a long-term view needs to be taken, and that more general emphasis by adults working with young children on making aspects of teaching and learning, particularly reasoning, more explicit may be as beneficial as any particular programme. Similarly, McGuinness (1999) emphasizes the benefits of creating and supporting dispositions for good thinking, and an atmosphere where talking about thinking is actively pursued. In Chapter 6 Carr's ideas about positive dispositions as being the inclination to be 'ready, willing and able' (Carr 2001:21) were discussed. Perkins and Tishman (http://pzweb.harvard.edu./Research/PatThk.htm) emphasize the key importance of children being ready, willing and able to think.

Philosophy for Children

What is Philosophy for Children?

Philosophy for Children (P4C), sometimes referred to as Philosophy with Children (PWC), is one of the most widely known types of intervention to support children's thinking. Philosophy for Children was the idea of Matthew Lipman in the United States (Lipman 1991, 2003, Lipman *et al*. 1980). Concerned at what he saw as the low levels of thinking skills of college students, in contrast to the questioning, enquiring minds of young children, he felt that action was necessary to tackle the issue from early in life. The aim of Philosophy for Children is 'to promote excellent thinking: thinking that is creative as well as logical, inventive as well as analytical' (Lipman 1991:35). He further describes excellent thinking as 'multidimensional', combining critical thinking, creative thinking and 'caring thinking', a mode he suggests is usually seen as 'falling in the affective rather than the cognitive camp' (Lipman 2003:201), but which he sees as of equal importance to the other two modes. Similar aims underpin the work of others who have developed ideas of philosophical thinking with children. In the United Kingdom, one of the best-known advocates is Robert Fisher, who suggests that it exposes children to 'the skills and habits of higher order thinking' (Fisher 2001:67).

Looked at in relation to McGuinness's earlier categorization of interventions, Lipman suggests that Philosophy for Children steers a middle path between the two very different models that thinking is either best taught through specific subjects or best approached through an autonomous course in thinking. He suggests that this middle path involves directing the skills learned in the independent course to the 'basic' skills of reading and writing.

He believes that, in so doing, children will then transfer the added critical reflectiveness of their reading and writing to other subjects and areas of learning (Lipman 2003). Other advocates, including Costello (2000), Fisher (1998) and Haynes (2002) all emphasize the potential transferability of thinking as a result of a philosophical approach. The principal vehicle for the development of this critical reflection is discussion, drawing on ideas of Socratic dialogue. It is seen as closely related to Vygotskian principles (Fisher 1990, Lewis and Rowley 2002) and to sociocultural concepts such as Rogoff's (2003) idea of guided participation (Lipman 2003).

The practice of philosophy with children

Lipman's approach to supporting children's thinking was to develop a series of stories, for use with children of different ages. Each story features characters who are depicted discussing ideas. For example, when turn taking comes up as part of the story, characters are shown discussing underlying principles of sharing and reciprocity. The stories intended for young children focus on the practice of reasoning and inquiry skills whereas those for older children move on to underlying principles and broader application (Lipman 1991). A typical session devoted to children's thinking begins with the reading of such a story, or part of it. Lipman suggests that this story reading is shared, with children being allowed to 'pass' if they do not wish to read aloud. Costello (2000) suggests that the practice of 'passing', which may tend to be done by less confident readers, can serve to make these children feel less participant, and alienate them from the activity. With younger children, this may be particularly the case. In Costello's view, the reading is best done by the adult. The adult then asks the children for their comments, what they would like to discuss about the story and the questions they want to ask, using open-ended questions and prompts, such as 'What puzzles you? What interests you? What do you like about this passage?' (Costello 2000:41–2). As a result of this, a particular topic is selected for exploration by the group, facilitated by the adult. The aim is to create a community of enquiry, or 'habitat' (Lipman 2003:157) for thinking, in which there is a readiness to reason, mutual respect and an absence of indoctrination (Lipman et al. 1980). Rules for discussion are developed, including listening, turn taking and not interrupting (Fisher 1990), showing respect for others and the avoidance of ridicule (Haynes 2002).

Lipman, and others such as Fisher (1990, 1998, 2001) have focused the discussions in the community of enquiry around specially written stories from which moral and philosophical points are drawn and debated. Costello (2000) suggests the value of video material with young children. Haynes broadens the possible range of stimuli, emphasizing the value of 'carefully structured exploration of a variety of narratives found in story, myth, poetry, news, drama, music, painting, photography' (2002:45). Adult choices from these stimuli are made on the basis of their power 'to express ambiguity, to produce puzzlement, or to evoke a deep response' (Haynes 2002:22). This includes the use of picture books, for example, of the kinds suggested in Chapters 5 and 8, which may include multilayered, parallel and ambiguous narratives. Haynes summarizes the process of such philosophical enquiry, pointing out that it should be seen as a flexible process, admitting diversions and discussion over often long periods of time:

- getting started: this may involve discussion of rules, meditation or silence as preparation;
- sharing a stimulus to prompt enquiry;

- pause for thought: children may think alone, in groups, and they may draw or write notes;
- questioning: questions are recorded for everyone to see;
- connections: links are made between questions, in the process of which children draw distinctions;
- choosing a question to begin enquiry: the adult needs to ensure that this is a fair, inclusive process;
- building on each other's ideas: discussion;
- recording discussion: notes, webs, concept maps, for all to see;
- closure and review: summarizing what has been discussed; 'Resolution is rare – new questions are more common' (Haynes 2002:30). This aspect includes reflection on the process.

(Adapted from Haynes 2002:29–30)

The discussions use the children's own generated questions as starting points, a factor which Papaleontiou-Louca (2003) suggests involves a high degree of metacognitive involvement. Haynes concurs, believing that 'Philosophical enquiry addresses the ground of metacognition as part of the ground of philosophy' (2002:45). The role of the adult in managing the discussion is to both listen responsively and intervene tactfully, to treat all children's contributions as legitimate, to encourage risk-taking and speculation and to avoid pursuing their own interests (Haynes 2003). Fisher emphasizes the importance of good feedback to the children, in ways which demonstrate that adults are not looking for 'right answers' (1990:170).

Discussions will, in Fisher's view, often revolve around some key themes: fairness, freedom, friendship, truth, knowledge and judgement (1990:174). This has obvious similarities with the three themes of friendship, fairness and fantasy which Paley (1986) identifies as so important to children. As MacNaughton and Williams (2004) suggest, such philosophical discussions often have moral and ethical dimensions. Paley's work often seems to implicitly combine such issues. A good example is her initiative of presenting the children with a new classroom rule: 'You can't say you can't play' (1993), to avoid the exclusion of some children from play. A brief extract of the children's discussion is shown in Box 10.1. Costello (2000) also emphasizes the relationship of philosophical thinking to the development of citizenship in children.

Is it philosophy?

While this is not the place for protracted discussion about whether or not young children can engage in philosophy, it is worth highlighting that there are differing views about this issue. White (2002), commenting on the growth in popularity of programmes under this umbrella term, points out that encouraging children's questions is undoubtedly valuable, but that not all questions are philosophical ones, and that merely asking questions does not make a child into a philosopher. Haynes, reflecting on this idea of the philosophical potential of questions, asks whether questions such as 'How do cats kiss?, Why do men have nipples?, How are rivers made?' (Haynes 2002:82), all asked by 4- and 5-year-olds, belong in philosophy. Costello (2000) relates the arguments of, among others, Mary Warnock and Roger Scruton, that philosophy is not an appropriate subject for study by children, and best left until adulthood. Lipman agrees that merely talking, or asking questions, does not constitute

Box 10.1 You can't say you can't play

Paley introduces a rule into the kindergarten that stipulates 'You can't say you can't play' to any child who wants to join in your game. The following is a very brief exitract from one of her discussions with the children about this rule.

ANGELO: Let anybody play if someone asks.
LISA: But then what's the whole point of playing?
NELSON: You just want Cynthia.
LISA: I could play alone. Why can't Clara play alone?
ANGELO: I think that's pretty sad. People that is alone they has water in their eyes.
LISA: I'm more sad if someone comes that I don't want to play with.
PALEY: Who is sadder? The one who isn't allowed to play or the one who has to play with someone he or she doesn't want to play with?
CLARA: It's more sadder if you can't play.
LISA: The other one is the same sadder.

(Paley 1993:19–20)

philosophy, and suggests that these need to be converted into particular forms of discussion and dialogue, incorporating reasoning, drawing inferences, testing for consistency and comprehensiveness, and learning to think independently (Lipman 2003). He, along with others such as Fisher (1990, 2001) and Haynes (2002, 2003) emphasizes that these are all things that children can do. Costello argues against the idea that these types of discussion in young children are 'pre-philosophical', for the same reasons that we would no longer talk of children's understanding in mathematics as 'pre-mathematical'.

Critiques and evaluations of philosophy with children

As suggested earlier, Coles and Robinson (1991a) and McGuinness (1999) both provide favourable reports on Lipman's work. Wilson (2000) also reports evidence of improvement in intellectual performance and on creativity measures, although this is in children aged 10–13 years. Fisher reports evidence that his programme, *Stories for Thinking* (Fisher 1996), has a positive effect on 'children's self-esteem and self-concept as thinkers and learners, the fluency and quality of children's questioning, the quality of their thinking, their ability to listen to others and engage effectively in class discussion' (Fisher 2001:71) among others. More widely, Trickey and Topping (2004) report positive findings from ten studies, although they do emphasize the difficulty of collecting reliable data. They conclude: 'given certain conditions, children can gain significantly in measurable terms both academically and socially through this type of interactive process' (2004:375). Looking particularly at evidence from settings which have introduced philosophy with young children, Haynes suggests that the children are more able to generate alternative explanations for hypothetical situations and to make links between thoughts and feelings in different hypothetical situations (2003:6).

Specific criticisms of philosophy for children include Fisher's (1998) suggestion that the specially written novels may lack literary style, and that the absence of pictures, seen by

Lipman as important for avoiding prescriptive imagery, means that 'dimensions of meaning to a story' (Fisher 1998:117) may be lacking. Whalley (1991) points to the potential drawback, if only Lipman's original stories are used, of cultural and linguistic bias, given that they were written for an American market. He also highlights a wider potential criticism, that only one philosophical viewpoint is represented in Lipman's work. Lewis and Rowley suggest that philosophy for children approaches have tended to overemphasize 'question raising', above 'question understanding and question focusing' (2002:55), and that more attention may need to be paid to ensuring that children understand the question under discussion. They suggest that this may be particularly important in the early years.

Creative and critical thinking

Initially, it is worth looking at these aspects of young children's thinking together, not because critical and creative thinking are one and the same thing, far from it, but because they are interdependent, and can work together in complementary ways (Lipman 2003), and are often considered, along with problem-solving (later in this chapter) as 'higher level' mental activities (Wilson 2000). In addition, they may both be key aspects in areas such as problem-solving, and, more generally, in children's play.

How can critical and creative thinking be distinguished? A major problem here is the wide variety of definitions and attributes suggested by the literature. White, for example, comments on the 'confusedness' (2002:129) of much writing about creativity and creative thinking. A wide range of terms are often used. Critical thinking is frequently referred to as convergent, and concerned with deductive reasoning, while creative thinking is often described as lateral thinking (de Bono 1991), or divergent thinking, and concerned with inductive reasoning and exploring ideas. De Boo refers to creative thinking as 'hypothetical', or 'intuitive' (1999:60), and critical thinking as 'reflective' (1999:64). The National Advisory Committee on Creative and Cultural Education (NACCCE) talk of 'generative and evaluative thinking' (1999:31), and suggest that 'creative thinking always involves some critical thinking' (1999:31). Rodd suggests creative and critical thinking can be described in the following ways:

> *Creative thinking* – the ability to produce original and divergent solutions problems. Involves
> - fluency – the ability to propose many solutions;
> - flexibility – the ability to see a problem, issue or incident from different perspectives;
> - originality – the ability to produce novel ideas.
>
> *Critical thinking*
> Involves
> - observation
> - comparison
> - explanation
> - prediction.

(Rodd 1999:351)

Problem-solving, looked at later, is, for Fisher (1990), where both creative thinking and critical thinking come together, in the application of solving problems. He suggests that creative thinking is good for generating new ideas, many of which may ultimately not be useful (as with Noam's thinking in Box 10.2). He believes that it is then the role of critical thinking to help children to learn to identify their most powerful ideas. While de Boo (1999) agrees that problem-solving is about application, he differs somewhat from Fisher in suggesting that critical thinking is primarily about metacognitive strategies. However we define the terms, there are areas of overlap and common concern and ways in which children's experiences of solving problems may support the development of their critical and creative thinking and vice versa. The labelling of thinking as either 'creative' or 'critical' may be an oversimplification and have its roots in our understanding of the functions of the left and right hemispheres of the brain (Fisher 1990).

Box 10.2 Noam, aged 5, and Richard Feynman

The first extract features Noam, and the second is an episode from the life of Richard Feynman, the nuclear physicist. Are there similarities in the thinking of Noam and Feynman? What is the relationship of knowledge and interest to their creative thinking?

Noam:
A 5-year-old is being interviewed on the subject of heat, using pictures and objects as stimuli.

TEACHER: What will happen if we put this (pan of milk) on the cooker?
NOAM: It will go all bubbly.
TEACHER: Why will it go all bubbly?
NOAM: Because the hot of the cooker...
TEACHER: But how does the hotness get into the milk?
NOAM: It goes all over bottom and it makes a little gap and it squeezes through the hole and gets into the milk.
TEACHER: So the heat makes a hole in the saucepan?
NOAM: You can't see it, it's too really...sort of...(indicates sliding around with his hands).
TEACHER: Anything else?
NOAM: (thinks) No. Oh, if it had holes the milk would fall through (shrugs).

(de Boo 1999:53)

Richard Feynman:
I was in the cafeteria and some guy, fooling around, throws a plate in the air. As the plate went up in the air I saw it wobble, and I noticed the red medallion of Cornell on the plate going around. It was pretty obvious to me that the medallion went around faster than the wobbling. I had nothing to do so I started to figure out the motion of the rotating plate.

I discover that when the angle is very slight, the medallion rotates twice as fast as the wobble rate – two to one. It came out of a complicated equation! The I thought, 'Is there some way I can see in a more fundamental way, by looking at the forces or the dynamics, why it's two to one?'

The diagrams and the whole business that I got the Nobel Prize for came from that piddling around with the wobbling plate.

(Feynman 1986:173–4)

Creative thinking

An important starting point here is drawing a clear distinction between creative thinking and creativity. Creative thinking, while a part of creativity, is not interchangeable with it (Jones and Wyse 2004). Thus, the focus here is on a discussion of creative thinking. What the two share, however, is their applicability to the widest range of human activity. Too often 'creativity' is located within the arts (NACCCE 1999). For example, while The Curriculum Guidance for the Foundation Stage in England emphasizes that 'being creative enables children to make connections between one area of learning and another and so extend their understanding' (DfEE 2000:116), it describes creative development as an 'area of learning (that) includes art, music, dance, role play and imaginative play' (2000:116). This is unsatisfactory for two very important reasons. First, this suggests that aspects such as science and maths are not 'creative', and thus do not involve creative thinking (and Box 10.2 clearly shows this not to be the case!), and, second, it appears to limit vital forms of representation and meaning-making such as role-play and art to creative activity.

Defining creative thinking

Meadows (1993) suggests that a key problem in identifying and supporting creative thinking lies in the lack of consistency and precision of any definition. Looking back at some of the terms identified earlier, creative thinking is often described as 'divergent' thinking, and classically measured by tests such as asking participants how many uses they can think of for an object such as a brick. The greater the number of uses, the higher the score. As Cohen points out, however, not all suggested uses are necessarily evidence of creative thinking: 'If someone said one use of a brick was as a snack, they would be loopy, poking fun, or just wrong' (2002:143). In addition, he asks whether coming up with 15 uses for a brick is necessarily more creative than coming up with 3 good ones. Both Cohen (2002) and Meadows (1993) emphasize that it may be quality not quantity of divergent thinking performance which predicts creative thinking. Quantity, Meadows suggests, is important 'if it stems from a willingness to postpone self-censorship, and provides material for further development' (1993:191), that is, if it contributes to flexibility and fluidity of thinking. So, a useful starting principle might be that creative thinking is both 'original and appropriate' (Fisher 1990:31).

The idea of imagination as part of creative thinking is discussed by a number of writers. Claxton suggests that imagination, fantasy and entering into 'imaginative scenario(s)' (1999b:96) are related to creative thinking. White, while suggesting that cultivating the imagination cannot be an aim of education by itself, nevertheless believes that cultivating children's powers to imagine is important for intellectual autonomy, self-understanding, empathy, learning to frame hypotheses and even sense of humour (2002).

The NACCCE definition of 'creativity' as 'imaginative activity fashioned so as to produce outcomes that are both original and of value' (1999:29) brings together both ideas of originality and imagination. It also adds another element, in suggesting that creative thinking is applied, and that the production of outcomes is important. White (2002) suggests that it is these outcomes – whether they are tangible things or ideas – which are the outward evidence of creative thinking.

Are there characteristic stages in creative thinking?

The term 'stages' here does not imply a developmental path through which people might progress over time. Rather, it is concerned with possible stages in the exercise of any kind of creative thinking. Both Meadows (1993) and Claxton (1998, 1999b) outline a series of stages which they suggest are characteristic of 'the creative process' (Meadows 1993:195), although as Meadows emphasizes, we do not have enough data to confirm or refute their significance as a possibly cyclic process of creative thinking. These are:

- Familiarization (Meadows) or preparation (Claxton): information gathering, acquiring expertise – 'Some of this activity is highly purposeful and analytical. Some of it might be much more leisurely and receptive' (Claxton 1999b:163).
- Incubation (Claxton) or 'letting it lie fallow' (Meadows 1993:195): an intuitive process that works best when an impasse in understanding has been reached (Claxton 1999b).
- Insight (Meadows) or illumination (Claxton): a moment or reaction which suggests an answer. This might be abrupt, but may also be slow and subtle (Claxton 1999b).
- Verification (Claxton) or working out and testing the solution (Meadows).

(Adapted from Claxton 1998, 1999b and Meadows 1993)

Claxton believes that different elements of this process may be facilitated by different types of interactions and contexts. He suggests that the first, preparation, stage is often highly social, and even collaborative. Ideas are tested out with others, and discussed, with members of the group bringing different thoughts and experiences to the situation. The second, incubation, stage may be much more solitary, allowing individuals the chance to introspect, reflect and develop their own viewpoints. He suggests that this can help to avoid too swift a convergence on a solution. Lloyd and Howe's (2003) research with children of 4 and 5 years of age shows a positive association between solitary active play (solitary pretence and functional play with objects) and divergent thinking. They speculate that the time to think things over and replay experiences, and possibly generate further possibilities, in privacy, may be important in supporting divergent thinking skills. Claxton suggests that time, 'soft thinking' (1998, 1999b) and even boredom are key elements in creative thinking.

Supporting creative thinking: some implications for practice

In her analysis of creative thinkers, Meadows (1993) identifies a number of attitudes that may be common to them. Among these are choosing challenges rather than avoiding them, valuing appropriateness, tolerance of risk and the ability to both confront uncertainty and enjoy complexity. Claxton (1999b) suggests that the ability to tolerate and manage uncertainty is an important feature of creative thinking. This implies a significant role for the kinds of emotional qualities, such as self-efficacy, self-esteem and mastery, discussed in Chapter 3. Hypothesizing and making leaps of the imagination require confidence on the thinker's part and a willingness to take risks. This has clear implications for practice, requiring a supportive, 'learner inclusive' (Craft and Jeffrey 2004) environment in which it is 'okay' to make mistakes. The effects of stress and pressure to perform may contribute to a narrowing of focus, and more interest in 'getting it right' rather than in taking risks and coming up with ideas and outcomes of originality and value (Claxton 1999b). The NACCCE cites the psychologist Carl Jung: 'The creative mind plays with the object it loves' (Jung cited in NACCCE 1999:30). It is this emotional commitment which may be important in sustaining adults and children in taking risks, if they view it as of interest and value for them.

This emotional aspect also implies that creative thinking may not be general – none of us is emotionally committed to everything, and most of us have particular interests, which motivate us more. Meadows illustrates this task- or domain-specificity in creative thinking, citing writers and artists, for example, as creative in particular, but not all, fields. Only some people, she suggests, are creative thinkers in a range of fields – da Vinci, Freud or Piaget, for example (Meadows 1993). This is worth remembering alongside Whitebread's (2000a) conclusion that interventions for supporting children's thinking seem to be most successful when they are embedded in contexts meaningful to the children – those contexts may be very different for individual children, and an important implication for practice will be to provide opportunities for the development of creative thinking in a wide range of contexts and 'subject' areas. Singer (1973) views pretend play and make-believe of all kinds as facilitatory for creative and flexible thinking. Box 10.2 features contexts that may be important for the protagonists in both parts. Noam, at 5, is hypothesizing on the basis of both previous knowledge and immediate stimuli. His thinking is original, but, as de Boo (1999) points out, he also rejects the theory he comes up with, continuing perhaps then to search for a more appropriate idea. The deep interest, and outcome, of Feynman's thinking in the second part of Box 10.2 is clear.

Critical thinking

Defining critical thinking

As with creative thinking, the concept of critical thinking can prove to be a rather fuzzy one. Lipman observes that 'it has come to denote *any* thinking that, when applied to an instance of thinking, could make it more efficient and reliable' (2003:56, emphasis in original). He describes 31 different characterizations (see 2003:56–8) before concluding that a number of key terms, including 'impartial, accurate, careful, clear, truthful, abstract, coherent and practical' (2003:58) summarize the majority of these positions. For Lipman, the idea of practicality is an important one. Critical thinking is practical in that it can be applied to both abstract and concrete issues. De Boo (1999) positions critical thinking as a metacognitive process, suggesting that it is concerned with our ability to assess the effectiveness of our thinking. It differs, he believes, from problem-solving in this respect, in that the latter he suggests is more to do with evaluating our methods of investigating or our conclusions. Popularly, as noted earlier, critical thinking is often equated with convergent thinking, in which the principle is convergence on one right answer. As Cohen (2002) points out, this principle underpins much testing, particularly of the IQ variety. As such, convergent thinking can only be a part of a wider category of critical thinking.

Supporting critical thinking: some implications for practice

Fisher suggests that the two most important processes in critical thinking are:

1   learning how to question, when to question, and what questions to ask;
2   learning how to reason, when to use reasoning, and what reasoning methods to use.

(Fisher 1990:65–6)

Looking at Fisher's first point, in Chapter 7 children's own efforts to make sense of the world, their questions and 'intellectual search' (Tizard and Hughes 2002) were seen as significant in supporting their thinking. De Boo (1999) suggests the value of posing open-ended questions which encourage speculation and investigation. Like de Boo, Fisher (1990) also emphasizes the value of adult modelling of such questions, suggesting that, through them, the vocabulary of analysis can be introduced to children. To use some of Lipman's (2003) definitional words, questions can highlight what it might mean to be clear, accurate, or careful in one's thinking. Adult modelling may support their use by children in their own questions. In a similar way, the use of metacognitive prompts and reference to the language of thinking, for example, 'was that a good way for you to decide?', or 'what do you need to think about next?' will be valuable (Swartz 2000). Box 10.3 illustrates this at one nursery school, where staff decided to focus on using particular words *about* thinking and learning in their interactions with the children and encouraged the children to use them themselves. Bruner (1987) emphasizes that these kinds of metacognitive processes and critical thinking can be successfully 'taught' to young children.

Most importantly, though, will be the provision of opportunities for children to question and explore their own ideas, to think aloud, as Vygotsky (1986) proposes, in an environment which supports this process. Forman suggests that the way to help children to ask good questions is to help them to reflect on the facts as they know them, until they discover something new to question (1989). He suggests that this supports the formulation of questions that really arise from the child's own current understanding. He recommends the value of symbolic representation such as children's drawing, as a way of representing their understanding and as the basis of this kind of reflection, supported by other people. As Richetti and Sheerin (1999) suggest, the ultimate aim is for the questioning to reside with the children, not the adults.

Fisher's second point, that critical thinking requires learning how to reason, is related to creative thinking in that both are underpinned by hypothesizing. Children's early hypotheses tend to be inductive, that is, they rely on single ideas, which may or may not conform to the 'received model' (Selley 1999), as we saw in Chapter 8. As their experience grows, children tend to begin to have some general principles, or hypotheses that support them in thinking deductively (de Boo 1999). Young children's abilities in this area will

Box 10.3 The language of thinking

In the nursery, recounted by a member of staff:
While playing a game with Archie which involved throwing a ball into a tube I said 'I'm going to have to practice because I'm useless at this.'
ARCHIE: You'll have to practice and practice or you won't be able to do it.

This followed an earlier comment from Carl:
CARL: You have to practice to learn or you wouldn't know how to do it then.

'Practice' was one of the 'thinking skills' words staff had been using, these comments show Archie and Carl's use of it in appropriate contexts.

Reproduced with permission of Pat Gura and Ann Bridges, and the staff, children and parents of Vanessa Nursery School

Box 10.4 David, aged 2½ years, at a parent and toddler group

David joins the worker, Helen, at a table, and starts to colour in a picture of a car using a blue crayon.

DAVID: My dad's got a blue car.

HELEN: Has he, so has mine.

DAVID: You got a dad?

HELEN: Yes

DAVID: But you're too big for a dad. (At this point David's mother comes and sits next to him. He looks up at her.) This lady's got a dad.

MUM: Has she? That's nice, most people do have dads.

DAVID: But she's too big.

MUM: But I'm bigger than her I've got a dad.

DAVID: Have you? Who's that?

MUM: Grandad

DAVID: But he's granded, not dad.

MUM: He's your grandad, but he's my dad.

DAVID: Oh. (He does not say anything for a while.)

DAVID: So even big people have dads.

depend, to some extent, on a number of factors, including first-hand experience, their confidence in the language of discussion, the attitudes and support of those around them and the kinds of stimuli in their environment (de Boo 1999). We are more familiar with the idea of deduction as a feature of the kinds of detective stories featuring Sherlock Holmes-type figures, but, as Box 10.4 shows, even very young children can question and reason deductively.

As with young children's creative thinking, the part played by emotion may be significant. Just as taking risks in one's thinking may require a sense of self-worth, so challenging one's own thinking, and thinking critically about the ideas and beliefs one has, may also be potentially damaging to one's self-esteem. An environment that supports children's confidence in being self-critical will be important, alongside the development of appropriate ways of challenging the ideas of others. We looked in Chapter 3 at the value of children's experiences in managing negotiation and conflict, and at how practitioners in Reggio Emilia provide children with models of negotiation, discussion and argument as a way of supporting their emotional and cognitive development. These ideas are central to the development of critical thinking skills too. Claxton (1999b) suggests that the development of dispositions to engage in what may often be hard thinking, can help children not only to persevere when the going gets tough, but also to recognize the kinds of issues and situations that may, or may not, warrant such thinking.

It was suggested that creative thinking will often be task- or domain-specific (Meadows 1993). Gardner (1993b) emphasizes that critical thinking will be no different in this respect. McKendree *et al.*, looking particularly at the role of representation in critical thinking, suggest that children's 'native abilities' (2002:65) in reasoning will be context dependent. As before, then, starting from contexts which are within children's experience, and which have meaning for them, will be valuable. Play contexts may be valuable here, both co-operative and solitary.

Creative and critical thinking and play

How do critical and creative thinking relate to young children's play? It is useful to look at the ideas discussed earlier in relation to the taxonomy of children's play outlined by Hutt (1979) and Hutt *et al.* (1989). A very simplified version of this Piagetian-influenced categorization, showing only the three main subdivisions, is shown in Figure 10.1. Of these three, the subdivision of games with rules 'occupies a special intermediate position' (Hutt *et al.* 1989:225), with games often having their own conventions, usually socially constrained and highly ritualized. What is worth considering in the context of children's thinking are the parts played by the two chief subdivisions of ludic and epistemic behaviour.

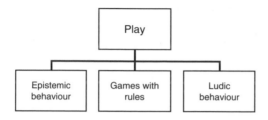

Figure 10.1 A taxonomy of children's play.
Source: Simplified from Hutt 1979.

What are the features of epistemic behaviour? First of all, it is concerned with the acquisition of knowledge, information and skills, and is relatively independent of mood state (Hutt *et al.* 1989). It may involve exploration, the acquisition of skills, and problem-solving and is particularly characteristic of playing with something new and exploring ideas of 'what can it do?' Its associations with critical thinking are readily apparent. Ludic behaviour, by contrast, is 'essentially diversive, that is, concerned with self-amusement' (Hutt *et al.* 1989:222), and is much more mood dependent, related to playing for the fun of it. The two major categories of ludic behaviour are symbolic, or fantasy, play, involving representation and pretence, and repetitive play, involving the rehearsal of skills and concepts already acquired. It is characterized by more of a sense of mastery and exploring ideas of 'what can I do with it?'. Thus, it has much in common with what has been described as creative thinking.

In their play children will move in and out of these two types of behaviour. Presented with a new idea, or novel material, for example, children's first actions may be to explore it, to find out what it can do, to investigate and 'problem solve' with it. Having explored its properties, children may feel more at ease, and more confident about trying out new, divergent ideas for the material – in many ways engaging in more advanced problem solving! Sylva *et al.* (1976) demonstrated that, in a problem-solving activity, in contexts where children were given opportunities to play with materials, they subsequently outperformed another group 'taught' how to use the materials in ways which would help them to solve the given problem. Not only that, but the group that had the experience of play were both more inventive in the strategies they used and more persistent in their attempts to solve the problem.

Think of children faced with clay for the first time, for example. Initially, they may explore its properties and what it can do – can you squeeze it, roll it into a ball, stretch it, does it break, what happens when you sit on it? This exploratory phase is often then followed by the creation of artefacts, – figures, pots, tiles, animals, model buildings and so on – divergent creations that attempt to address the question 'what can I do with it?'. As a result, children often then develop a deeper understanding of the material, developing critical judgement about what, for them, are the 'best' ways of solving problems about how to join pieces of clay together, how to stop it crumbling or how to make a good pot.

As Tyler (1991) suggests, both ludic and epistemic behaviour are important, and work together, in complementary ways, much like creative and critical thinking. Too much emphasis on epistemic behaviour may ensure much new learning, but may not help children to use their knowledge and understanding in novel and creative ways, and to transfer that learning to new situations. Overemphasis on the ludic aspects of behaviour may not support children in acquiring fresh knowledge (Tyler 1991). Similarly, creative thinking can help children to think of many ways to solve a problem, in novel ways, but thinking critically may be what is needed to support them in deciding which of these is the best 'fit' for a particular problem. Fisher suggests:

> Most problems require both types of thinking. Creativity is not just a question of creating new solutions to problems, but of creating better solutions and this requires critical judgement. To find an original solution to a logically complex problem can require creative powers of invention.
>
> (Fisher 1990:33)

Problem-solving

What is problem-solving and why does it matter?

Problem-solving is a goal-directed activity. The goal may be chosen by ourselves, or we may be set it by someone else. For Meadows (1993), problem-solving is what you do when you work towards that goal, but either do not have a routine way of getting there, or an obstacle like lack of skill or knowledge means that a previously possible solution does not work. For Fisher (1990) and de Boo (1999), this involves the application of both critical and creative thinking, which, unlike problem-solving, may be engaged in for their own sakes. Problem-solving for them is the point where critical thinking and creative thinking are applied in a process which culminates in a product of some kind. That product may be a tangible object or design or it may be a mental solution.

Problems come in many forms, ranging from 'life-threatening' to 'minor irritant' (Fisher 1990:100). They may be physical, requiring a baby to work out the best way of retrieving the teddy that is just beyond their reach. Other types of problem are inherently more social. These may involve both positive and negative strategies, for example, the use of aggression to solve conflict (Siegler *et al.* 2003), negotiation in sharing toys or in role taking in pretend play. Other types of problem are more symbolic, requiring the manipulation of signs and symbols in areas such as mathematics. Much of this activity may be unconscious, not reserved for special 'problem-solving' occasions. Bailey and Farrow suggest that 'The significant point is that organisms are always *actively* (though not necessarily consciously) involved in exploring their environment, seeking information from it in species-typical ways, and attempting to solve the problems it throws up' (1998:270). This has much in common with a position identified by Bereiter and Scardamalia as 'learning as problem solving'

(1989:364), which they link to information processing theorists (see Chapter 2), and which argues that all learning can be seen as a kind of problem-solving. The problem with this position, they suggest, is that learning varies considerably in the extent to which it poses problems for people. Much everyday learning is relatively *un*problematic. Can this still be seen as problem-solving?

While much problem-solving does occur in everyday, real-life situations, and is part of the cultural contexts in which we live, problem-solving is also used as a learning tool in early years settings and schools. Crucial features of real-life problems are that they are often ill-defined and multifaceted, amenable to no single or final solution (Fisher 1990). In this, they are often (but not necessarily) different to the types of problems 'set' for children to solve in nurseries and schools. As discussed later in the chapter, this may be important for children's interest and motivation in tackling the problem as defined.

Why does problem-solving matter? What benefits might it have for young children? Given the context of this book, do children become better thinkers as a result of engaging in problem-solving? The view that children are problem-solvers is a central tenet of a number of theorists, including Piaget and Bruner (see Chapter 2). Problem-solving is linked by Bronson (2000a), DeLoache and Brown (1987) and Wood (1998), among others, to the development of aspects such as self-regulation (see Chapter 5). Fisher (1990) suggests a reciprocal relationship between problem-solving and thinking, viewing problem-solving as helping to develop children's thinking, at the same time that it is also supported by it. Hope also relates this to learning, asserting that 'when we solve a problem we learn something new' (2002:265). For Meadows (1993) problem-solving is important because the world is not predictable. If this is the case, it implies that problem-solving, as a generalized skill, may be valuable, an issue which is considered later in the text. MacNaughton and Williams (2004) cite research pointing to a number of ways in which problem-solving may contribute to children's holistic development. In particular, in the context of thinking they suggest that it can help develop initiative and creativity, mathematical thinking and that it supports resilience and children's confidence in working things out for themselves.

How do children's problem-solving skills develop?

Children are, in many important respects, engaged in solving problems from early in life, in self-initiated and self-directed ways, 'in situations where there is no external pressure to improve or change, no obvious guidance, and no feedback other than their own satisfaction' (DeLoache and Brown 1987:111). They are constantly puzzling about how the world around them works, and about how they themselves can make things happen. At 3 months they know that their own actions can influence events (Gopnik *et al.* 1999) and from about 6 months onwards, they engage in 'sophisticated voluntary actions' (Karmiloff-Smith 1994:186) which imply goal-directed behaviour, already suggested as a defining feature of problem-solving. A critical part of this process will be the formulation of plans to reach whatever goal is identified. For young children, planning and action will often occur simultaneously (Gura 1992), but, gradually, the ability to plan in advance of action will develop. As children get older, they are able to create more complex plans, which take a greater number of factors into account and which have more steps (Thornton 2002).

The simplest planning strategy, used by adults, children and species such as chimpanzees (Karmiloff-Smith 1994) is that of trial and error. While it is very characteristic of the approach of young children to problem-solving, Thornton (2002) points out that it is by no

Box 10.5 Thomas, aged 3 years 8 months, in the nursery garden

Thomas is in the garden. He has a plant pot tray, a 'stompalong' (child's plastic stilt) and a short piece of plastic pipe. He experiments with the three items, piling them on top of one another, trying out different combinations in an attempt to find in which order the three things will balance. Eventually, he places the plant pot tray first, then the plastic stilt, and finally he places the pipe into the upturned, open end of the stilt.

THOMAS: There! That's a perfect fit.

means a primitive strategy that we develop away from, but one which we continue to use throughout life. What may change over time are the ways in which the strategy is employed. Young children, for example, 2- and 3-year-olds, may try out different solutions to a problem, but in no particular order, and may often repeat themselves. Adults and older children tend to approach trial and error as a problem-solving strategy more systematically and may also try a broader range of possibilities. Both of these characteristics mean that older children are more likely to be successful than younger ones, even in trial and error strategies (Thornton 2002). Box 10.5 shows a boy engaged in this trial and error process in his experimentations with shape, size and balance.

The ability to plan may be a crucial element in problem-solving. Meadows (1993) identifies a number of ways in which more expert problem-solvers may have more sophisticated planning strategies than novices. Note here, as before, that the emphasis is not on this necessarily being a function of age alone but the extent of the expert's knowledge and experience in the particular domain involved. She suggests that expert problem-solvers are more skilled at means-end analysis, that is, in selecting actions which lead to the achievement of the goal. For anything but the simplest of problems, this may include setting up sub-goals. For example, in painting a picture my first sub-goal might be to collect together paints, paper and brushes before I can begin to paint. As Meadows (1993) points out, in many instances young children do not always need to put such sub-goals into effect, because an adult does this preliminary work, in this case putting out materials (and sometimes even supplying the picture to be painted, but that is another matter!). This suggests the value of developing practical approaches which increasingly give the responsibility for such activity to the children themselves, in order for them to have opportunities to develop skill in structuring their plans.

Other aspects that Meadows suggests may be different between experts and novices include the extent of their knowledge of the subject of the problem, their ability to interpret how that knowledge needs to be used, how flexible their plans are, memory capacity and their experience in potentially helpful metacognitive activities (Meadows 1993). Thornton (2002) emphasizes that this skill in identifying which factors are (or are not) relevant to a problem, and which strategies may be most effective, is only possible in situations where we have knowledge and expertise. To sum up here, the development of children's knowledge about a specific problem context will play an important part in determining whether they can plan in a systematic way or whether they will need to rely on trial and error. It is useful to refer back here to the discussion in Chapter 8 on the role of experience and expertise in conceptual development.

Different models to explain the development of problem-solving in young children

While there is much consensus about aspects such as the role of trial and error, planning and knowledge in children's problem-solving skills, there are also some key differences in the models used to describe its development. DeLoache and Brown suggest a 'general acquisition mechanism' (1987:115) or sequence of stages which may be common when children approach a problem. Describing both the behaviour of children aged $1\frac{1}{2}$–$3\frac{1}{2}$ years in nesting a set of cups and children aged 4–7 years in train track play, they suggest that there is a progressive sequence over time in the strategies children use to correct their errors in construction. This sequence has some similarities to Piaget's stage model of cognition. Children progress from trying to correct their errors in construction by:

1   exerting physical force without changing any of the elements: for example, brute force in trying to make a larger cup fit into a smaller one;
2   making limited changes in a part of the problem set: local correction, for example, taking out one piece of the track and trying to make it fit, while ignoring the rest;
3   considering and operating on the problem as a whole: for example, a consideration of the whole set of cups, and multiple relationships.

(Adapted from DeLoache and Brown 1987)

The first stage was characteristic of the youngest children in each group, with the final stage of more 'advanced correction strategies' (DeLoache and Brown 1987:112) only being used by the older children in each group. Both age groups displayed similar approaches in that they spontaneously monitored the success of their own goal-directed efforts, and attempted to correct their errors.

Thornton suggests that the 'traditional model' (2002:135) that new and powerful strategies replace older ones as children develop may be fundamentally wrong. The use of microgenetic study (study of the same children repeatedly over short periods of time), she suggests, reveals that older and weaker strategies are not replaced, but continue to be used alongside newer, more sophisticated strategies, often for considerable lengths of time. In addition, these newer, more powerful strategies do not necessarily grow out of the older ones, and may be unconnected with them (Thornton 2002). Siegler's overlapping waves theory was looked at in Chapter 2. Thornton (2002) suggests that it provides a useful model here, with children using different strategies at the same time, and even for the same problem. In a particular situation, a young child's choice of strategy will depend on its history in the child's experience. Each experience provides more feedback, with particular strategies gradually becoming more closely associated with success in particular contexts. Smith et al. (2003) suggest that a key factor here is the environment, and the ways in which this creates a context in which children realize the importance of particular strategies. They also suggest that this model may be most likely in contexts where children have 'a moderate amount of experience at a task' (Smith et al. 2003:428). When children (and adults) are very familiar with a task, they suggest, they will have established, and will consistently use, the most appropriate strategy they have. In very novel situations, similarly, strategy use will tend to be more restricted, as people do not yet have enough knowledge of the context. When people are at the stage of developing their understanding of a situation, they may try out a number of different problem-solving strategies at the same time.

Look now at the episode described in Box 10.6, which shows Mark using a range of problem-solving strategies, including hypothesizing, trial and error, metacognitive knowledge and even physical force, in his own, self-initiated and self-directed activity.

Box 10.6 Mark, aged 3 years 8 months, at the water tray in a community preschool

Mark is playing alone at a transparent water tray. He slots a length of thin flexible tubing inside the neck of a bottle, fits a funnel into the tubing and takes a deep breath. Holding the neck of the bottle he uses a large jug to pour water slowly down the funnel and tubing into the bottle. He repeats this several times with varying degrees of accuracy, shaking the bottle each time. He pauses and stares blankly at the water. He then lifts the bottle higher and tries the same activity. This time the water spills before reaching the funnel.

MARK: Oh no. (He looks puzzled, and continues pouring the water, readjusting his position.)

Removing the tubing, he pours the water out of the bottle. He reaches for a wider piece of blank tubing and tries to slot it into the neck of the bottle. He tries banging the tubing over the neck, and then twisting it in a screwing motion. With a frown he gives up.

He picks up a thin rigid tube and a different jug. Holding it at the top, he rests the end of the tube on the base of the water tray. He watches the top of the tube intently as he pours water accurately down it. He then lifts the tube above the water and watches it flowing out of the bottom. He repeats this sequence several times.

He pauses, and looks puzzled. He suddenly crouches down and looks underneath the water tray, seeming confused. He reaches out to touch the base in several places. He then stands back up, and looks closely down one end of the tubing, placing it near to his eye. As he does this some water drips from the tube. He then puts the opposite end of the tube to his eye.

Mark develops 'a complex interaction between strategy and declarative knowledge' (Meadows 1993: 87). Metacognitive strategies are apparent, first, as Mark constructs a theory, based on previous experience, that objects can be screwed or banged to make them fit; second, in his search for an explanation as to why he did not see the water coming out of the tube again. He knows the water has not just disappeared; so it is logical that he would see it come out again. Finally, Mark concludes that the water must be either under the trough or alternatively still in the tube. Mark's observations lead to conflicting ideas about how water behaves when changing the height of the tube. He searches for clues to extend and test his hypotheses.

Abridged and reproduced with permission of Janet Roberts

Some implications for practice in supporting young children's problem-solving

Strategies and processes

There is, as we have seen, considerable debate about whether there are general problem-solving strategies which can be taught or whether much critical and creative thinking and problem-solving is task- or domain-specific (Meadows 1993). Whitebread nevertheless identifies some processes which he believes are 'involved in solving any problem' (2000a:156). These are:

- understanding and representing the problem (including identifying what kinds of information are relevant to its solution);
- gathering and organizing relevant information;
- constructing and managing a plan of action;
- reasoning, hypothesis testing and decision-making;
- using various problem-solving tools (drawings, maps and other representations).

(Whitebread 2000a:156–7)

Fisher (1990) and MacNaughton and Williams (2004) also add to these the importance of children reviewing and evaluating what has been done. However, while such general processes may be identifiable, they do not form a 'recipe' for problem-solving, and attempts to teach procedures at the expense of understanding 'do not foster (and may inhibit) the development of strategies for regulating one's own problem solving' (Wood 1998:294).

Knowledge and experience in meaningful contexts

While concurring with Whitebread that there are problem-solving strategies which can be applied in many different situations, Meadows (1993) emphasizes the crucial importance of these being set in meaningful, useful contexts. These experiences provide children with opportunities for developing knowledge, both declarative (knowing that) and procedural (knowing how), and expertise, and a bigger repertoire of problems on which to draw (Whitebread 2000a). This emphasis on the value of knowledge and experience links to Tizard and Hughes (2002) in Chapter 8, as well as to all of the theoretical positions outlined in Chapter 2. Gura suggests that, in relation to block play, experience and developing expertise go hand in hand, leading to more complex representation and problem-solving:

> Our own study shows a direct link between exploratory activity with blocks, ie materials-mastery play, and the ability to use them with increasing fluency and *flair* in creating representations covering a wide range of content. This involves a great deal of problem-solving as children work out which aspects of the object or experience they want to represent can be done with blocks, and how.
>
> (Gura 1992:118, emphasis in original)

Play of all kinds provides valuable contexts for the development of problem-solving. Sociodramatic pretend play, in particular, may have a reciprocal relationship with problem-solving (Bergen 2002), and provide opportunities for meaning-making, role-taking and negotiation, supportive of problem-solving (Hope 2002).

Looked at more widely, the sociocultural context will also play a part here. The problems that young children spontaneously want to solve in their lives arise as part of their cultural context, and may even determine what is seen as a 'problem' (Hope 2002).

Whose problem is it?: choice and direction in problem-solving

The relationship between child- and adult-initiated activity in early childhood settings is a subject of considerable debate, much of which is outside the scope of this book. In the context of children's thinking, Siraj-Blatchford *et al.* (2002) found that the 'excellent' and 'good' settings in their study tended to have an equal balance between adult-led and child-initiated activity. In our research, those working with children aged 3 and 4 tended to suggest a balance which placed more emphasis on activities that were mostly child chosen, while those practitioners working with 4- and 5-year-olds were more likely to favour an equal division between child chosen and adult-led activities (Robson and Hargreaves 2005). Siraj-Blatchford *et al.* (2002) also found that the percentage of adult-initiated activities also increased, as a function of the age of the children. This may be attributable to a number of factors, but the tendency for increasing formalization of the curriculum, and of children's activities, and the requirement to move children 'through a predetermined series of narrowly defined goals and targets' (Hendy and Whitebread 2000:251) as they go through school will play a part here in determining what is seen as appropriate. As Hendy and Whitebread (2000) observe, this may not be conducive to a classroom atmosphere in which initiative and the ability to think for oneself as a child is likely to flourish.

Is there a relationship between choice and 'ownership' and children's problem-solving and thinking skills? De Boo cites research which suggests that, when children are presented with a problem to solve, they give fewer and less varied responses than when they identify and solve their own problems (Tuma and Reif 1980, cited in de Boo 1999). Looking at children's play activities as contexts for thinking, Siraj-Blatchford *et al.* suggest that 'freely chosen play activities often provide the best opportunities to extend children's thinking' (2002:12). Segar (2004) studied groups of children aged 3–5 years in English nursery and reception classes. She found similar levels of persistence at tasks in individual children, whether they were child- or adult-initiated, suggesting that the children were prepared, in most instances, to 'go along with' whatever was asked of them. What differed were the levels of involvement of the children, with child-initiated tasks consistently associated with higher levels of involvement than those initiated by adults. Laevers (1999) suggests that involvement is an outward sign of intense mental activity in a child.

Fisher (1990:122) suggests that it is the child's experience and environment which should provide the catalyst for problem-solving. Such a statement, however, can be interpreted in a number of ways. In Reggio Emilia, for example, long-term projects arise out of the children's expressed interests and concerns. A similar approach is outlined in Katz and Chard (2000). See, for example, the inspiration for *The Crowd*, a project undertaken by children and adults in Reggio Emilia, which is briefly outlined in Box 10.7.

A common approach in many early childhood settings is to use familiar contexts for young children as vehicles for the development of problem-solving skills, often linking this with wider learning intentions and planning. Belle Wallace outlines a model known as *TASC: Thinking Actively in a Social Context*, which 'sets out a framework for the development of a problem-solving and thinking skills curriculum' (2002:8). This approach is intended to develop such skills in an integrated way across all activities and areas of the

Box 10.7 The Crowd, Reggio Emilia

Just back from the summer vacation, talking with his friends and a teacher, Gabriele commented on a summer evening he remembers:

GABRIELE: In the evening, it was full of people, people walking up and people walking down. You couldn't see anything, just people, legs, arms and heads.

Staff decided to explore other children's images of crowds:

- When there's a lot of people, they make a lot of noise.
- It's a carpet of people that walks and moves.
- Everybody passes by with their shoulders all squeezed together.
- I was right in the middle. When there's lots and lots of people, it's a real big problem because you can get lost.
- Crowds at night are real dangerous because it's dark.

One girl drew people all going in the same direction. To explore this, and other ideas, staff thought of as many different ways and situations in which the children could test out their thinking. The children went out into the town square, projected images of crowds onto a wall at the centre, drew each other from muiltiple perspectives, made paper and card models of themselves and put them together as 'crowds', and explored spaces of different sizes, being part of a crowd. Two final representations, one in clay, and one graphic, resulted from the children's self-directed, collaborative activity.

(Adapted from Reggio Children 1996:142–55)

curriculum, using a number of skills, conceptualized as a cyclic 'wheel', which are designed to guide the actions of practitioners in their work with children:

- gather/organize: find out what children know, show how ideas link, stimulate children's questions, focus on questions to explore;
- identify: explain/demonstrate the task, discuss what is needed;
- generate: ask for learners' ideas, add ideas, discuss ways of finding out and recording;
- decide: look at feasibility of ideas, share tasks among group;
- implement: use variety of activities and finding out and recording skills;
- evaluate: check if goal was achieved, think about improvements, discuss group co-operation;
- communicate: share with others and encourage communication;
- learn from experience: reflect on process, state what has been learned, look for uses in other lessons.

(Adapted from Wallace 2002:18–19)

Chandler (2004), noting the use of *TASC* in one school, records a teacher's comment that the *TASC* wheel gave the children a structure for their thinking, which can nevertheless be used flexibly, either in whole or in part, depending on circumstances. The examples provided by Wallace (2002) include ideas for work in classes for children between 3 and 7 years, around topics such as 'Our Teddy Bears Picnic', 'What do we know about buildings?' and 'How could we develop our field?', linked to the class's medium-term planning, and involving a number of areas of the curriculum.

Lambert (2000) suggests that such an approach, which starts from curriculum intentions identified by the adults in the setting, may be problematic for young children precisely because the focus is on problems prescribed by the curriculum, rather than on ones that the children spontaneously want to solve, arising from their real-life experiences. The procedures involved may often be divorced from real-world procedures. She suggests that the kinds of problems children are often interested in solving differ in many respects from those 'given' to them as exercises. Among the differences she suggests are ones of goal difference, the amount of information available and the solutions and answers required. In settings, she suggests, the goal is generally predetermined by the curriculum, specific information needed to solve the problem may be given and there may be one solution or one answer. By contrast, she suggests that in life children spontaneously discover or select their own goals, the amount of information available will differ, and often be very diverse, and solutions may be equally diverse. She emphasizes that, in her view, problems in settings tend not to be related to real-life problems.

While the differences that she proposes may not apply to all 'problem-solving' approaches, including *TASC*, her comparisons are useful, in pointing to possible ways in which there may be differences between the reasoning and problem-solving strategies that children use in adult-initiated and child-initiated activities. She suggests that an approach which starts from the child's interests is 'aligned with how children in the first years of school simply prefer to think' (Lambert 2000:37).

Time and space

Giving sufficient, uninterrupted, time to children's problem-solving supports them in developing deeper understandings and more complex knowledge about the problems they are addressing (Lambert 2000). In addition, children will need to know that this time is available. Gura (1992), looking at children's blockplay, for example, comments on the way in which a 'hit and run' attitude seemed to develop among children where lack of time prevented them from embarking on sustained play which develops over a period of time. Practitioners in our research suggested that this was one of the biggest challenges they faced, but they emphasized the importance they placed upon both time for activity and time for children to talk about their thinking (Robson and Hargreaves 2005).

Relationships, attitudes and dispositions

Children's attitudes and dispositions, including their interest, motivation and confidence, will be crucial to their success in problem-solving (Fisher 1990). The impact of stress and pressure may be to lessen children's creativity in problem-solving (Claxton 1998).

This suggests a number of key aspects of the role of adults in their interactions with young children. Most importantly, relationships between adults and children which are 'responsive and reciprocal' (Carr 2001) seem to promote greater persistence at activities and co-operation with others (Claxton 1999b). Other, more direct benefits to children's problem-solving seem to be related to adult modelling of problem-solving (Bronson 2000a, Gura 1992, Mercer 2000), adult suggestions of problem-solving strategies (Bronson 2000a) and joint adult–child participation in problem-solving activities (Bronson 2000a, Gura 1992). Discussions between adults and children in problem-solving activities provide opportunities for adult examples of strategy use that children can then use in their private speech, in the way Vygotsky describes (1986), as well as providing a forum for discussion about how children are thinking about, and trying to solve, problems (Mercer 2000, Wood 1998). Adult diagnosis of children's problem-solving processes is facilitated by direct involvement with activities, allowing for both discussion and direct observation. The pitfalls of adult questions were looked at in Chapter 7, and Gura (1992) suggests the value of non-evaluative comments, rather than questions, for finding out about children's problem-solving. Box 10.8 shows the importance of joint adult–child participation and discussion, while also highlighting the importance of supporting children's interactions with one another.

Playing together and alone

Children's interactions with one another will have an important impact upon their problem-solving skills. In Chapter 7 the value of co-operative and collaborative activity, particularly in pairs, was discussed. In the context of problem-solving, children in friendship pairs are

Box 10.8 Six children, including Angelina, aged 3 years 9 months, Jake, aged 3 years 3 months and Hollie, aged 3 years 5 months, making peppermint creams in the nursery, with Cathy, a practitioner

---

Each child has their own bowl and spoon, and, before the point at which we join the activity, the children, working with Cathy, have explored the ingredients, and measured out icing sugar into their bowls. Jo, another staff member, is nearby.

CATHY: When we make icing to ice our biscuits we add water but today we are making peppermint creams so we have different ingredients. Look and see what else we can add to bind the icing sugar and make it stick together.

ANGELINA AND JAKE: Cream!

JAKE: Yukky cream. (He makes a face and others laugh. They take it in turns to pour the cream. Jake puts too much cream in his bowl.)

CATHY: Jake, it's a bit too runny, what do you think you should do to make it thicker?

JAKE: More cream.

CATHY: Are you sure?

JAKE: Yes. (He pours more cream in. He then turns tearfully to another member of staff.) It's still runny Jo.

JO: That happened to me once but when I put more icing sugar in it made it thicker.

JAKE: Oh. (He adds three more spoonfuls of sugar.)

HOLLIE: Well done, Jake, that's nicer, it's smooth now. Clever Jake, aren't you Jake. Jake nods and smiles, and adds two more spoonfuls of sugar.

JAKE: It's getting thicker (whispered).

What could have been a negative learning experience became for him a positive experience of collaborative adult/child problem solving, and can be seen as part of a process of developing a positive disposition towards learning. Jake's self-esteem was raised by Hollie's praise of his accomplishment and provided him with the confidence to proceed.

Abridged and reproduced with permission of Jo Short

more successful in problem-solving activities than non-friends (Smith *et al*. 2003), a phenomenon which seems to be related to their willingness to discuss and constructively evaluate their solutions together. Even where they are not friends, children in novice–expert pairs who are prepared to exchange and resolve differences of opinion show significant improvements in their performance in problem-solving tasks. Katz and Chard (2000) suggest that this improvement even carries over into other tasks. In larger groups, the thinking of both children and adults contributes to 'a larger, more meaningful whole' (Project Zero and Reggio Children 2001:247). Developing children's ability to both take feedback from others, and to give constructive, in-depth feedback of their own, can help children to think about problems and solutions in new ways (Gura 1992).

Children's solitary play may also support problem-solving, by allowing children time and space to reflect privately (Lloyd and Howe 2003). Lloyd and Howe believe that such solitary play is not necessarily a more immature form of play, as has often been asserted. They suggest the importance of creating opportunities and spaces for children to play together, or alone, as they choose, while emphasizing the importance of helping 'reticent' children to engage with their physical and social environment.

Implications for practice – a final summary

The points set out here provide an overall summary and conclusion for the chapter, and, in many ways, for the book as a whole:

- The importance of an environment where questioning and risk-taking in thinking are encouraged (Claxton 1999b, De Boo 1999).
- Interventions aimed at supporting children's thinking are most effective when they are set in contexts which are meaningful for children. Such contexts will be different for individual children (McKendree *et al*. 2002, Whitebread 2000a).
- The importance of experience for feeding young children's thinking (Fisher 1990).
- Pretence and make-believe may be particularly valuable for problem-solving, developing creative thinking, negotiation and talk about mental states (Bergen 2002, Singer 1973).
- Children's self-initiated activities may often provide the best contexts for problem-solving and extending their thinking (Lambert 2000, Siraj-Blatchford *et al*. 2002).
- Giving sufficient, uninterrupted, time to children's problem-solving supports the development of deeper understanding and more complex knowledge (Lambert 2000).
- The value of supporting the development of children's personal reflections, both on their own ideas and representations and on those of others.
- The value of adult use and modelling of metacognitive strategies, including identifying what you don't know, generating questions, thinking aloud and problem-solving (Fisher 1990, Mercer 2000, Swartz 2000).
- Adult–child joint problem-solving may be valuable for supporting metacognition and problem-solving (Bronson 2000a). However, when adults get involved children may sometimes be more likely to say that they cannot do something. When working with other children, they may be less likely to question their ability and often gain confidence through mimicking another child (Whitebread *et al*. 2005).
- The most effective response from an adult to a child asking for help may be to direct them to another child who has competence or expertise in the area. Often just watching another child supports metacognitive development (Whitebread *et al*. 2005).

- Children in friendship pairs are more successful in problem-solving activities than non-friends (Smith *et al.* 2003). Even where they are not friends, children in novice–expert pairs can show significant improvements in their performance in problem-solving tasks (Katz and Chard 2000).
- Children's solitary play may support problem-solving, by allowing children time and space to reflect privately (Lloyd and Howe 2003).
- Adult diagnosis of children's thinking may be facilitated by their direct involvement in children's activities, their discussions with children, and their use of non-evaluative comments to probe understanding (Gura 1992).

Further reflection

1   In your view, are thinking skills transferable and generalizable? Can children be supported in developing such transferable thinking skills? If so, how, in your view, can this be done?

2   Costello (2000:3) clearly sets out the arguments 'for' and 'against' the teaching of philosophical thinking to young children. The chief arguments against the teaching of philosophy to young children are that it is not 'real' or 'serious' philosophy, and that children will not be able to understand it. What is your response to this? If you disagree, what arguments would you offer in favour of philosophy for young children?

3   What problems have you solved this week? How did you tackle them? Are there similarities, or do you approach different kinds of problems in different ways?

Further reading

Developing 'good' thinking, and models for teaching thinking

Claxton, G. (1998, 1999b)
Coles, M.J. and Robinson, W.D. (1991a)
Costello, P. (2000)
Fisher, R. (1990, 2001)
Haynes, J. (2002)
Lipman, M. (2003)
McGuinness, C. (1999)
Meadows, S. (1993) pp. 333–42
Swartz, R.J. *et al.* (1998, 2000)
Thinking Skills Review Group (2004)

Creative thinking, critical thinking and problem solving

de Boo, M. (1999) chapters 3 and 6
Claxton, G. (1998, 1999b)
DeLoache, J. and Brown, A. (1987)
Fisher, R. (1990) chapters 2, 3 and 4
Gura, P. (1992) chapter 7
Hope, G. (2002)

Karmiloff-Smith, A. (1994) pp. 121–5, 186–93
Lambert, E.B. (2000)
Meadows, S. (1993) pp. 87–92, 190–6
Project Zero and Reggio Children (2001)
Reggio Children (1996)
Thornton, S. (2002) chapter 6
Wallace, B. (2002)
Whitebread, D. (2000a)

Websites

A brief selection of some useful websites

21st Century Learning Initiative: http://www.21learn.org

Cambridgeshire Independent Learning in the Foundation Stage: www.educ.cam.ac.uk/cindle

Childrenthinking: www.childrenthinking.co.uk

Dialogue Works: www.dialogueworks.co.uk

Institute for the Advancement of Philosophy for Children (IAPC): http://cehs.montclair.edu/academic/iapc

Making Learning Visible: http://pzweb.harvard.edu/mlv

National Center for Teaching Thinking (USA): http://www.nctt.net

Project Zero: http://pzweb.harvard.edu

Scottish Education Forum on Teaching Thinking Skills: http://www.scotland.gov.uk/library3/education/ftts-00.asp

Sightlines Initiative: www.sightlines-initiative.com

Society for the Advancement of Philosophical Enquiry and Reflection in Education (SAPERE): www.sapere.net

Teaching Thinking (Robert Fisher): www.teachingthinking.net

Tuckswood First School: www.creative-corner.co.uk/schools/tuckswood/home.html

Bibliography

Abbott, L. and Moylett, H. (eds) (1999) *Early Education Transformed*, London: Falmer Press.

Adey, P. and Shayer, M. (1994) *Really Raising Standards: Cognitive Intervention and Academic Achievement*, London: Routledge.

Ainsworth, M.D.S., Blehar, M.C., Waters, E. and Wall, S. (1978) *Patterns of Attachment*, Hillsdale, NJ: Erlbaum.

Alderson, P. (2005) 'Children's Rights: A New Approach to Studying Childhood', in *Understanding Early Childhood* (ed.) H. Penn, Maidenhead: Open University Press, pp. 127–41.

Alderson, P. and Morrow, V. (2004) *Ethics, Social Research and Consulting with Young People*, London: Barnardo's.

Anning, A. and Edwards, A. (1999) *Promoting Children's Learning from Birth to Five*, Buckingham: Open University.

Anning, A. and Ring, K. (2004) *Making Sense of Children's Drawings*, Maidenhead: Open University Press.

Arnheim, R. (1969) *Visual Thinking*, Berkeley, CA: University of California Press.

Arnold, C. (1999) *Child Development and Learning 2–5 Years*, London: Hodder and Stoughton.

Astington, J. (1994) *The Child's Discovery of the Mind*, London: Fontana.

—— (1998) 'Theory of Mind goes to School', *Educational Leadership*, 56(3): 46–9.

Astington, J.W. and Baird, J.A. (2004) 'Why Language Matters for Theory of Mind', *International Journal of Behavioral Development, Supplement Newsletter Number 1 Serial Number 45*, 28(3): 7–9.

Athey, C. (1990) *Extending Thought in Young Children: A Parent Teacher Partnership*, London: Paul Chapman.

Bailey, R. (2002) 'Playing Social Chess: Children's Play and Social Intelligence', *Early Years*, 22(2): 163–73.

Bailey, R. and Farrow, S. (1998) 'Play and Problem-solving in a New Light', *International Journal of Early Years Education*, 6(3): 265–75.

Baron-Cohen, S. (1995) *Mind Blindness*, Cambridge, MA: MIT Press.

—— (2004) *The Essential Difference: Men, Women and the Extreme Male Brian*, London: Penguin.

Barratt-Pugh, C. and Rohl, M. (2000) *Literacy Learning in the Early Years*, Buckingham: Open University Press.

Bartholomew, L. and Bruce, T. (1993) *Getting to Know You*, London: Hodder and Stoughton.

Bartsch, K. and Wellman, H.M. (1995) *Children Talk About the Mind*, Oxford: Oxford University Press.

Baumeister, R.F., Campbell, J.D., Krueger, J.I. and Vohs, K.D. (2005) 'Exploding the Self-Esteem Myth', *Scientific American*, 292(1): 70–7.

Bayley, R. (2002) 'Learning Styles', *Early Years Educator*, Supplement, 4: 5.

Bell, M.A. and Wolfe, C.D. (2004) 'Emotion and Cognition: An Intricately Bound Developmental Process', *Child Development*, 75(2): 366–70.

Bennett, N. and Dunne, E. (1992) *Managing Classroom Groups*, London: Simon and Schuster.

Bereiter, C. and Scardamalia, M. (1989) 'Intentional Learning as a Goal of Instruction', in *Knowing, Learning and Instruction* (ed.) L.B. Resnick, Hillsdale, NJ: Lawrence Erlbaum Associates.

Bergen, D. (2002) 'The Role of Pretend Play in Children's Cognitive Development', *Early Childhood Research and Practice*, 4:1. Online. Available at: <http://ecrp.uiuc.edu/v4n1/bergen.html> (accessed 10 February 2005).

Bidell, T.R. and Fischer, K.W. (1992) 'Cognitive Development in Educational Contexts: Implications of Skill Theory', in *Neo-Piagetian Theories of Cognitive Development* (eds) A. Demetriou, M. Shayer and A. Efklides, London: Routledge, pp. 11–30.

Blackburn, S. (2003) 'State of Mind', Review of *The Blank Slate*, in *New Scientist*, 24 May 2003: 24.

Blagg, N., Ballinger, M. and Gardner, R. (1988) *Somerset Thinking Skills Course*, Oxford: Basil Blackwell.

Blakemore, S.-J. (2005) 'Life before Three. Play or Hot-housing?', *RSA Journal*, February: 36–9.

Blakemore, S.-J. and Frith, U. (2000) *The Implications of Recent Developments in Neuroscience for Research on Teaching and Learning*. Online. Available at: <http://www.tlrp.org/pub/acadpub/Blakemore2000.pdf> (accessed 24 February 2005).

—— (2005) *The Learning Brain*, Oxford: Blackwell.

Bowlby, J. (1969) *Attachment and Loss. Volume 1: Attachment*, London: Hogarth Press.

Bredekamp, S. (1987) *Developmentally Appropriate Practice in Early Childhood Education Programs Serving Children from Birth Through Age 8*, Washington, DC: National Association for the Education of Young Children.

Bretherton, I. (ed.) (1984) *Symbolic Play: The Development of Social Understanding*, New York: Academic Press.

Broadhead, P. (1997) 'Promoting Sociability and Cooperation in Nursery Settings', *British Educational Research Journal*, 23(4): 513–31.

—— (2004) *Early Years Play and Learning: Developing Social Skills and Cooperation*, London: RoutledgeFalmer.

Bronfenbrenner, U. (1979) *The Ecology of Human Development*, Cambridge, MA: Harvard University Press.

Bronson, M. (2000a) *Self-regulation in Early Childhood: Nature and Nurture*, New York: The Guilford Press.

—— (2000b) 'Recognizing and Supporting the Development of Self-Regulation in Young Children', *Young Children*, 55(2): 32–7.

Brooker, L. (2002) *Starting School – Young Children Learning Cultures*, Buckingham: Open University.

Brooks, M. (2004) 'Drawing: The Social Construction of Knowledge', *Australian Journal of Early Childhood*, 29(2): 41–9.

Brown, A. and DeLoache, J.S. (1983) 'Metacognitive Skills', in *Early Childhood Development and Education* (eds) M. Donaldson, R. Grieve and C. Pratt, Oxford: Blackwell, pp. 280–9.

Brown, W. (2000) Review of *The Myth of the First Three Years* (John T. Bruer), *Early Childhood Research Quarterly*, 15(2): 269–73.

Browne, E. (1994) *Handa's Surprise*, London: Walker Books.

Bruer, J.T. (1998) 'Brain Science, Brain Fiction', *Educational Leadership*, November, 14–18.

—— (1999) *The Myth of the First Three Years: A New Understanding of Early Brain Development and Lifelong Learning*, New York: Free Press.

Bruner, J.S. (1960) *The Process of Education*, Cambridge, MA: Harvard University Press.

—— (1966) *Towards a Theory of Instruction*, New York: Norton.

—— (1986) *Actual Minds, Possible Worlds*, Cambridge, MA: Harvard University Press.

—— (1987) 'The Transactional Self', in *Making Sense*, (eds) J. Bruner and H. Haste, London: Methuen, pp. 81–96.

—— (1988) 'Vygotsky: A Historical and Conceptual Perspective', in *Language and Literacy from an Educational Perspective, Volume 1, Language Studies* (ed.) N. Mercer, Milton Keynes: Open University Press, pp. 86–98.

Bruner, J.S. and Haste, H. (eds) (1987) *Making Sense*, London: Methuen.

Bruner, J.S., Jolly, A. and Sylva, K. (eds) (1976) *Play*, Harmondsworth: Penguin.

Bryant, P. (1997) 'Mathematical Understanding in the Nursery School Years', in *Learning and Teaching Mathematics: An International Perspective* (eds) T. Nunes and P. Bryant, Hove: Psychology Press, pp. 53–67.

Butterworth, G. and Harris, M. (1994) *Principles of Developmental Psychology*, Hove: Lawrence Erlbaum.

Cahill, L. (2005) 'His Brain, Her Brain', *Scientific American*, 292(5): 22–9.

Carey, S. (1985) *Conceptual Change in Childhood*, Cambridge, MA: MIT Press.

Carr, M. (1992) *'Maths for Meaning: Tracing a Path for Early Mathematics Development'*, *SAME Papers 1992*, Hamilton, New Zealand: University of Waikato Centre for Science and Mathematics Research and Longman Paul.

—— (1998) *Assessing Children's Learning in Early Childhood Settings*, Wellington, New Zealand: New Zealand Council for Educational Research.

—— (2001) *Assessment in Early Childhood Settings*, London: Paul Chapman.

Case, R. (1992) 'The Role of Central Conceptual Structures in the Development of Children's Scientific and Mathematical Thought', in *Neo-Piagetian Theories of Cognitive Development* (eds) A. Demetriou, M. Shayer and A. Efklides, London: Routledge, pp. 52–64.

Catherwood, D. (1999) 'New Views on the Young Brain: Offerings from Developmental Psychology to Early Childhood Education', *Contemporary Issues in Early Childhood*, 1(1): 23–35.

Cattell, R.B. (1971) *Abilities: Their Structure, Growth and Action*, Boston, MA: Houghton-Mifflin.

Central Advisory Council for Education (CACE) (1967) *'Children and Their Primary Schools'* (The Plowden Report), London: HMSO.

Chak, A. (2001) 'Adult Sensitivity to Children's Learning in the Zone of Proximal Development', *Journal for the Theory of Social Behaviour*, 31(4): 383–95.

Chandler, S. (2004) *How TASC (Thinking Actively in a Social Context) Helped to Ensure Rapid School Improvement*, Paper presented at National Teacher Research Panel Second Conference, Birmingham, National Exhibition Centre, March. Online. Available at: <http://www.standards.dfes.gov.uk/innovation-unit/investigation/teacherresearch2/ntrp> (accessed 4 January 2005).

Chomsky, N. (1957) *Syntactic Structures*, The Hague: Mouton.

Chukovsky, K. (1963) *From Two to Five*, Berkeley, CA: University of California Press.

Clark, A. (2005) 'Spaces to Play', Paper presented to British Association for Early Childhood Education, London Branch, London, January.

Clark, A. and Moss, P. (2001) *Listening to Young Children: The Mosaic Approach*, London: National Children's Bureau and Joseph Rowntree Foundation.

Claxton, G. (1998) *Hare Brain, Tortoise Mind*, London: Fourth Estate.

—— (1999a) *Sure Start Brighter Future*, British Association for Early Childhood Education Conference Lecture, Westminster, London: 9 June.

—— (1999b) *Wise Up: The Challenge of Life Long Learning*, London: Bloomsbury.

Claxton, G. and Carr, M. (2004) 'A Framework for Teaching Learning: The Dynamics of Disposition', *Early Years*, 24(1): 87–97.

Clements, D.H. (2004) 'Geometric and Spatial Thinking in Early Childhood Education', in *Engaging Young Children in Mathematics: Standards for Early Childhood Mathematics Education* (eds) D.H. Clements and J. Sarama, London: Lawrence Erlbaum, pp. 267–97.

Clements, D.H. and Sarama, J. (eds) (2004) *Engaging Young Children in Mathematics: Standards for Early Childhood Mathematics Education*, London: Lawrence Erlbaum.

Cohen, D. (2002) *How the Child's Mind Develops*, London: Routledge.

Cole, M. (1996) *Cultural Psychology: A Once and Future Discipline*, Cambridge, MA: Belknap Press.

—— (2005) 'Cultural-Historical Activity Theory in the Family of Socio-Cultural Approaches', *International Journal of Behavioral Development, Supplement Newsletter Number 1 Serial Number 47*, 29(3): 1–4.

Cole, M. and Scribner, S. (1978) 'Introduction', in *Mind in Society*, by L. Vygotsky, Cambridge, MA: Harvard University Press.

Cole, M., Gay, J., Glick, J.A. and Sharp, D.W. (1971) *The Cultural Context of Learning and Thinking*, London: Methuen.

Cole, P.M., Martin, S.E. and Dennis, T.A. (2004) 'Emotion Regulation as a Scientific Construct: Methodological Challenges and Directions for Child Development Research', *Child Development*, 75(2): 317–33.

Coles, M. (1996) 'The Magicfying Glass: What We Know of Classroom Talk in the Early Years', in *Listening to Children Think: Exploring Talk in the Early Years* (eds) N. Hall and J. Martello, London: Hodder and Stoughton, pp. 1–17.

Coles, M.J. and Robinson, W.D. (eds) (1991a) 'Teaching Thinking: What Is It? Is It Possible?', in *Teaching Thinking: A Survey of Programmes in Education* (eds) M.J. Coles and W.D. Robinson, London: Bristol Classical Press, pp. 9–24.

—— (1991b) *Teaching Thinking: A Survey of Programmes in Education*, London: Bristol Classical Press.

Cooper, H. (2002) *History in the Early Years*, London: RoutledgeFalmer.

—— (ed.) (2004) *Exploring Time and Place through Play*, London: David Fulton.

Corrie, L. (2000) 'Neuroscience and Early Childhood? A Dangerous Liaison', *Australian Journal of Early Childhood*, 25(2): 34–40.

Costa, A.L. (1991) (ed.) *Developing Minds*, Alexandria, VA: Association for Supervision and Curriculum Development.

Costello, P.J.M. (2000) *Thinking Skills and Early Childhood Education*, London: David Fulton.

Craft, A. and Jeffrey, B. (2004) 'Creative Practice and Practice which Fosters Creativity', in *Supporting Children's Learning in the Early Years* (eds) L. Miller and J. Devereux, London: David Fulton, pp. 105–12.

Crystal, D. (1998) *Language Play*, London: Penguin.

Csikszentmihalyi, M. (1979) 'The Concept of Flow', in *Play and Learning* (ed.) B. Sutton-Smith, New York: Gardner Press, pp. 257–74.

Cutting, A.L. and Dunn, J. (1999) 'Theory of Mind, Emotion Understanding, Language, and Family Background: Individual Differences and Interrelations', *Child Development*, 70(4): 853–65.

Dahlberg, G., Moss, P. and Pence, A. (1999) *Beyond Quality in Early Childhood Education and Care: Postmodern Perspectives*, London: Falmer.

Dawes, L., Mercer, N. and Wegerif, R. (2000) *Thinking Together*, Birmingham: Questions Publishing Company.

de Bono, E. (1991) 'The CoRT Thinking Program', in *Developing Minds* (ed.) A.L. Costa, Alexandria, VA: Association for Supervision and Curriculum Development, pp. 27–32.

de Boo, M. (1999) *Enquiring Children, Challenging Teaching*, Buckingham: Open University.

—— (ed.) (2000a) *Science 3–6: Laying the Foundations in the Early Years*, Hatfield: Association for Science Education.

—— (2000b) 'Why Early Years Science?', in *Science 3–6: Laying the Foundations in the Early Years*, (ed.) M. de Boo, Hatfield: Association for Science Education, pp. 1–6.

DeLoache, J.S. and Brown, A.L. (1987) 'The Early Emergence of Planning Skills in Children', in *Making Sense* (eds) J. Bruner and H. Haste, London: Methuen, pp. 108–30.

Demetriou, A., Shayer, M. and Efklides, A. (eds) (1992) *Neo-Piagetian Theories of Cognitive Development*, London: Routledge.

Dennison, P.E. and Dennison, G. (1994) *Brain Gym: Teacher's Edition Revised*, Ventura: Edu-Kinesthetics Inc.

Department for Education and Employment (DfEE) (2000) *Curriculum Guidance for the Foundation Stage*, London: HMSO.

Dockett, S. (1998) 'Constructing Understandings through Play in the Early Years', *International Journal of Early Years Education*, 6(1): 105–16.

Donaldson, M. (1978) *Children's Minds*, Glasgow: Fontana/Collins.

—— (1992) *Human Minds*, London: Penguin.

Donaldson, M., Grieve, R. and Pratt, C. (1988) (eds) *Early Childhood Development and Education*, Oxford: Blackwell.

Dowling, M. (2000) *Young Children's Personal, Social and Emotional Development*, London: Paul Chapman.

—— (2002) 'How Young Children Learn', *Early Education*, Summer.

Driver, R. (1983) *The Pupil as Scientist?* Milton Keynes: Open University Press.

Duckworth, E. (1987) *'The Having of Wonderful Ideas' and Other Essays on Teaching and Learning*, New York: Teachers College Press.

Duffy, B. (1998) *Supporting Creativity and Imagination in the Early Years*, Buckingham: Open University Press.

Dunn, J. (1987) 'Understanding Feelings: The Early Stages', in *Making Sense* (eds) J. Bruner and H. Haste, London: Methuen, pp. 26–40.

—— (1988) *The Beginnings of Social Understanding*, Oxford: Blackwell.

—— (1993) *Young Children's Close Relationships: Beyond Attachment*, London: Sage.

—— (2004a) *Children's Friendships*, Oxford: Blackwell Publishing.

—— (2004b) 'Commentary: Broadening the Framework of Theory-of-Mind Research', *International Journal of Behavioral Development, Supplement Newsletter Number 1, Serial Number* 45, 28(3): 13–14.

—— (2005) *'Relationships and Children's Discovery of the Mind'*, British Academy/British Psychological Society Annual Lecture, London, 5 April.

Dunn, J., Brown, J., Slomkowski, C., Tesla, C. and Youngblade, L. (1991) 'Young Children's Understanding of Other People's Feelings and Beliefs: Individual Differences and Their Antecedents', *Child Development*, 62: 1352–66.

Dunn, J., Cutting, A.L. and Fisher, N. (2002) 'Old Friends, New Friends: Predictors of Children's Perspective on Their Friends at School', *Child Development*, 73(2): 621–35.

Dweck, C.S. (2000) *Self-Theories: Their Role in Motivation, Personality and Development*, Hove, East Sussex: Psychology Press.

Edwards, C., Gandini, L. and Forman, G. (1998) *The Hundred Languages of Children*, 2nd edn, Westport, CT: Ablex.

Edwards, S. (2003) 'New Directions: Charting the Paths for the Role of Sociocultural Theory in Early Childhood Education and Curriculum', *Contemporary Issues in Early Childhood*, 4(3): 251–66.

—— (2005) 'Children's Learning and Developmental Potential: Examining the Theoretical Informants of Early Childhood Curricula from the Educator's Perspective', *Early Years*, 25(1): 67–80.

Eliot, L. (1999) *What's Going On in There?* London: Allen Lane.

Ellis, S. and Kleinberg, S. (2000) 'Exploration and Enquiry', in *Science 3–6: Laying the Foundations in the Early Years* (ed.) M. de Boo, Hatfield: Association for Science Education, pp. 15–27.

Escobedo, T.H. (1999) 'The Canvas of Play: A Study of Children's Play Behaviors While Drawing', in *Play and Culture Studies, Volume 2* (ed.) S. Reifel, Stamford, CA: Ablex Publishing, pp. 101–22.

Farr Darling, L. (2002) 'Moles, Porcupines, and Children's Moral Reasoning: Unexpected Responses', *Early Years*, 22(2): 91–103.

Feynman, R. (1986) *Surely You're Joking, Mr Feynman!*, London: Counterpoint.

Fisher, J. (ed.) (2002) *The Foundations of Learning*, Buckingham: Open University Press.

Fisher, R. (1990) *Teaching Children to Think*, Oxford: Basil Blackwell.

—— (1996) *Stories for Thinking*, Oxford: Nash Pollock.

—— (1998) *Teaching Thinking: Philosophical Enquiry in the Classroom*, London: Cassell.

—— (2001) 'Philosophy in Primary Schools: Fostering Thinking Skills and Literacy', *Reading*, 35(2): 67–73.

—— (2005) *Thinking Skills*. Online. Available at: <teachingthinking.net/Thinkskills.htm> (accessed 6 June 2005).

Flavell, J.H. (1977) *Cognitive Development*, Englewood Cliffs, NJ: Prentice Hall.

Flavell, J.H. and Hartman, B.M. (2004) 'What Children Know About Mental Experiences', *Young Children*, 59(2): 102–8.

Flavell, J.H., Flavell, E.R. and Green, F.L. (2001) 'Development of Children's Understanding of Connections Between Thinking and Feeling', *Psychological Science*, 12(5): 430–2.

Fleer, M. (1996) 'Theories of "Play": Are They Ethnocentric or Inclusive?', *Australian Journal of Early Childhood*, 21(4): 12–17.

Fogarty, R. (1999) 'Architects of the Intellect', *Educational Leadership*, November, 76–7.

Foote, R.C. and Holmes-Lonergan, H.A. (2003) 'Sibling Conflict and Theory of Mind', *British Journal of Developmental Psychology*, 21: 45–58.

Forman, G.E. (1989) 'Helping Children Ask Good Questions', in *The Wonder of It: Exploring How the World Works* (ed.) B. Neugebauer, Redmond, WA: Exchange Press, pp. 21–4.

—— (1999) 'Instant Video Revisiting: The Video Camera as a "Tool of the Mind" for Young Children', *Early Childhood research and Practice*, 1(2). Online. Available at: <http://ecrp.uiuc.edu/v1n2/forman.html> (accessed 10 February 2005).

France, P. (1986) 'The Beginnings of Sex Stereotyping', in *Untying the Apron Strings* (eds) N. Browne and P. France, Milton Keynes: Open University Press, pp. 49–67.

Frost, R. (1915) 'The Death of the Hired Man', *North of Boston*, New York: Henry Holt.

Furrow, D. (1984) 'Social Intelligence and Processing Speed at 2 Years of Age', *Child Development*, 55: 355–62.

Gardner, H. (1983) *Frames of Mind*, London: Heinemann.

—— (1991) *The Unschooled Mind*, London: Fontana.

—— (1993) *Multiple Intelligences: The Theory in Practice*, New York: Basic Books.

—— (1998) 'A Multiplicity of Intelligences', *Scientific American Presents*, 9(4): 18–23.

—— (1999) *The Disciplined Mind*, New York: Simon and Schuster.

Garvey, C. (1977) *Play*, Glasgow: Fontana.

Gelman, R. and Gallistel, C.R. (1978) *The Child's Understanding of Number*, Cambridge, MA: Harvard University Press.

Gerhardt, S. (2004) *Why Love Matters*, London: Routledge.

Gibbs, N. (1995) 'The EQ Factor', *Time Magazine*, October 2: 60–6.

Giffin, H. (1984) 'The Coordination of Meaning in the Creation of a Shared Make-believe Reality', in *Symbolic Play: The Development of Social Understanding* (ed.) I. Bretherton, New York: Academic Press.

Gifford, S. (2004a) 'Between the Secret Garden and the Hothouse: Children's Responses to Number Focused Activities in the Nursery', *European Early Childhood Education Research Journal*, 12(2): 87–100.

—— (2004b) 'A New Mathematics Pedagogy for the Early Years: in Search of Principles for Practice', *International Journal of Early Years Education*, 12(2): 99–115.

Gold, K. (2002) 'Pick a Brain', *Times Educational Supplement: Friday Section*, 20 September.

Goldschmied, E. and Jackson, S. (2004) *People under Three*, 2nd edn, London: Routledge.

Goleman, D. (1996) *Emotional Intelligence*, London: Bloomsbury.

—— (1999) *Working with Emotional Intelligence*, London: Bloomsbury.

Gopnik, A., Meltzoff, A. and Kuhl, P. (1999) *How Babies Think*, London: Weidenfeld and Nicolson.

Goswami, U. (2004) 'Neuroscience, Education and Special Education', *British Journal of Special Education*, 31(4): 175–81.

Gregory, R.L. (1977) 'Psychology: Towards a Science of Fiction', in *The Cool Web: The Pattern of Children's Reading* (eds) M. Meek, A. Warlow and G. Barton, London: Bodley Head, pp. 393–8.

Griffiths, J. (2003) 'Do Little Children Need Big Brains?', *Early Education*, Summer: 7–8.

Gura, P. (ed.) (1992) *Exploring Learning: Young Children and Blockplay*, London: Paul Chapman.

Hall, N. and Abbott, L. (eds) (1991) *Play in the Primary Curriculum*, London: Hodder and Stoughton.

Hall, N. and Martello, J. (eds) (1996) *Listening to Children Think*, London: Hodder and Stoughton.

Hall, N. and Robinson, A. (2003) *Exploring Writing and Play in the Early Years*, 2nd edn, London: David Fulton.

Halliday, M.A.K. (1985) *An Introduction to Functional Grammar*, London: Edward Arnold.

Harding, J. and Meldon-Smith, L. (2000) *How to Make Observations and Assessments*, London: Hodder and Stoughton.

Harris, P.L. (1989) *Children and Emotion*, Oxford: Blackwell.

Hartley, D. (1993) *Understanding the Nursery School*, London: Cassell.

Haste, H. (1987) 'Growing into Rules', in *Making Sense* (eds) J. Bruner and H. Haste, London: Methuen, pp. 163–95.

Hatano, G. (2004) 'Commentary: Socializing and Relativizing ToM', *International Journal of Behavioral Development, Supplement Newsletter Number 1, Serial Number* 45, 28(3): 15–16.

Hatano, G. and Inagaki, K. (1992) 'Desituating Cognition through the Construction of Conceptual Knowledge', in *Context and Cognition* (eds) P. Light and G. Butterworth, London: Harvester, pp. 115–33.

Haynes, J. (2002) *Children as Philosophers*, London: RoutledgeFalmer.

—— (2003) 'Philosophising with Young Children', *Early Education*, Summer: 5–6.

Heal, C. and Cook, J. (1998) 'Humanities: Developing a Sense of Place and Time in the Early Years', in *A Curriculum Development Handbook for Early Childhood Educators* (ed.) I. Siraj-Blatchford Stoke on Trent: Trentham Books, pp. 121–36.

Heath, S.B. (1983) *Ways with Words*, Cambridge: Cambridge University Press.

Hedegaard, M. (2005) 'A Cultural-Historical Perspective on Children's Cognitive Development', *International Journal of Behavioural Development, Supplement Newsletter Number 1, Serial Number 47*, 29(3): 12–15.

Hendy, L. and Whitebread, D. (2000) 'Interpretations of Independent Learning in the Early Years', *International Journal of Early Years Education*, 8(3): 243–52.

Hickey, D.T. (1997) 'Motivation and Contemporary Socio-constructivist Instructional Perspectives', *Eductional Psychologist*, 32(3): 175–93.

Hindle, D. and Smith, M.C. (1999) *Personality Development: A Psychoanalytic Perspective*, London: Routledge.

Hohmann, M. and Weikart, D. (1995) *Educating Young Children: Active Learning Practices for Preschool and Childcare Programs*, Ypsilanti, MI: High/Scope Education Research Foundation.

Holland, P. (2003) *We Don't Play with Guns Here*, Maidenhead: Open University Press.

Hoodless, P. (1996a) 'Children Talking About the Past', in *Listening to Children Think* (eds) N. Hall and J. Martello, London: Hodder and Stoughton.

—— (1996b) *Teaching of History in the Primary School 69: Time and Timelines in the Primary School*, London: The Historical Association.

Hope, G. (2002) 'Solving Problems: Young Children Exploring the Rules of the Game', *The Curriculum Journal*, 13(3): 265–78.

Hughes, M. (1986) *Children and Number*, Oxford: Basil Blackwell.

Hughes, M. and Grieve, R. (1988) 'On Asking Children Bizarre Questions', in *Early Childhood Development and Education* (eds) M. Donaldson, R. Grieve and C. Pratt, Oxford: Blackwell, pp. 104–14.

Hughes, M. and Westgate, D. (1988) 'Re-appraising Talk in Nursery and Reception Classes', *Education 3–13*, 16(2): 9–15.

Hutchins, P. (1997) *Titch*, London: Red Fox.

Hutt, C. (1979) 'Exploration and Play (#2)', in *Play and Learning* (ed.) B. Sutton-Smith, New York: Gardner Press, pp. 175–94.

Hutt, J., Tyler, S., Hutt, C. and Christopherson, H. (1989) *Play, Exploration and Learning: A Natural History of the Preschool*, London: Routledge.

Inkpen, M. (1993) *Kipper's Birthday*, London: Hodder Children's Books.

Isaacs, S. (1930) *Intellectual Growth in Young Children*, London: Routledge and Kegan Paul.

James, A. and Prout, A. (eds) (1997) *Constructing and Reconstructing Childhood: Contemporary Issues in the Sociological Study of Childhood*, London: Falmer Press.

Johnson, A. (2000) 'Language and Thought', in *Childhood Studies* (eds) J. Mills and R. Mills, London: Routledge, pp. 97–111.

Johnson, S. (2001) *Teaching Thinking Skills*, Impact No.8, London: Philosophy of Education Society of Great Britain.

Jones, R. and Wyse, D. (2004) *Creativity in the Primary Curriculum*, London: David Fulton.

Karmiloff-Smith, A. (1994) *Baby It's You*, London: Ebury Press.

Katz, L. and Chard, S. (2000) *Engaging Children's Minds*, 2nd edn, Norwood, NJ: Ablex.

Katz, L.G. (1998) 'What Should Young Children Be Doing?' *American Educator*, Summer 1988: 29–45.

Kellogg, R. (1969) *Analyzing Children's Art*, Palo Alto, CA: Mayfield Publishing Company.

Kenner, C., Wells, K. and Williams, H. (1996) 'Assessing a Bilingual Child's Talk in Different Classroom Contexts', in *Listening to Children Think: Exploring Talk in the Early Years* (eds) N. Hall and J. Martello, London: Hodder and Stoughton, pp. 117–30.

Kuhn, D. (2000) 'Does Memory Development Belong on an Endangered Topic List?', *Child Development*, 71(1): 21–5.

Laevers, F. (ed.) (1994) *The Leuven Involvement Scale for Young Children* (Manual and video) Experiential Education Series, No.1, Leuven: Centre for Experiential Education.

—— (1999) 'The Project Experiential Education: Well-Being and Involvement Make the Difference', *Early Education*, Spring.

—— (2000) 'Forward to Basics! Deep-level-learning and the Experiential Approach', *Early Years*, 20(2): 20–9.

Lambert, E.B. (2000) 'Problem-solving in the First Years of School', *Australian Journal of Early Childhood*, 25(3): 32–8.

Lave, J. and Wenger, E. (1992) *Situated Learning: Legitimate Peripheral Participation*, Cambridge: Cambridge University Press.

Learning and Skills Research Council (LSRC) (2004) *Should We Be Using Learning Styles? What Research Has To Say To Practice*, London: Learning and Skills Development Agency.

Leat, D. (1999) 'Rolling the Stone Uphill: Teacher Development and the Implementation of Thinking Skills Programmes', *Oxford Review of Education*, 25(3): 387–403.

LeDoux, J. (1998) *The Emotional Brain*, London: Phoenix.

—— (2003) *Synaptic Self*, London: Penguin.

Lee, V.L. and Das Gupta, P. (1995) *Children's Cognitive and Language Development*, Milton Keynes: Open University in association with Blackwell Publishers.

Lewis, L. and Rowley, C. (2002) 'Issues Arising in the Use of Philosophical Enquiry with Children to Develop Thinking Skills', *Education 3–13*, June: 52–5.

Light, P. and Butterworth, G. (1992) *Context and Cognition*, London: Harvester.

Lipman, M. (1991) 'Philosophy for Children', in *Developing Minds* (ed.) A.L. Costa, Alexandria, VA: Association for Supervision and Curriculum Development, pp. 35–8.

—— (2003) *Thinking in Education*, Cambridge: Cambridge University Press.

Lipman, M., Sharp, A.M. and Oscanyan, F.S. (1980) *Philosophy in the Classroom*, Philadelphia, PA: Temple University Press.

Lloyd, B. and Howe, N. (2003) 'Solitary Play and Convergent and Divergent Thinking Skills in Preschool Children', *Early Childhood Research Quarterly*, 18: 22–41.

Lofdahl, A. (2005) ' "The Funeral": A Study of Children's Shared Meaning-Making and Its Developmental Significance', *Early Years*, 25(1): 5–16.

Lowenfeld, V. and Brittain, W. (1982) *Creative and Mental Growth*, 7th edn, New York: Macmillan.

McCaldon, S. (1991) 'In the Olden Days', in *Play in the Primary Curriculum* (eds) N. Hall and L. Abbott, London: Hodder and Stoughton, pp. 61–70.

MacDonald, A.R., Hargreaves, D.J. and Miell, D. (eds) (2002) *Musical Identities*, Oxford: Oxford University Press.

McGuinness, C. (1999) *'From Thinking Skills to Thinking Classrooms'* (Research Report 115), London: DfEE.

McKendree, J., Small, C., Stenning, K. and Conlon, T. (2002) 'The Role of Representation In Teaching and Learning Critical Thinking', *Educational Review,* 54(1): 57–67.

Maclellan, E. (1997) 'The Importance of Counting', in *Teaching and Learning Early Number* (ed.) I. Thompson, Buckingham: Open University, pp. 33–40.

MacNaughton, G. (2003) *Shaping Early Childhood*, Maidenhead: Open University Press.

MacNaughton, G. and Williams, G. (2004) *Teaching Young Children*, Maidenhead: Open University Press.

Marnat, M. (1974) *Klee*, London: Spurbooks.

Matthews, J. (1994) *Helping Children to Draw and Paint in Early Childhood*, London: Hodder and Stoughton.

—— (2003) *Drawing and Painting: Children and Visual Representation*, London: Paul Chapman Publishing.

Mayall, B. (1996) *Children, Health and the Social Order*, Buckingham: Open University Press.

Meade, A. and Cubey, P. (1995) *Thinking Children*, Wellington, New Zealand: New Zealand Council For Educational Research.

Meadows, S. (1993) *The Child as Thinker*, London: Routledge.

Medcalf-Davenport, N.A. (2003) 'Questions, Answers and Wait-time: Implications for Assessment of Young Children', *International Journal of Early Years Education*, 11(3): 245–53.

Meek, M., Warlow, A. and Barton, G. (eds) (1977) *The Cool Web: The Pattern of Children's Reading*, London: Bodley Head.

Meins, E. (1997) *Security of Attachment and the Social Development of Cognition*, Hove: Psychology Press.

Mercer, N. (2000) *Words and Minds*, London: Routledge.

Midgeley, M. (2003) 'It's All In the Mind', Review of *The Blank Slate*, in *The Guardian Review*, 21 September: 10.

Miller, L (1999) 'Babyhood: Becoming a Person in the Family', in *Personality Development: A Psychoanalytic Perspective* (eds) D. Hindle and M.V. Smith, London: Routledge.

Miller, L. and Devereux, J. (eds) (2004) *Supporting Children's Learning in the Early Years*, London: David Fulton in association with Open University.

Milner, P. and Carolin, B. (eds) (1999) *Time to Listen to Children: Personal and Professional Communication*, London: Routledge.

Ministry of Education, New Zealand (1996) *Te Whariki: Early Childhood Curriculum*, Auckland: New Zealand Learning Media Ltd.

Moore, C. (2004) *George and Sam*, London: Penguin Viking.

Morrow, V. (1999) 'It's Cool . . .' Cos You Can't Give Us Detentions and Things, Can You?!', in *Time to Listen to Children: Personal and Professional Communication* (eds) P. Milner and B. Carolin, London: Routledge, pp. 203–15.

Motluk, A (2002) 'You Are What You Speak', *New Scientist*, 30 November: 34–8.

Moyles, J.R. (1989) *Just Playing: The Role and Status of Play in Early Childhood*, Milton Keynes: Open University Press.

—— (ed.) (1994) *The Excellence of Play*, Buckingham: Open University Press.

Moyles, J., Adams, S. and Musgrove, A. (2002) *SPEEL Study of Pedagogical Effectiveness in Early Learning* (Research Report 363), London: DfES.

Munn, P. (1997) 'Children's Beliefs about Counting', in *Teaching and Learning Early Number* (ed.) I. Thompson, Buckingham: Open University Press, pp. 9–19.

Murphy, P. (ed.) (1997) *Making Sense of Science Study Guide*, Buckingham: SPE/Open University.

Naito, M. (2004) 'Is Theory of Mind a Universal and Unitary Construct?' *International Journal of Behavioral Development, Supplement Newsletter Number 1, Serial Number 45*, 28(3): 9–11.

National Advisory Committee on Creative and Cultural Education (NACCCE) (1999) *All Our Futures*, Sudbury: Department for Education and Employment.

National Oracy Project (1990) *Teaching, Talking and Learning in Key Stage 1*, York: National Curriculum Council.

Navarra, J. (1955) *The Development of Scientific Concepts in a Young Child*, Westport, CT: Greenwood.

Nelson, K. (2004) 'Commentary: The Future of ToM lies in CoM', *International Journal of Behavioral Development, Supplement Newsletter Number 1, Serial Number 45*, 28(3): 16–17.

Neugebauer, B. (ed.) (1989) *The Wonder of It: Exploring How the World Works*, Redmond, WA: Exchange Press.

Nimmo, J. (1998) 'The Child in Community: Constraints From the Early Childhood Lore', in *The Hundred Languages of Children* (eds) C. Edwards, L. Gandini and G. Forman, Westport, CT: Ablex, pp. 295–312.

Nunes, T. (1995) 'Mathematical and Scientific Thinking', in *Children's Cognitive and Language Development* (eds) V. Lee and P. Das Gupta, Milton Keynes: Open University in association with Blackwell Publishers, pp. 189–229.

—— (2005) 'What We Learn in School: The Socialization of Cognition', *International Journal of Behavioral Development, Supplement Newsletter Number 1, Serial Number 47*, 29(3): 10–12.

Nunes, T. and Bryant, P. (eds) (1997) *Learning and Teaching Mathematics: An International Perspective*, Hove: Psychology Press.

Nutbrown, C. (1999) *Threads of Thinking: Young Children Learning*, London: Paul Chapman.

Organisation for Economic Cooperation and Development (OECD) (2001) *Preliminary Synthesis of the First High Level Forum on Learning Sciences and Brain Research*, New York: Sackler Institute, OECD-CERI.

Paley, V.G. (1981) *Wally's Stories*, Cambridge, MA: Harvard University Press.

—— (1986) 'On Listening to What the Children Say', *Harvard Educational Review*, 56(2): 122–31.

—— (1993) *You Can't Say You Can't Play*, Cambridge, MA: Harvard University Press.

—— (2004) *A Child's Work*, Chicago: University of Chicago Press.

Palmer, J. (1994) *Geography in the Early Years*, London: Routledge.

Papaleontiou-Louca, E. (2003) 'The Concept and Instruction of Metacognition', *Teacher Development*, 7(1): 9–30.

Pascal, C. and Bertram, T. (1997) *Effective Early Learning*, London: Hodder and Stoughton.

—— (1999) 'Accounting Early for Lifelong Learning', in *Early Education Transformed* (eds) L. Abbott and H. Moylett, London: Falmer Press.

Pellicano, E. and Rhodes, G. (2003) 'The Role of Eye-Gaze in Understanding Other Minds', *British Journal of Developmental Psychology*, 21: 33–43.

Penn, H. (2005) *Understanding Early Childhood*, Maidenhead: Open University Press.

Perkins, D.N. (1992) *Smart Schools*, New York: Free Press.

—— (1994) *'The Intelligent Eye: Learning to Think by Looking at Art'*, *Occasional Paper 4*, Santa Monica, CA: The Getty Center for Education in the Arts.

Perner, J. (2004) 'Tracking the Essential Mind', *International Journal of Behavioral Development, Supplement Newsletter Number 1, Serial Number 45*, 28(3): 4–7.

Peterson, C.C. (2004) 'Journeys of Mind: ToM Development in Children with Autism, Sensory or Motor Disabilities', *International Journal of Behavioral Development, Supplement Newsletter Number 1, Serial Number 45*, 28(3): 11–13.

Piaget, J. (1950) *The Psychology of Intelligence*, London: Routledge and Kegan Paul.

—— (1952) *The Child's Conception of Number*, London: Routledge and Kegan Paul.

—— (1959) *The Language and Thought of the Child*, London: Routledge and Kegan Paul.

—— (1962) *Play, Dreams and Imitation in Childhood*, London: Routledge and Kegan Paul.

Piazza, G. and Barozzi, A. (2001) 'The City of Reggio Emilia', in *Making Learning Visible: Children as Individual and Group Learners*, Project Zero and Reggio Children, Reggio Emilia, Italy: Reggio Children.

Pinker, S. (1994) *The Language Instinct*, London: Penguin.

—— (1997) *How the Mind Works*, London: Penguin.

—— (2002) *The Blank Slate*, London: Penguin.

Pollard, A. (1997) *Reflective Teaching in the Primary School*, London: Cassell.

Pound, L. (2003) *Supporting Musical Development in the Early Years*, Buckingham: Open University Press.

—— (2004) 'Born Mathematical?' in *Supporting Children's Learning in the Early Years* (eds) L. Miller and J. Devereux, London: David Fulton in association with Open University, pp. 137–44.

Pramling, I. (1988) 'Developing Children's Thinking about Their Own Thinking', *British Journal of Educational Psychology*, 58: 266–78.

Pramling Samuelson, I. (2004) 'How Do Children Tell Us about Their Childhoods?', *Early Childhood Research and Practice*, 6: 1. Online. Available at: <http://ecrp.uiuc.edu/v6n1/pramling.html> (accessed 10 February 2005).

Prentice, R. (1994) 'Experiential Learning in Play and Art', in *The Excellence of Play* (ed.) J. Moyles, Buckingham: Open University Press, pp. 125–35.

Project Zero and Reggio Children (2001) *Making Learning Visible: Children as Individual and Group Learners*, Reggio Emilia, Italy: Reggio Children.

Project Zero Patterns of Thinking Project. Online. Available at: <http://pzweb.harvard.edu./Research/PatThk.htm> (accessed 27 September 2002).

Raban, B., Ure, C. and Waniganayake, M. (2003) 'Multiple Perspectives: Acknowledging the Virtue of Complexity in Measuring Quality', *Early Years*, 23(1): 67–77.

Reggio Children (1996) '*The Hundred Languages of Children*' (exhibition catalogue), Reggio Emilia, Italy: Reggio Children.

Reifel, S. (ed.) (1999) *Play and Culture Studies, Volume 2*, Stamford, CA: Ablex.

Resnick, L.B. (ed.) 1989) *Knowing, Learning and Instruction*, Hillsdale, NJ: Lawrence Erlbaum Associates.

Revell, P. (2005) 'Each to Their Own', *Education Guardian*, 31 May: 6–7.

Richetti, C. and Sheerin, J. (1999) 'Helping Students Ask the Right Questions', *Educational Leadership*, 57(3): 58–62.

Rinaldi, C. (1998) 'Projected Curriculum Constructed Through Documentation–Progettazione: An Interview with Lella Gandini', in *The Hundred Languages of Children* (eds) C. Edwards, L.Gandini and G. Forman, Westport, CT: Ablex, pp. 113–25.

Roberts, R. (2002) *Self Esteem and Early Learning*, 2nd edn, London: Paul Chapman.

Robertson, A. (2004) 'Let's Think! Two Years On', *Primary Science Review*, 82: 4–7.

Robson, S. and Hargreaves, D.J. (2005) 'What do Early Childhood Practitioners Think About Young Children's Thinking?' *European Early Childhood Education Research Journal*, 13(1): 81–96.

Rodd, J. (1999) 'Encouraging Young Children's Critical and Creative Thinking Skills', *Childhood Education*, 75(6): 350–5.

Rogoff, B. (1990) *Apprenticeship in Thinking: Cognitive Development in a Social Context*, Oxford: Oxford University Press.

—— (2003) *The Cultural Nature of Human Development*, Oxford: Oxford University Press.

Romaine, S. (2004) 'Bilingual Language Development', in *The Child Language Reader* (eds) K. Trott, S. Dobbinson and P. Griffiths, London: Routledge, pp. 287–303.

Scherer, M. (1999) 'The Understanding Pathway. A Conversation with Howard Gardner', *Educational Leadership*, November, 12–16.

Scoffham, S. (2003) 'Teaching, Learning and the Brain', *Education 3–13*, 31(3): 49–58.

Segar, S. (2004) 'If We Want Deep Level Learning We Cannot Do Without Involvement', unpublished thesis, University of Surrey Roehampton.

Selley, N. (1999) *The Art of Constructivist Teaching in the Primary School*, London: David Fulton Publishers.

Sharman, C., Cross, W. and Vennis, D. (2004) *Observing Children*, 3rd edn, London: Continuum.

Sharp, J. (ed.) (2002) *Primary Science: Teaching Theory and Practice*, Exeter: Learning Matters.

—— (2002) 'Children's Ideas', in *Primary Science: Teaching Theory and Practice* (ed.) J. Sharp, Exeter: Learning Matters, pp. 25–37.

Siegler, R.S. (1998) *Children's Thinking*, 3rd edn, Upper Saddle Ridge, NJ: Prentice Hall.

—— (2000) 'The Rebirth of Children's Learning', *Child Development*, 71(1): 26–35.

Siegler, R., DeLoache, J. and Eisenberg, N. (2003) *How Children Develop*, New York: Worth.

Singer, J.L. (1973) *The Child's World of Make-believe: Experimental Studies of Imaginative Play*, New York: Academic Press.

Siraj-Blatchford, I. (ed.) (1998) *A Curriculum Development Handbook for Early Childhood Educators*, Stoke on Trent: Trentham Books.

Siraj-Blatchford, I., Sylva, K., Muttock, S., Gilden, R. and Bell, D. (2002) '*Researching Effective Pedagogy in the Early Years*' (Research Report 356), London: DfES.

Smith, A. (1998) *Accelerated Learning in Practice*, Stafford: Network Educational Press.

Smith, A. and Call, N. (1999) The ALPS Approach: Accelerated Learning in Practice, Stafford: Network Educational Press.

Smith, P.K., Cowie, H. and Blades, M. (2003) *Understanding Children's Development*, 2nd edn, Oxford: Blackwell.

Sperling, R.A., Walls, R.T. and Hill, L.A. (2000) 'Early Relationships Among Self-Regulatory Constructs: Theory of Mind and Pre-School Children's Problem Solving', *Child Study Journal*, 30(4): 233–53.

Sternberg, R.J. (1985) *Beyond IQ. A Triarchic Theory of Human Intelligence*, Cambridge: Cambridge University Press.

—— (1986) *Intelligence Applied. Understanding and Increasing Your Intellectual Skills*, Orlando, FL: Harcourt Brace Jovanovich.

Storr, A. (1993) *Music and the Mind*, London: Harper Collins.

Sutherland, P. (1992) *Cognitive Development Today: Piaget and his Critics*, London: Paul Chapman.

Sutton-Smith, B. (ed.) (1979) *Play and Learning*, New York: Gardner Press.

Swan, S. and White, R. (1994) *The Thinking Books*, London: Falmer Press.

Swartz, R.J. (2000) *Towards Developing and Implementing A Thinking Curriculum*. Online. Available at: <http://www.nctt.net/hongkongaddress.html> (accessed 7 December 2002).

Swartz, R.J., Fischer, S. and Parks, S. (1998) *Infusing the Teaching of Critical and Creative Thinking into Secondary Science: A Lesson Design Handbook*, Critical Thinking Books and Software. Online. Available at: <http://www.nctt.net/infusion_chapter1.html> (accessed 22 February 2005).

Sylva, K., Bruner, J.S. and Genova, P. (1976) 'The Role of Play in the Problem-solving of Young Children 3- to 5-years-of-age', in *Play, Its Role in Development and Evolution* (eds) J.S. Bruner, A. Jolly and K. Sylva, Harmondsworth: Penguin.

Sylva, K., Roy, C. and Painter, M. (1980) *Childwatching at Playgroup and Nursery School*, London: Grant McIntyre.

Sylwester, R. (1998) 'Art for the Brain's Sake', *Educational Leadership*, 56(3): 31–5.

Szarkowicz, D.L. (2000) 'When They Wash Him They'll Know He'll be Harry: Young Children's Thinking About Thinking within a Story Context', *International Journal of Early Years Education*, 8(1): 71–82.

Talay-Ongan, A. (2000) 'Neuroscience and Early Childhood: A Necessary Partnership', *Australian Journal of Early Childhood*, 25(2): 28–33.

Thinking Skills Review Group (2004) *Thinking Skills Approaches to Effective Teaching and Learning: What is the Evidence for Impact on Learners?*, London: EPPI-Centre.

Thompson, I. (ed.) (1997) *Teaching and Learning Early Number*, Buckingham: Open University Press.

Thornton, S. (2002) *Growing Minds*, Basingstoke: Palgrave Macmillan.

Tizard, B. and Hughes, M. (2002) *Young Children Learning: Talking and Thinking at Home and at School*, 2nd edn, London: Fontana.

Trawick-Smith, J. (1998) 'A Qualitative Analysis of Metaplay in the Preschool Years', *Early Childhood Research Quarterly*, 13(3): 433–52.

Trepanier-Street, M. (2000) 'Multiple Forms of Representation in Long-Term Projects', *Childhood Education*, Fall: 18–25.

Trevarthen, C. (1995) 'The Child's Need to Learn a Culture', *Children and Society*, 9(1): 5–19.

—— (2002) 'Origins of Musical Identity: Evidence from Infancy for Musical Social Awareness', in *Musical Identities* (eds) R.A.R. MacDonald, D.J. Hargreaves and D. Miell, Oxford: Oxford University Press, pp. 21–38.

Trickey, S. and Topping, K.J. (2004) ' "Philosophy for Children": a Systematic Review', *Research Papers in Education*, 19(3): 365–80.

Trott, K., Dobbinson, S. and Griffiths, P. (eds) (2004) *The Child Language Reader*, London: Routledge.

Tyler, S. (1991) 'Play in Relation to the National Curriculum', in *Play in the Primary Curriculum* (eds) N. Hall and L. Abbott, London: Hodder and Stoughton, pp. 10–28.

Umek, L.M. and Musek, P.L. (2001) 'Symbolic Play: Opportunities for Cognitive and Language Development in Preschool Settings', *Early Years*, 21(1): 55–64.

Valanides, N., Gritsi, F., Kampez, M. and Ravanis, K. (2000) 'Changing Pre-school Children's Conceptions of the Day/Night Cycle', *International Journal of Early Years Education*, 8(1): 27–39.

Vygotsky, L. (1976) 'Play and Its Role in the Mental Development of the Child', in *Play* (eds) J.S. Bruner, A. Jolly and K. Sylva, Harmondsworth: Penguin, pp. 537–54.

—— (1978) *Mind in Society*, Cambridge, MA: Harvard University Press.

—— (1986) *Thought and Language*, Cambridge, MA: MIT Press.

Waddell, M. (1989) *Once There Were Giants*, London: Walker Books.

Wadsworth, P. (1997) 'Document 9: Children's Ideas in Science', in *Making Sense of Science Study Guide* (ed.) P. Murphy, Buckingham: SPE/Open University.

Wall, K. (2004) *Autism and Early Years Practice*, London: Paul Chapman.

Wallace, B. (2002) *Teaching Thinking Skills Across the Early Years*, London: David Fulton.

Watson, L. (1997) 'Children's Misconceptions and Conceptual Change', *Australian Journal of Early Childhood*, 22(2): 12–16.

Wellman, H.M. (2004) 'Theory of Mind: Developing Core Human Cognitions', *International Journal of Behavioral Development, Supplement Newsletter Number 1, Serial Number 45*, 28(3): 1–4.

Wellman, H.M. and Liu, D. (2004) 'Scaling of Theory-of-Mind Tasks', *Child Development*, 75(2): 523–41.

Wellman, H.M., Cross, D. and Watson, J. (2001) 'Meta-Analysis of Theory-of-Mind Development: The Truth About False Belief', *Child Development*, 72(3): 655–84.

Wells, G. (1987) *The Meaning Makers*, Sevenoaks: Hodder and Stoughton.

—— (1999) *Dialogic Inquiry: Towards a Sociocultural Practice and Theory of Education*, Cambridge: Cambridge University Press.

Whalley, M.J. (1991) 'Philosophy for Children', in *Teaching Thinking: A Survey of Programmes in Education* (eds) M.J. Coles and W.D. Robinson, London: Bristol Classical Press, pp. 66–76.

White, J. (2002) *The Child's Mind*, London: RoutledgeFalmer.

Whitebread, D. (2000a) 'Teaching Children to Think, Reason, Solve Problems and Be Creative', in *The Psychology of Teaching and Learning in the Primary School* (ed.) D. Whitebread, London: RoutledgeFalmer, pp. 140–64.

—— (ed.) (2000b) *The Psychology of Teaching and Learning in the Primary School*, London: Routledge Falmer.

Whitebread, D., Anderson, H., Cotlman, P., Page, C., Pasternak, D.P. and Mehta, S. (2005) 'Developing Independent Learning in the Early Years', *Education 3–13*, 33(1): 40–50.

Whitehead, M. (2002) *Developing Language and Literacy with Young Children*, 2nd edn, London: Paul Chapman.

—— (2004) *Language and Literacy in the Early Years*, 3rd edn, London: Sage.

Willig, J. (1990) *Children's Concepts and the Primary Curriculum*, London: Paul Chapman.

Wilson, V. (2000) '*Education Forum on Teaching Thinking Skills*', Report. Online. Available at: <http://www.scotland.gov.uk/library3/education/ftts-00.asp> (accessed 6 June 2005).

Wolfe, P. and Brandt, R. (1998) 'What Do We Know from Brain Research?', *Educational Leadership*, November: 8–13.

Wood, D. (1998) *How Children Think and Learn*, 2nd edn, Oxford: Blackwell.

Wood, D. and Wood, H. (1996) 'Vygotsky, Tutoring and Learning', *Oxford Review of Education*, 22(1): 5–16.

Wood, D.J., Bruner, J.S. and Ross, G. (1976) 'The Role of Tutoring in Problem-solving', *Journal of Child Psychology and Psychiatry*, 17: 89–100.

Wood, E. and Attfield, J. (2005) *Play, Learning and the Early Childhood Curriculum*, London: Paul Chapman.

Index